ISLAM'S MESSAGE

Islam's Message

MUZAFFAR HUSAIN

ANMOL PUBLICATIONS PVT. LTD.
NEW DELHI - 110 002 (INDIA)

ANMOL PUBLICATIONS PVT. LTD.
4374/4B, Ansari Road, Daryaganj
New Delhi - 110 002
Ph.: 23261597, 23278000
Visit us at: www.anmolpublications.com

Islam's Message

First Published, 2004

ISBN 81-261-2007-X

PRINTED IN INDIA

Published by J.L. Kumar for Anmol Publications Pvt. Ltd., New Delhi - 110 002 and Printed at Mehra Offset Press, Delhi.

Contents

Preface

Islam is a universal religion. It's a leading light for the whole mankind. Holy Quran addresses all the human beings and not only the believers. In the same way Holy Prophet is mercy for all the worlds, not the Muslims in this world alone.

Islam's message is eternal. It guides man to lead a pious and successful life in this world and to attain salvation in the world hereafter, thus becoming an achiever. Islam, as a complete faith offers a perfect code of conduct to its followers.

Islam is not only a philosophy like some other religions. It is a practical way of life, which makes living in this world easier and full of rewards in the next world.

Islam's message is of peace, transquility and contentment for all those, who desire to lead a disciplined life for improving their lot. This message is for all the people, all the lands and all the times.

Holy Prophet was a great scholar and teacher. He, himself preached Islam first and trained an army of preachers, who took his message to far off places and virtually, it was spread to all corners of the contemporary world. This message is now reaching new destinations, not only Western Europe but USA and Canada too.

This work is aimed at making people understand the essence of Islam and receive its message to come to the right track. The undersigned is confident that this modest effort of his would be able to spread Islam's Message to larger extents. And that must be an achievement.

—Editor

1

Introduction

In order to understand the primary doctrines of the religion of Mohammed, the first great point to examine is the true significance of the word Islam, for on this hinge some of the most important points are involved in the science of religion. Salm (salama, in the first and fourth conjugations) means in the first instance to be tranquil, at rest, to have done one's duty, to have paid up, to be at perfect peace, and, finally, to hand one's self over to Him with whom peace is made. The noun derived from it means peace, greeting, safety, salvation. The word thus implies absolute submission to God's will—as generally assumed—neither in the first instance, nor exclusively, but means, on the contrary, one who strives after righteousness with his own strength.

The essence of the great principles thus embodied in Islam is set forth in the second chapter of the Koran:—"There is no doubt in this book. A guidance to the pious, who believe without seeing (or in the Unseen), who observe the prayers, and distribute (charity) out of what we have bestowed on them; and who believe in that which We have commissioned thee with, and in that We commissioned others with, before thee, and who have assurance in the life to come;—these have received the direction of their Lord."

The principal bases on which the entire system of the Islamic laws is built, are, firstly (1) a belief in the unity, immateriality, power, mercy and supreme love of the Creator; (2) charity and brotherhood among mankind; (3) subjugation of the passions; (4) the outpouring of a grateful heart to the Giver of all gifts; and (5) accountability for human actions in another existence. The grand and noble conceptions, expressed in the Koran, of the power and love of the Deity surpass everything of their kind. The Unity of God, His immateriality, His majesty, His mercy form the constant and never ending theme of the most eloquent and soul-stirring passages. The flow of life, light and spirituality never ceases. But throughout, there is no trace of dogmatism. Appeal is made to the inner consciousness of man, to his intuitive reason alone.

But in order to elucidate more fully the distinctive character of Mohammed's teachings regarding the Divinity, a brief glance at the state of opinion among the various religious sects in Arabia, will not be amiss.

Among the heathen Arabs, the idea of Godhead varied according to the culture of the individual or of the clan. With some it rose (comparatively speaking) to the "divinisation" or deification of nature; among others it fell to simple fetishism, the adoration of a piece of dough, a stick, or a stone. Some believed in a future life; others had no idea of it whatever. The heathen Arabs had their groves, their oracle-trees, their priestesses like the Syro-Phoenicians. Phallic worship was not unknown to them; and the generative powers received adoration, like the hosts of heaven, under monuments of stone and wood. The wild denizens of the desert, then as now, could not be impervious to the idea of some unseen hand driving the blasts which swept over whole tracts, or forming the beautiful visions which rose before the traveller to lure him to destruction. But above all, there floated an intangible, unrealised conception of a superior Deity, the Lord of All.

The Jews, those great conservators of the monotheistic idea, as they have been generally regarded in history, probably might have assisted in the formation of this conception. But they themselves showed what strange metamorphosis can take place in the thoughts of a nation, when not aided by a historical and rationlistic element in their religious code.

The Jews had entered Arabia at various times, and under the pressure of various circumstances. Naturally, the ideas of the different bodies of emigrants, refugees or colonists would vary much. The ideas of the men driven out by the Assyrians or Babylonians would be more anthropomorphic, or anthropopathic, than of those who fled before Vespasian, Trojan, or Hadrian. The characteristics which had led the Israelites repeatedly to lapse into idolatry in their original homes, when seers were in their midst to denounce their backslidings, would hardly preserve them from the heathenism of their Arab brothers. With an idea of "the God of Abraham, "they would naturally combine a materialistic conception of the deity, and hence we find them rearing "a statue representing Abraham with the ram beside him, ready for sacrifice," in the interior of the Kaaba.

Amongst the later comers, the Shammaites and the Zealots formed by far the largest proportion. Among them, the worship of the law verged upon idolatry, and the scribes and Rabbins claimed a respect almost approaching adoration. They believed themselves to be the guardians of the people, the preservers of law and tradition, "living exemplars and mirrors, in which the true mode of life, according to the law, was preserved." They looked upon themselves as the "flower of the nation," and they were considered, through their intercourse with God, to possess the gift of prophecy. In fact, by their people as well as by themselves, they were regarded as the prime favourites of God. The veneration of the Jews for Moses went so far, says Josephus, that they reverenced his name next to that of God; and this veneration they transferred to Ezra, the Restorer of national life and law, under the Kyanian dynasty.

Besides, the mass of the Jews had never, probably, thoroughly abandoned the worship of the Teraphim, a sort of household gods in a human form, consulted on all occasions as domestic oracles, or regarded perhaps more as guardian penates. This worship must have been strengthened by contact with the heathen Arabs.

The Christian had a nobler exemplar before him. The teachings of the Prophet of Nazareth should have elevated him to a purer conception of the deity. But six centuries has surrounded that noble figure with those myths which, in opposition to his own words, resolved him into a manifestation—an hypostasis—of the Godhead. The vulgar masses, unable to comprehend or realise this wonderful mixture of Neopythagorianism, Platonism, Judaeo-Hellenistic philosophy, and the teachings of Jesus,—reverted to the primitive worship of relics and of a tinselled goddess, who represented the pure Mother of Jesus. But this degradation of human reason was not confined to the Christians of Arabia. Even at the Council of Nice, which definitely settled the nature of Jesus, there were men who held that besides "God the Father," there were two other Gods—Christ and the Virgin Mary.

Against all the absurdities we have described above, the life-aim of Mohammed was directed. Addressing, with the voice of Truth, inspired by deep communion with the God of the universe, the fetish worshippers of the Arabian tribes on one side, and the followers of degraded Christianity and Judaism on the other, Mohammed, that "master of speech," as he has been so nobly called, never out of the province of reason, and made them all blush at the monstrousness of their beliefs. Mohammed, the grand apostle of the unity of god, thus stands forth in history in noble conflict with the retrogressive tendency of man to associate other beings with the Creator of the universe.

Ever and anon in the Koran occur passages, fervid and burning, like the following:—

"Your God is one God; there is no God but He, the most merciful. In the creation of the heaven and earth, and the alternation of night and day, and in the ship which saileth on the sea; laden with what is profitable to mankind; and in the rain water which God sendeth from heaven quickening against the dead earth, and the animals of all sorts which cover its surface; and in the change of winds, and the clouds balanced between heaven and earth,—are signs to people of understanding; yet some men take idols beside God, and love them as with the love due to God." What a depth of sympathy towards those benighted people do these words convey. Again:—"It is He who causeth the lightning to appear unto you, (to strike) fear and (to raise) hope; and formeth the pregnant clouds. The thunder celebrateth His praise, and the angels also.... He launches his thunderbolts, and striketh therewith whom He pleaseth while they dispute concerning Him. It is He who of right ought to be invoked; and those (the idols) whom they invoke besides Him, shall not respond to them at all: otherwise than as he, who stretcheth forth his hands to the water that it may ascend to his mouth, when it cannot ascend (thither)." "He hath created the heaven and the earth to (manifest His) justice. Far be that from Him which they associate with Him. He hath created man. . . . and behold he is a professed disputer. He hath likewise created the cattle for you. And they are likewise a credit unto you, when they come trooping home at evening time or are led forth to pasture in the morn.. And He hath subjected the night and day to your service; and the sun, and the moon, and the stars are all bound by his laws... It is He who hath subjected the sea unto you, and thou seest the ships ploughing the deep... and that ye might render thanks. Shall He therefore who createth be as he who createth not? Do ye not therefore take heed? If ye were to reckon up the blessings of God, ye shall not be able to compute their number; God is surely gracious and merciful. He knoweth that which ye conceal and that which ye publish. But those (the idols) whom ye invoke, besides the Lord, create nothing, but are themselves created. They are dead and not living."

And so this wonderful book goes on, appealing to the noble feelings of man,—his inner consciousness and his moral sense, in order to prove and manifest the enormity of idolatrous beliefs. There is scarcely a chapter which does not contain some fervid passages on the power, mercy, and unity of God. Occasionally, however, come denunciations on the Christians and the Jews, for the superstitious rites they practised in defiance of the warnings of their teachers. The fire of religious zeal, which had burned in the bosoms of Isaiah and Jeremiah, was rekindled in the breast of another and a far greater man. He denounces; but above the wail, the cry of agony at the degradation of humanity, is heard the voice of hope, sounding through eternity.

The Koran severly censures the Jews for their "worship of false gods and idols" and for their exaggerated reverence for the memory of Ezra: the Christians, for their adoration of Jesus and his mother.

> "Hast thou not seen those to whom a portion of the Scriptures have been given? They believe in false gods and idols. They say to the unbelievers, they are better directed in the right way than those that believe (the Moslems)." The Jews say, Ezra is the son of God; the Christians say, Christ is the son of God... May God resist them. How infatuated they are! They take their priests and their monks for their lords besides God.... They seek to extinguish the light of God with their mouths."
>
> The Jews and the Christians say, We are the children of God, and His beloved." Many of those unto whom the scriptures have been given, desire to render you again unbelievers, after ye have believed... Be constant in prayer, and give alms; and what good ye have sent before you for your souls, ye shall

find it with God." They say. Verily none shall enter paradise, except those who are Jews or Christians... Say, Produce your proof if ye speak the truth. Nay, but he who directeth himself towards God, and doth that which is right, he shall have his reward with his Lord."

"O' ye who have received the scriptures exceed not the just bounds in your religion; neither say of God otherwise than the truth. Verily, Christ Jesus the son of Mary is the apostle of God, and his Word. Believe therefore in God and His apostles and say not. There are three Gods; forbear this. . . Chirst doth not proudly disdain to be a servant unto God."

The following passage shows the feeling with which such religious conceptions were regarded:—

They say the God of Mercy hath begotten a son (or issue). Now have ye uttered a grievous thing; and it wanteth but little that the heaven should be torn open, and that the earth cleave asunder, and the mountains fall down, for that they attribute children unto the Merciful, whereas it is not meet for God to have children. Verily, there is none in heaven or on earth, but shall approach the Merciful as his servant. He encompasseth them.."

But the inspired Preacher does not confound the good with the bad. His mission is to proclaim the truth, and he must give all men their due.

"Yet they are not all alike, there are of those who have received the scriptures, upright people; they mediate on the signs of God in the night season, and worship; they believe in God, and the last day; and command that which is just; and forbid that which is unjust, and zealously strive to excel in good works; these are of the righteous."

The mercy of the Almighty is one of the grandest themes of the Koran. The very name Ar-Rahman by which God is often distinguished and invoked, expresses a deep, all-penetrating conviction regarding the mercy of the Deity.

The grand central figure of Mohammed rises before our view, clothed in all the majesty of prophetic greatness. King, chief, magistrate, and spiritual guide, he rules the heart of men with his heaven-inspired genius. Men gather from all quarters of the globe to listen to his wonderful words, which breathe energy and force and infuse new life into the dormant heart of Humanity. It was an age of earnestness and faith, marked by the uprise of the Soul against the domination of aimless, lifeless philosophy. It proved the utter futility of inane talk when in collision with active principles.

2

Pre-Islamic Days

In order to appreciate thoroughly the achievements of Mohammed (May peace be upon him) in the moral world, it is necessary to take a rapid survey of the religious and social conditions of the nations of the earth about the time of the Islamic dispensation. For we must fully recognise that the causes which had led to the advent of the Great Prophet of Nazareth, in the reign of Augustus, acted with greater force during the reigns of the degenerate emperors who occupied the throne of the Caesars, at the period of Mohammed's appearance.

In the dim twilight of history we see, or fancy, strange figures and strange scenes enacted on the high table land of Bactria, appropriately styled "the mother of countries. Several dans are gathered together on that plateau: having just emerged from savageness into barbarism, they are becoming alive to the sense of an Universal Ideality. Innumerable idealities are taking the place of the natural objects, hitherto worshipped with fear and trembling. With some of these ancient dwellers on the earth, the host of abstractions and personifications of the powers of Nature are subordinated to two comprehensive Principles: Light and Darkness. The sun, the bright harbinger of life and light, becomes the symbol of a beneficent Divinity, whose power, though held in check, is eventually to conquer the opposing principle of Evil and Darkness. With others, the idealities which they now impress on the fetish they worshipped before, merge in each other; at one time standing forth as distinct personal entities, at another time resolving themselves into a hylozoic whole.

Through the darkness which yet shroud this primeval home of mankind, we can see the dim traces of a religious conflict between the two divisions of the Aryan family, which has left its mark in the deep imprecations heaped by the Vedic hymn-singer on the head of the half mythic, half historical Persic hero, Djaradashti of the Vedas, the first Azar and Zardahusht of the Iranians The western dualistic clans are successful, and drive their half polytheistic, half pantheistic brethren across the Paropamisadae. The darkness which hitherto enshrouded the homes of our ancestors, now clears a little; we see the Eastern Aryans bust into India, driving before them the black aboriginal races; massacring and enslaving them. History repeats itself strangely!

The tide of Aryan conquest continued flowing eastward and southward for centuries. The Aryan colonies were naturally acted upon by the fetishism of the races whom they conquered or among whom they settled; until at last the gross inhuman Sakti worship was produced on the one hand, and the degrading sensualism of Krishna on the other. In the parts, however, which formed the core of the Aryan nation, the thoughts and feelings brought from their native home continued forages to exercise an influence. But soon they were to lose what remained. In the enjoyment of peace and plenty, cut-off from the energetic life of their brothers of the West, always exposed to the voluptuous influences of a morbidly fertile imagination, and without possessing a system of positive morality embodied in effectual laws, the Aryan settlers lost the spiritual belief of their forefathers.

They indeed obtained a code; but it represented the ideas which prevailed in an age of gross materialism.

A revolt ensued, arising from revolutionary and negative instincts acting on one Hindu mind. But Buddhism, with all its grand aspirations, never pretended to be a religion. Essentially adapted to the recluse, it never acquired a tangible hold on the masses; and its failure under the most favourable circumstances sealed its fate in India as a religious system.

On the expulsion of Buddhism from Hindustan, Brahmanism regained its supremacy. The temples became the haunts of debauchery and crimes. Immorality was sanctioned by religion. The demons of destruction and lust became the two favourite objects of popular worship. The revolting orgies of Ashtaroth and Moloch were enacted, under ether names and aspects.

Popular Faiths

The social life of the masses was miserable beyond conception. The condition of women, even during that vague and mythic period which passes under the name of the Vedic age, was not so favourable as some writers on India would fain represent to us now. She formed the prize in gambling and feats of athletics. She was the drudge of the house, and had to accept as many husbands as there were brothers in the family. But she arrived at the depth of degradation under Brahmanic domination. The contempt with which the Brahmanic legislator speaks of women, and the complete servitude to which he subjects them are astounding beyond expression.'

In describing the religious condition of Persia, the empire of the great Chores, we have to enter into more minute details. The proximity of the country to the birthplace of Islam and the powerful influence it has always exercised on Mahommedan thought, not to speak of the character and tone it communicated to Christianity and Judaism, make Persia a most important object of study.

The Aryan race had split into two sections by the migration of one branch across the Paropamisadae; and of the other, towards the great settlements of their Semitic brethren.

As in the Eastern branch, so also among the Western Aryans, the idea of divinity had acquired a degree of consistency and definiteness, probably under the hands of some heaven-inspired genius. The same influences, however, which led to the degradation of the Aryans, were rife among the Iranians. They had either displaced or subjugated the old Turanian tribes who had preceded them in the work of colonization, and the extreme materialism of these Turanians did not fail to degrade the yet undeveloped idealism of their Iranian neighbours. The frequent contact of the followers of Afrasiab and Kai-Kaus, in the field and the hall, exercised a lasting effect on the Persic faith. The complex system of celestial co-ordination which was prevalent among the Assyrians, also left its mark on the Iranians, under the domination of the Peshdadian or Perso-Assyrian sovereigns. Under these influences, the Western Aryans soon found the level of their neighbours The symbolical worship probably in vogue among the early emigrants, became degraded into pyrolatry.

The captivity of the Hebraic tribes and their long exile near the seats of Persian domination, most probably gave impetus to that religious reform which occurred during the reign of Darius Hystaspes. There was mutual action and reaction. The Israelites impressed on renovated Zoroastrianism a deep and abiding conception of a Divine Personality overshadowing the universe. They received from the Iranians the conception of a celestial hierarchy, and the idea of a duality of principles in the creation of good and evil. Thenceforth it is not the Lord who puts a lying spirit into the mouths of evil-doers;Satan, like Ahriman, from this time takes a prominent part in the religious and moral history of the Hebrews.

The reforms effected by the historic Zoroaster, under Darius Hystaspes, seem to have continued in full force for some centuries But his religion at last met with the fate which appears to be the end of every system which does not possess the homogeneity, the practicality, the human sympathy amongst its professors, the absence of all esoteric feelings, which is needful for an universal creed.

The swarms of conquerors, who passed like a whirlwind over the face of that beautiful country before the time of Mohammed, destroyed all social and moral life. The Macedonian conquest with the motley hordes which followed on its footsteps; the influx of all the dregs of Lesser Asia, Cilicians, Tyrians, Pamphylians, and various others, half Greeks half Asians, obeying no moral law; the hasty and reckless temper of the conqueror himself, all led to the debasement of the pure Zoroastrian faith. The Mobeos, the representatives of the national life, were placed under the ban of persecution by the drunken foreigner, the aim of whose life was to he'lenize Asia. Under the Seleucidae, the process of denationalization went on apace. Antiochus Epiphanes, the man who hated the monotheistic Jews, was not likely to allow the idealistic Zoroastrians to remain in peace. Even the rise of the Parthian dynasty tended to accelerate the ruin and decline of Zoroastrianism. In settled and quiet parts it became mixed with the old Sabaeism of the Medes and the Chaldeans, or, where kept alive in its pristine character, it was confined to the hearts of some of those priests who had taken refuge in the inaccessible recesses of their country. Last sad representatives of a dying faith! Around them clustered the hopes of a renovated religious existence under the auspices of the Sassanide dynasty. How far the brilliant aspirations of Ardishir Babekan (Artaxerxes Longimanus), the founder of the new empire, were realized is a matter of history.

The political autonomy of Persia, its national life, was restored; but the social and religious life were lost beyond the power of rulers to restore. The teachings of yore lived perhaps in books; but in the hearts of the people, they were as dead as old Gushtasp or Rustam. The degradation was already complete when Artaxerxes Mnemon (Bahman Ardishir) introduced among the Persians the worship of that androgynous being Mithra, the Persian counterpart of the Chaldean Mylitta or Anaitis, and the concomitant phallic cultus. The climax was reached when Mazdak, in the beginning of the sixth century of the Christian era bade all men to be partners in riches and women, just as they are in fire, water and grass; private property was not to exist; each man was to enjoy or endure the good and bad lots of tills world. The lawfulness of marriage with sisters and other blood-relations had already been recognised by Mago-Zoroastrianism. The proclamation of this frightful communism revolted some of the nobler minds, even among the Persians. The successor of Zoroaster, as Mazdak styled himself, was put to death; but his doctrines had taken root, and from Persia they spread over the West.

All these evils betokened a frightful depravation of moral life and foreshadowed the speedy extinction of the nation in its own iniquities. This doom, though staved off for a tame by the personal character of Kesra Anushirvan, after his death became more and more inevitable. But a Master had already appeared, destined to change the whole aspect of the world.

The series of disasters which one after another had befallen the doomed nation of Moses had culminated in the wars of Titus and of Hadrian. The house of Israel was a total wreck; its members were fugitives on the face of the earth, seeking shelter far and wide, but carrying everywhere their indomitable pride, their rebellious hardness of heart denounced and reprehended by an endless succession of Prophets. The Jews, in their safe retreats in foreign lands, re-enacted the scenes of past times. The nation lived in hope, but the hope was mixed with rigid uncompromising bigotry on the one hand and a voluptuous epicureanism on the other. Jesus had come and gone without producing much visible effect upon them. The Child of his age, he came as the messenger of universal brotherhood and love. In the midst of a proud and exclusive race, he trod the paths of humility and mildness; kind and gentle to his immediate followers, devoted to the cause of all, he left behind him the impress of an elevated self-denying spirit. The want of firmness such as had enabled Moses to strike awe into the hearts of a back sliding rebellious race, made Jesus a victim to the vengeance of the vested interests of his day.

The greatest and by far the most gifted of the disciples of Jesus, was Paul. In spite of the promise attached to the "effusion of the Holy Ghost," it was found necessary that there should be "someone defender of the Gospel who, versed in the learned arts, might be able to combat the Jewish doctors and the pagan philosophers with their own arms. For this purpose Jesus himself, by an extraordinary-voice from heaven, had called to His service a thirteenth apostle, whose name was Saul (afterwards Paul), and whose acquaintance both with Jewish and Grecian learning was very considerable,"' in which the other apostles were sadly wanting. St. Paul indeed did wonders for the Christian Church. He infused into the simple teachings of his Master the most mysterious principles of Neopythagorganism, with its doctrine of intelligences, and its notion of the triad, borrowed from the far East.

The jealousy between the home and the foreign, the Judaical and the anti-Judaical party, was shown in the curious though well-known antipathy of the two Apostles, Peter and Paul. The Ebionites most probably represented the beliefs of the original companions of the prophet Jesus. He had conversed with them familiarly, and "in all the actions of rational and animal life," had appeared to them as of the same nature as themselves. They had marked him grow from infancy to youth and from youth to manhood; they had seen him increase in stature and wisdom. Their belief was tempered by their knowledge of him as a man. The depravation of ideas from this original faith, through various intermediate phases like those of the Docetes, the Marcionites, the Patripassians and various others, to the decisions of the Council of Nice forms a continuous chain. The strangers who had never beheld the manhood, could easily embrace the divinity of Jesus, to which, whether polytheists or philosophers, Greeks or Barbarians, they were already predisposed by their belief, in aeons and emanations.

Reigning Chiefs

With the apparent conversion of Constantine, Christianity became the dominant power in the Roman Empire. The fate of paganism was sealed. Its downfall, though staved off for a time by the greatest and most sincere of the Roman emperors, had become inevitable. Says Gibbon, "the Christians, in peace and piety, might have enjoyed their solitary triumph. But the principle of discord was alive in their bosom, and they were more solicitous to explore the nature than to practise the laws of their founder. We have no heart to enter into the details of their intestine quarrels; their murders, their massacres; the fulsomeness of the language in which they wrangled about the nature of their great Teacher, and of his mother; the terrible denunciations they heaped on each other; we have no heart to dilate upon the dark deeds practised in the court of Byzantium under the sanction of the Church; nor is there any need to do more than merely direct the attention to the quarrels of the monophysites and the monothelites, or to the questions that rent the Christian world with the darkest of all passions, the passion which animates all monopolists, whether spiritual or temporal. Suffice it for us to give a summary of the Christianity of those days in the words of an apologist and a Christian.

"The Bishop of Constantinople was the passive victim, the humble slave, or the factious adversar of the Byzantine Emperor:

rarely exercised a lofty moral control upon his despotism. The lower clergy, whatever their more secret beneficent or sanctifying workings on society, had sufficient power, wealth and rank, to tempt ambition or to degrade to intrigue; not enough to command the public mind for any great salutary purpose; to repress the inveterate immorality of an effete age; to reconcile jarring interests, to mould together hostile races: in general they ruled, when they did rule, by the superstitious fears, rather than by the reverence and attachment of a grateful people. They sank downward into the common ignomace, and yielded to that worst barbarism—a worn-out civilisation. Monasticism withdrew a great number of those who might have been energetic and useful citizens, into barren seclusion and religious indolence; but except when the monks formed themselves, as they frequently did, into fierce political orpolemic factions, they had little effect on the condition of society. They stood aloof from the world—the anchorites in their desert wildernesses, the monks in their jealously-barred convents; and secure, as they supposed, of their own salvation, left the rest of mankind to inevitable perdition."'

Lawlessness was thus the order of the day among the Christians. Instead of taking an example from the lessons of piety, gentleness and humanity inculcated by their great Master, they were animated by the fiercest animosity against each other and against the outside world.

Outside Arabia

The countries included in Asiatic Turkey westward of the Euphrates, devastated alternately by the Parthians and the Romans and then by the Persians and the Byzantines, presented a scene of utter desolation. The moral misery of the people was surpassed by their social ruin. The followers of Jesus, instead of alleviating, intensified the evil. Mago-Zoroastrianism combating with a degraded Christianity in Maesopotamia; the Nestorians engaged in deadly conflict with the orthodox party, the earlier contests of

Montanus and the prophetesses, had converted Western Asia into a frightful Aceldama.

The whirlwinds of conquest which had passed over Africa; the massacres, the murders, the lawlessness of the professors and teachers of the Christian religion, had destroyed every spark of moral life in Egypt and in the African provinces of the decaying empire. In Europe the condition of the people was, if possible, even more miserable. In broad day, under the eyes of the ministers of religion and the people, Narses, the benefactor of his country, was burnt alive in the market-place of Constantinople.' In the streets of Rome, under the eyes of the Exarch, the partisans of rival bishops waged war, and deluged churches with the blood of Christians.

The Jews, chased successively from their native homes by the Assyrians, the Greeks and the Romans, had found among the Arabs safety and protection. But they had brought with their religion the bitter spirit of strife which had caused perhaps the greater portion of their misfortunes. The Nestorians and the Jacobite Christians had also founded colonies in Arabia. The deadly rivalry between these two creeds to dominate over Arabia occasioned sanguinary wars in the most fertile provinces. Magism and Sabaeism had also their representatives among the Arabs, and especially among the Himyarites. But the majority of the people were addicted to fetishism of the grossest type. Animals and plants, the gazelle, the horse, the camel, the palm-tree, inorganic matter like pieces of rock, stones, etc. formed the principal objects of adoration. The idea of a Supreme Divinity, however, was not unrecognised; but its influence was confined to an inappreciable few who, escaping from the bondage of idolatry, betook themselves to a philosophical scepticism more or less tinged with the legendary notions, religious and secular, of their neighbours the Sabeans, the Jews, or the Christians. Among these, some distinctly recognised the conception of a supreme Godhead, and, revolting at the gross materialism of their day, waited patiently for the appearance of a Deliverer who, they felt convinced in their hearts, would soon appear.

Whether the introduction of idolatry in Mecca was late or ancient is wholly irrelevant to the question. The broad fact remains that idolatry was deep-rooted among the Arabs.

Human sacrifices were frequent. Each tribe had its particular idols and particular temples; and often there used to arise sanguinary conflicts between the followers or the worshippers of rival temples. But the prestige of the Kaaba stood unimpeached among all. Even the Jews and the Sabeans sent offerings there. The custody of this tmeple was an object of great jealousy among the tribes, as it conferred on the custodians the most honourable functions and privileges in the sight of the Arabs. At the time of Mohammed's birth, this honour was possessed by his family, and his grandfather was the venerable chief of the theocratic commonwealth which was constituted round the Kaaba.

Such was the moral and religious condition of the Arabs Neither Christianity nor Judaism had succeeded in raising them in the scale of humanity. "After five centuries of Christian evangelisation," says Muir, "we can point to but a sprinkling here and there of Christians—the Bani Harith of Najran; the Bani Hanifa of Yemama; some of the Bani Tay at Tayma; and hardly any more Judaism, vastly more powerful, had exhibited a spasmodic effort of prosefytism under Dzu Nowas; but, as an active and converting agent, the Jewish Faith was no longer operative. In fine, viewed thus in a religious aspect, the surface of Arabiahad been now and then gently rippled by the feeble efforts of Christianity; the stemerinfluences of Judaism had been occasionally visible in a deeper and more troubled current; but the tide of indigenous idolatry and of Ishmaelite superstition, setting from every quarter with an unbroken and unebbing surge towards the Kaaba, gave ample evidence that the faith and worship of Mecca held the Arab mind in a thraldom, rigorous and undisputed.

Politically, the divisions and jealousies of the tribes, combined with the antagonistic feelings which actuate done against the other religious arid race-differences, had enabled the Assyrians, the Babylonians, the Greeks, the Persians and the Abyssinians to become masters of various provinces in the North, in the East, and in the South-West. The Abyssinians had even gone so far as to invade Hijaz with the intention of destroying the national temple. But their power was broken before Mecca by the sturdy patriotism of Abd-ul-Muttalib. After twenty years' oppression, they were driven out of Yemen by a nauve prince, the celebrated Saif, son of Dhu'l-yezen, with the assistance of Persia. On his assassination by the Christians, the sovereignty he had enjoyed under the auspices of the great Anushirvan passed entirely into Persian hands, and Yemen became tributary to Persia.

Besides the direct domination which the rival empires of Constantinople and Ctesiphon exercised over the various provinces of Arabia, two of the greatest chieftains, the kings of Ghassan and of Hira, divided their allegiance between the Caesar and the Chosroes; and the deadly wars, profitless and aimless, which Persian and Byzantine waged against each other, sucking out the life-blood of their people from mere lust of destruction, though often the right was on the side of the Zoroastrian than the Christian, the Ghassanide and Hirite stood face to face in hostile array, or locked in mortal combat.

The heterogeneous elements of which the Arabian peninsula was thus composed gave an extremely varied character to the folk-lore of the country. Among uncultured nations, the tendency always is to dress facts in the garb of legends. Imagination among them not only lends enchantment to the view, but magnifies distant objects.And the variety of culture multiplies legends, more or less based on facts. The Hamitic colonies of Yemen and of the south-west generally; the true Semites who followed in their footsteps, like the Aryans in the East; the Jews, the Christians, all brought their traditions, their myths, their legends with them. In the course of ages, these relics of the Past acquired a consistency and a character; but however unsubstantial in appearance, on analysis there is always to be found underlying them a stratum of fact. In the legend of Sheddad and his garden of lrem, we see in the hazy Past the reflexion of a mighty empire, which even conquered Egypt, –"of a wealthy nation, constructors of great buildings, with an advanced civilisation analogous to that of Chaldaea, professing a religion similar to the Babylonian; a nation in short, with whom material progress was allied to great moral depravity and obscene rites." In the traditional, half-legendary, half-historic destruction of the Adites and the Thamudites, we see the destructive fate which overwhelmed these Hamitic races before the Semitic tide, Assyrian and Arab.

The children of Jacob, flying from their ruthless enemies, brought their legends and traditions with them, and thus furnished their quota to the folklore of the peninsula. The last of the Semitic colonies who had entered Arabia were recognised by themselves as well as their neighbours as descended from Abraham; and tradition had handed down this belief and given it a shape and a character.

Manicheism, stamped out from Persia and the Byzantine dominions, had betaken itself to Arabia. The early Docetes, the Marcionites, the Valentinians, all had their representatives in this land of freedom. They all disseminated their views and traditions, which in course of time became intermixed with the traditions of the country. These Christians, more consistent in their views than their orthodox persecutors, believed that the God incarnate, or at least the Son of God, His Word, born in the bosom of eternity, an Emanation issuing from the Throne of Light, could not, did not die on the cross; that the words of agony which orthodox Christian traditions put into the mouth of Jesus, did not, and could not escape from his lips; in short, that the man who suffered on the cross was a different person from the Divine Christ who escaped from the hands of his persecutors and went away to the regions whence he had come.' This doctrine, however fanciful, was more consistent with the idea of the Sonship of Jesus; and in itself appears to have been based on some strong probabilities. The intense desire of Pilate, whom Tertullian calls a Christian, at heart, to save Jesus, even the unwillingness of Herod to incur more odium by the murder of the blessed Prophet of Nazareth; the darkness of the short hours when that great benefactor of humanity was led forth for the consummation of the frightful scenes which had continued all night long; the gloom which over shadowed the earth at the most awful part of this drama; all these coincident circumstances lend a strong probability to the belief that the innocent escaped and the guilty suffered.

Before the advent of Mohammed, all these traditions, based on fact though tinged by the colourings of imagination, must have become firmly embedded in the convictions of the people, and formed essential parts of the folk-lore of the country. Mohammed, therefore, when promulgating his faith and his laws, found these traditions floating among his people; he took them up and adopted them as the lever for raising the Arabs as well as the surrounding nations from the depth of social and moral degradation into which they had fallen.

3

Before Prophethood

Mohammed was born of noble parentage; the family of Hashim was the noblest amongst the Koreish; his grandfather Abd-ul-Muttalib was the custodian of the Kaaba. The same year which saw the destruction of the Abyssinian invaders, and which formed an epoch in the history of the Arabs,' witnessed the birth of Mohammed. He was born on the 12th of Rabi-ul-Awwal (Rabil), (now forming the third month of the Moslem calendar,) in the 40th year of the reign of Chosroes the Great, Kesra Anushirvan, the magnificent and successful rival of Justinian.

He missed all the parental care which forms the blessings of childhood. His father had died before he was born. He was bereft of his mother, when only six years of age. The charge of the orphan child fell to his grandfater, who loved him dearly. On his death-bed Abd-ul-Muttalib confided his young charge to his son Abu Taleb, a nuterine brother of Abdullah, the father of Mohammed.

In the house of Abu Taleb, Mohammed passed his early life. Endowed with the most amiable qualities, he won the affections of all who came in contact with him, A touching incident of the attachment subsisting between nephew and uncle is preserved by Moslem historians. Abu Taleb determined to make a journey to Syria, leaving Mohammed with his own children at Mecca. When

Abu Taleb was on the point of mounting his camel, Mohammed clasped his knees and cried, "O my uncle, take me with thee. "The heart of Abu Taleb melted within him and the little orphan nephew joined the commercial expedition of his uncle. They travelled together into Syria. During one of the halts, at a place called Busra, they met an Arab monk of the name of Bahira who, struck by the signs of future grandeur and intellectual and moral qualities of the highest type on the countenance of the orphan child of Abdullah, recognised in him the liberator and saviour of his country and people. He impressed his convictions on Abu Taleb, and enjoined him to guard his charge with the tenderest care from the paths of danger and the machinations of his enemies.

Very soon after, the sacrilegious wars of the Fijar broke out between the Koreish and the Bani-Hawazin which lasted with interruptions for nine years. In two of the contests Mohammed, though only fourteen or fifteen, accompanied his uncles in this tribal war; and proved himself a worthy descendant of the sturdy and patriotic defender of the Kaaba.

From this time till the twenty-fifth year of his age, Mohammed scarcely appears in public life. His kindliness of heart, and his gentleness of manners, combined with his fidelity, his honesty, his truth, and his unsullied character, had acquired for him the goodwill and affection of all his fellow-people, and the surname of al-Amin, "the True." In the twenty-fifth year of his age, Mohammed had occasion to travel once more into Syria, in charge of the merchandise of his kinswoman Khadija, a rich widow lady of the tribe of Koreish. The faithful prudence and exalted probity with which he discharged the trust reposed in him created a deep feeling of gratitude in the bosom of Khadija. A marriage was soon arranged between Mohammed and his noble kinswoman which was solemnised amidst universal approbation. The bride was given away by her own uncle, Amr ben Asad, her father Khuwailid having died before or during the wars of the Fijar.

This marriage acquired for Mohammed great consideration among his compatriots. He loved his wife devotedly and watched her with the most tender care. He managed her affairs and looked after her interests with unrivalled prudence. When Halima, his nurse, came to him and told him her poverty, he solicited for her the benevolence of Khadija, who gave the old and poor Bedouin woman a flock of forty sheep.' As long as Khadija lived, he never availed himself of the Arab custom of taking several wives. During her lifetime his love was unswerving; after her death he never recalled her memory but with the deepest emotion. Raised above the common cares of life by the gratitude and affection of Khadija, he devoted himself entirely to meditation and spiritual communion with God.

As yet Mohammed was a stranger to the outside world. He now added to his reputation among his fellow-men by taking a prominent part in the resuscitation of an old league called the Federation of the Fudhul (Hilf-ul-Fudhul), formed in ancient times for the repression of acts of lawlessness within the walls of Mecca. Such deeds of oppression and reckless audacity had become terribly frequent; and acts were done in broad daylight at which every soul possessed of a spark of humanity revolted and shuddered. This led to a new compact between four or five of the chief families of Mecca for the protection of the weak and the oppressed. Mohammed was one of the most prominent movers in this federation, the revival of which mainly resulted from his efforts.

In his thirty-fifth year, he settled by his decision a grave difficulty which had sprung up during the reconstruction of the Kaaba regarding the placing of the sacred stone, and which almost threatened to plunge the tribes into another of their ever recurring wars.

Pious Actions

But history will always remember him during this period for an act of patriotism the deep significance of which has been overlooked by all our historians excepting Ibn-Khaldun. Just before the reconstruction of the Kaaba, Mecca had been saved from a conspiracy to rob her of her independence. Othman, son of

Huwairith, an Arab who had embraced Christianity in the court of Constantinople, had come to Hijaz, backed by Byzantine gold, to throw Mecca into the hands of the Greeks. His design was exposed and the conspiracy proved abortive, Uefly through the exertions of Mohammed. The Western world lauds, till the heart grows sick, the successful exposure of Catiline by Cicero; the foul deed of Brutus assassinating his benefactor; or the murders committed by the two Athenian youths, as the greatest achievements in the history of freedom. But the merit of Mohammed, in saving his birthplace from falling under the yoke of the miserable despots of Byzantium, must always deserve the thanks of humanity. Mohammed had thus already served his country faithfully. He had tried also to discharge some of the debt of gratitude and obligation he owed his uncle Abu Taleb, by charging himself with the education of Ali, one of his sons. Abu Taleb who had a large family, had not the means of bringing them up as they deserved. Mohammed, rich by his alliance with Khadija, and Abbas, the brother of AbuTaleb, were the most opulent citizens of Mecca. During a severe famine which afflicted the country, Mohammed persuaded his uncle Abbas to adopt one of the sons of Abu Taleb, whilst he adopted another. Thus Abbas took Jafar; Ali; and Akil remained with their father. Mohammed had lost all his sons in early infancy. In the love of Alt, he found consolation for their loss; and the future marriage of the son of Abu Taleb with the youngest daughter of Mohammed, Fatima, sealed the bond of love and devotedness.

Mohammed had also about this time set an example to his fellow-citizens by an act of humanity hardly surpassed by any recorded in history. A young Arab of the name of Zaid, son of Harith, was made captive by a hostile tribe and sold to a nephew of Khadija, who presented him to her. Mohammed, struck by the gentleness of Zaid, asked him as a gift from Khadija; and the moment he was made over to him, Mohammed enfranchised the young boy. Sometime after, Zaid's father, who was tenderly attached to his son, came to Mecca in order to ransom him. Mohammed said to Zaid, he was free to remain with him or go with his father; and young Zaid preferred to remain with his benefactor.' But whether engaged in these acts of benevolence or in assisting his fellow-citizens to frustrate the plans of conspirators, or to settle public questions, the mind of Mohammed was always busy on the future destiny of his race. His two visits to Syria had opened to him a scene of moral and social misery beyond conception. Before him lay his own country, and he beheld his people sunk in absolute barbarism. His noble heart bled for degraded humanity. With the keen foresight of an inspired Teacher, he saw that every hope of social and political improvement rested on a moral regeneration.

Whether in the bosom of his family or in the depth of solitude, he passed his time in profound meditation. Solitude had indeed become a passion with him. Every year, the month of Ramadhan he spent with his family on the mount of Hira, devoting his time entirely to prayer and to the succour of the poor and famished wayfarers who came to him.' Here he often remained whole nights plunged in the profoundest thought, deep in communion with the unseen yet all-pervading God of the Universe. The poetry of the soul can go no further, when it is said, he heard even the stones and rocks and trees, calling on him to fulfil the task an Almighty Power was directing him to undertake. The mental visions and the apparitions of angels at these moments were the bright though gradual dawnings of those Truths with which he was to vivify the world. Often in the dark and benighted pathways of concrete existence, the soul of every great man has been conscious of unrealised yet not unseen influences, which have led to some of the happiest achievements of humanity. From Samuel, that ancient seer, wild and awful as he stands there, deep in the misty horizon of the Past, to Jesus in the wilderness pondering over the darksome fate of his people and the magnitude of his work, listening to the sweet accents of the God of Truth;—from Jesus to Mohammed in the solitude of his mountain-retreat,there is no break in the action of these Influences.In the still hours of the night, in the sweet calmness of the early dawn, in the depth of solitude when no human sympathy is near, a Voice comes to him from heaven gently as the sough of the gentlest breeze, "Thou art the Man, Thou art the Prophet of God;" or when wrapt in sleep, it comes in mighty waves, "Cry in the name of the Lord " The over-wrought mind at these moments raises a Vision before the eye, a Vision of the celestial ministrants who are believed to form the medium of intercommunication between the God of heaven and the man on earth. 'The Father of Truth chooses His own prophets, and He speaks to them in a voice stronger than the voice of thunder. It is the same inner voice through which God speaks to all of us". That voice may dwindle away, and become hardly audible; it may lose its divine accent and sink into the language of worldly prudence; but it may also from time to time assume its real nature with the chosen of God, and sound in their ears as a Voice from "Heaven."

We can appreciate the severe mental conflicts, the intensity of feeling, which wrung the heart of Mohammed, when we are told that before he had himself realised his Mission, he was almost driven to the verge of suicide, when a voice from within,—a Voice which proceeded from the Author of the Universe who had selected him for the salvation of his people—recalled him to his duty to mankind.

His was not the communion with God of those egoists who bury themselves in deserts or forests, and live a life of quietude for themselves alone. His was the hard struggle of the man who is led on-wards by a nobler destiny towards the liberation of his race from the bondage of idolatry. His destiny was unfolded to him, when wrapped in profound meditation, melancholy and sad, he felt himself called by that Voice from Heaven, which had called those who had gone before him, to arise and preach,—"O thou, enwrapped in thy mantle, arise and warn, and "glorify thy Lord." And he arose and girded himself for the work to which he felt himself called. Thenceforth his life is devoted to humanity. Preaching with unswerving purpose amidst frightful persecutions, insulted and outraged, he held on in his path of reproof and reform.

Faith in God

Khadija was the first to believe in him and his mission. When he had confided to her sorrowfully and despondingly, the early struggles which preceded the enlightenment of his mind by divine truths, she consoled him and expressed to him her belief that he would be the chosen one for regenerating his people. Now that his mission was revealed, she was the first to abandon the idolatry other people, and to join with him in purity of heart in offering up prayers to the All-Merciful.

In the beginning Mohammed opened his soul only to those who were attached to him, and tried to wean them from the gross practices of their fore -fathers. After Khadija, Ali was the first to believe in the mission of Mohammed. Often did the Prophet go into the depths of the solitary villages around Mecca, with his wife and young counsin, that they might together offer up their heartfelt thanks to the God of all nations for his manifold blessings Once they were surprised in the attitude of prayer by Abu Taleb, the father of Ali: And he said to Mohammed, "O son of my brother, what is this "religion that thou art following?" "It is the religion of God, of His angels, of His prophets and of our ancestor Abraham," answered the Prophet,"—"God has sent me to His servants to direct them towards the Truth; and thou, O my uncle, art the most worthy of all. It is meet that I should thus call upon thee, and it is meet that thou shouldn't accept the Truth and help in spreading it." "Son of "my brother," replied Abu Taleb, in the true spirit of the sturdy old Semite, "I cannot abjure the religion of my fathers; but by the Supreme God, "whilst I am alive none shall dare to injure thee." Then turning towards Ali, his son, the venerable patriarch enquired what religion was his: "O father," answered Ali, "I believe in God and His Prophet and go with him." "Follow him," said Abu Taleb, "he will invite thee to nothing but what is good."

Soon after Zaid, the son of Harith, who notwithstanding his freedom had cast in his lot with Mohammed, became a convert to the new faith. He was followed by a leading member of the Koreish community, of the name of Abdullah, son of Abu Kuhafa, who afterwards became famous in history as Abu-Bakr. His influence drew several other converts to the new faith, and the Prophet had the satisfaction of seeing his followers increase in number. It is a noble feature in the history of the Prophet of Arabia, and one which strongly attests the inspired character of his teachings and the intensity of his faith and trust in God, that his nearest relations, his wife, his beloved cousin, and intimate friends were most thoroughly imbued with the truth of his mission and convinced of his inspiration. Those who knew him best, who lived with him and noted all his movements, were his most sincere and devoted followers. If these men and women, noble, intelligent, and certainly not less educated than the fishermen of Galilee, had perceived the slightest sign of earthliness, deception, or want of faith in the Teacher himself, Mohammed's hopes of moral regeneration and social reform would all have been dashed to pieces in a moment. They braved for him persecutions and dangers; they bore up against physical tortures and mental agony caused by social excommunication, even unto death. Would they have done this, had they perceived the slightest backsliding in their master? But even if these people had not believed in Mohammed with such earnest faith and trust, it would furnish no reason for doubting the greatness of his work or the depth of his sincerity. For the influence of Jesus himself was least among his nearest relatives. His brothers never believed in him, and once they even went so far as to endeavour to obtain possession of his person, believing him to be out of his mind. Even his immediate disciples were not firm in their convictions. Perhaps this unsteadiness may have arisen from weakness of character, or it may have resulted, as Milman thinks, from the varying tone of Jesus himself; but that it is a fact is undeniable.This intense faith and conviction on the part of the immediate followers of Mohammed is the noblest testimony to the purity of his motives and the truth of his doctrine.

For three years he laboured thus, quietly to wean his people from the worship of idols. At last, he determined to assemble all his kinsmen in his house, in order to explain his mission to them. They came; but mocked his efforts, and taunted Abu Taleb about the enthusiasm of his son on behalf of Mohammed. Having thus failed to make any impression on his kinsmen, he commenced preaching openly to all his people. Little success attended these efforts. But his denunciations of their idols, his reproofs, his vehement exposure of the grossness of their worship lashed the Koreish into fury, as the reproofs of Jesus had roused the anger of the Jews in Sanhedrim before. Several times they sent deputations to AbuTaleb, asking him to stop his nephew from preaching against their religion. At first, Abu Tableb turned them away with soft and courteous words. But as Mohammed grew firmer in exposing the weakness of their idols, they expelled him from the Kaaba where he was preaching, and then came in a body to his uncle "We respect thy age and thy rank," said they, "but our respect for thee has bounds; and "verily, we can have no further patience with thy "nephew's abuse of our gods, and his ill-words against our ancestors; wherefore, do thou either prevent him from so doing, or thyself take part with him, so that we may settle the matter by fight, until one of the two parties is exterminated." Having thus spoken, they departed. Abu Taleb was unwilling to separate himself from his people, neither did he like abandoning his nephew to the tender mercies of the idolaters. Sending for Mohammed, he informed him of the speech of the Koreish, and begged him to renounce the task he had undertaken. Mohammed thought his uncle wished to with draw his protection: but his high resolve did not fail him. "Even at this moment," Firmly he replied: "O my "uncle, if they placed the Sun on my right hand, and "the Moon on my left, to force me to renounce my "work, verily I would not desist therefrom until God "made manifest His cause, or I perished in the attempt." "But the thought of desertion by his kind "protector overcame him." He burst into tears, and turned to depart. Then Abu Taleb called aloud: "Son of my brother, come back and he came. And Abu Taleb said: "Say whatsoever thou "pleasest; for by the Lord, I shall not abandon thee, "nay never.The Koreish made another attempt to persuade Abu Taleb to deliverup his nephew to them. They offered, in exchange, a young man of the family of Makhzum, but it was of no avail The declared intention of Abu Taleb to support his nephew excited their fury, and they renewed their menaces of violence. The venerable patriarch appealed to the sense of honour and pride of the Bani-Hashim, the kinsmen of Mohammed, to protect a distinguished member of their family from falling a victim to the hatred of rival clans. Abu Taleb's energetic appeal was nobly responded to by the Hashimites, with the exception of Abu Laheb, "the father of flame".

The fury of the Koreish, however, increased every day; and though, in the beginning, the powerful influence of Abu Taleb had the effect of warding off an immediate attempt on the life of Mohammed, yet the outrages, to which he and his disciples were exposed, were fearful. The hostile Koreish followed him wherever he went; they threw stones at him and his disciples when engaged in their devotions; they threw dirt on him during his meals. They stopped him from offering his prayers near the Kaaba. They organised a regular system of persecution; each family taking upon itself the task of strangling the new religion among its members. The hill of Ramdha and the place called Batha bacame thus the scenes of cruel tortures. The men or women whom the Koreish found abandoning the worship of their idol-gods, were exposed by them to the bumingheat of the desert, where when reduced to the last extremity by hunger and thirst, they were offered the alternative of adoring the idols or death. Some recanted; but the majority held firmly to their faith.They killed with excruciating torments Yasar and Samiya, his wife; they inflicted fearful tortures on Ammar, their son. Mohammed was often an eyewitness of the sufferings of his disciples, sufferings borne with patience and endurance as became martyrs in the cause of Truth. And these were not the only martyrs in the early history of Islam. Like the Pharisees tempting Jesus, the Koreish even came to Mohammed with temptations of worldly honour and worldly aggrandisement, in order to draw him from the path of his duty. One day, says the chronicler, he was sitting in the mosque of Hijr, at a little distance from an assembly of the opposing chiefs, when one of them, Otba, son of Rabia, came to him and said to the Prophet, "O son of my brother, thou art distinguished by thy qualities and thy descent. Now thou hast sown division among our people and cast dissension in our families; thou denouncest our gods and goddesses; thou dosttax our ancestors with impiety. We have a proposition to make to thee; think well if it will not suit thee to accept it." "Speak, "O father of Walid, said the Prophet, "I listen." "O son of my brother, if thou wishest to acquire riches by this affair, we will collect a fortune larger than is possessed by any of us; if thou desirest honours and dignity, we shall make thee our chief and shall not do a thing without thee; if thou desirest dominion, we shall make thee our King; and if the spirit (demon) which possesses thee cannot be overpowered, we will bring thee doctors and give them riches till they cure "thee."And when he had done, "Hast thou finished, O father of Walid," asked the Prophet. "Yes," replied he. "Then listen to me." "I listen," he said.

> "In the name of the most merciful God. This is a revelation from the most Merciful: a Book the verses whereof are distinctly explained, an Arabic Koran, for the instruction of people who understand; bearing good tidings, and denouncing threats: but the greater part of them turn aside, and hearten not thereto. And they say, "Our hearts are veiled from the doctrine to which thou invitest us; and there is a deafness in our ears, and a curtain between us and thee: wherefore act thou, as thou shall think fit; for we shall act according to our own sentiments" "Say, Verily I am only a man like you. It is revealed unto me that your God is one God: wherefore direct your way straight unto Him; and ask pardon of Him for what is past. And woe be to the idolaters; who give not the appointed alms, and believe not in the life to come! But as to those who believe and work righteousness, they shall receive an everlasting reward." When the Prophet finished this recitation, he said to Otba, 'Thou hast heard, now take the course which seemeth best to thee."

Profoundly afflicted by the persecution of his disciples, whose position every day became more and more unbearable, he advised them to go to Abyssinia and remain there, till some change for the better occurred in the feelings of the Koreish. Some immediately availed themselves of the advice, and sailed, to the number of fifteen, to the hospitable shores of Abyssinia. This is called the first Flight in the history of Islam. These emigrants were soon joined by many more of their fellow-sufferers and labourers in the cause of Truth, until their number amounted to eighty-two or eighty three men and eighteen women But the untiring hostility of the Koreish did not allow them rest or peace even here. The Koreish sent deputies to the King of Abyssinia (Najashi, Negus) to demand the delivery of these refugees in order to put them to death. They stated the chief charges against them to be their abjuration of the old religion and their adoption of a new one. The king sent for the exiles and enquired of them, whether what their enemies had stated was true "What is this religion for which you have abandoned your former faith?" asked the king, "and adopted neither mine nor that of any other people.".Jafar, son of Abu Taleb, and brother of Ali, acting as spokesman for the whole body of emigrants, spoke thus:—

> "O King, We were plunged in the depth of ignorance and barbarism—we adored idols; we ate dead bodies; and we spoke abominations; we disregarded every feeling of humanity, and the duties of hospitality and neighbourhood; we knew no law but that of the strong, when God raised among us a man, of whose birth, truthfulness, honesty and purity we were aware; and he called us to the Unity of God, and taught us not to associate anything with Him;he forbade us the worship of idols, and enjoined us to speak the truth; to be faithful to our trusts; to be merciful and to regard the rights of neighbours; he forbade us to speak evil of women, or to eat the substance of orphans; he ordered us to fly vices, and to abstain from evil; to offer prayers, to render alms, to observe the fast. We have believed in him, we have accepted his teachings and his injunctions to worship God and not to associate anything with Him. For this reason, our people have risen against us, have persecuted us in order to make us forgo the worship of God and to return to the worship of idols of wood, and other abominations. They have tortured and injured us, until finding no safety among them, we have come to thy country, and hope thou wilt protect us from their oppression."

The demands of the Koreish were scouted by the king, and the deputies returned in confusion to Mecca.

Here, we may pause for a moment in the course of our history, and recognise the deep significance of this touching episode. The words of Jafar contain a comprehensive summary of the entire teachings of Mohammed. No person has ever succeeded in equalling the burning enthusiasm of that man, pleading the cause of his fellow-religionists and persecuted kinsmen.

Whilst the disciples of Mohammed were seeking safety in other lands from the persecution of their enemies, he himself stood bravely at his post, and amidst every opprobrium, insult and outrage pursued his mission. Again they came to him with promises of honour and riches in order to seduce him from his duty; the reply was as before, full of life, full of faith.

> "I am neither desirous of riches, nor ambitious of dignity, nor of dominion; I am sent by God, who has ordained me to announce glad tidings unto you. I give you the words of my Lord; I admonish you. If you will accept what I bring you, there is happiness for you in this world and in the next; if you reject my admonitions, I shall be patient, and leave God to judge between you and me."

> They asked for miracles to prove his mission. Remark his reply. "God has not sent me to you to work wonders He has sent me to preach to you. If you will accept what I bring you, you will have happiness in this world and the next. If you reject my admonitions, I shall be patient, and God will judge between you and me."

The sublimity of these words have been hardly recognised even to the present day. Disclaiming every power of wonder working, Mohammed rests the truth of his divine commission entirely upon his teachings. "Listen to what say, and happy will be your lothere and hereafter" is his invariable appeal to his hostile and idolatrous people. "I am but a man like you,"he says, "but I bring you hope fill tidings."The answer he receives breathes a fierce animosity paralleled only by the darkest days of Arian or Pelagian presecution in Christendom. "Know this, O Mohammed," said they, "we shall never cease to stop "thee from preaching, till either thou or we perish."

Supported, however, by a firm conviction in Divine assistance, and upheld by the admonitions of the heavenly voice within, which he believed, in the sincerity of his heart, to be the voice of God, conveyed to him by the ministrators of heavenly mercy, he coutinued his preaching undeterred by the hostility of his enemies, or by the injuries they inflicted upon him. In spite of all opposition, however, slowly, but surely, the new teachings gained ground. The seeds of truth thus scattered could not fail to fructify. The wild Arab of the desert, the trading citizen of distant townships, who came to the national fair, heard the words of the strange man, whom his enemies thought possessed, listened to the admonitions, in which he poured forth his soul; listened with awe and wonder his denunciations of their divinities of wood and stone, and of their superstitions; and carried back to distant homes new light and new life, even unconsciously to themselves. The satires, the ill-names his enemies heaped upon Mohammed tended to make his words more extensively known. A Yathrebite wrote to the Koreish of Mecca, and holding up the examples of bygone ages, exhorted them not to become embroiled with civil dissensions and warfare. He also advised them to give a hearing to the new preacher:—

"An honourable man has adopted a certain religion, why persecute him? for it is only the Lord of the heavens who can read the heart of man! Follow the true religion: our eyes are fixed on you; they follow the right track who keep always in view the highest points."

About this time, also, Mohammed had the satisfaction of seeing his uncle, Hamza, and the well known Omar, both men of great energy, adopted his religion. Hamza, indeed, was the prototype of Ali in bravery, generosity, and chivalrous grandeur of character.

The accession of strength brought to the new faith, by the loss of Abu Taleb and Khadija, in the same year, (619-620A.C.). The venerable chief of the Bani-Hashim had stood faithfully by his nephew. For three consecutive years previous to his death he and his kinsmen—the children of Hashim and his brother, Muttalib,—had been beleaguered in their own quarter, and subjected to every privation by the Koreish in order to force them to deliver up Mohammed. This siege was the result of a regular league among the various families opposed to the Prophet. Reduced to the last extremities for want of provisions and water, the Bani-Hashim were only saved by the breaking-up of the league against them in consequence of external dissensions.

Abu Taleb did not survive this event many months; and in him Mohammed lost, not only the head of the family, who had kept it united, but a protector who had hitherto shielded him from the fury of his enemies. The death of Khadija was a loss equally severe. In the hard struggles of life; in the many afflictions and trials which he had to undergo. she was his sole comforter; and her death, following immediately upon that of Abu Taleb, fell heavily on Mohammed.

The death of Abu Taleb became the signal for the Koreish to redouble their persecutions. The family of Hashim, deprived of its head, could not afford an efficacious protection to Mohammed. The injuries and outrages to which he had been already exposed were renewed with increased fury.

Weighed down by the loss of his venerable protector and of his cherished wife, hopeless of turning the Koreish from idolatry, he determined to proceed to Tayef, and preach to its inhabitants the unity of God. Accompanied by his faithful servant Zaid, the son of Harith, he arrived among the Thakif. But, instead of making a favourable impression, his words roused their fury: they drove him from the city; and the rabble and the slaves followed, hooting and pelting him with stones until the evening, when they left him to pursue his way alone. Wounded and bleeding, footsore and weary, he betook himself to prayer under the shade of some palm trees, which afforded a welcome shelter to the thirsty and famished wayfarer. Raising his hands towards heaven, and with tears streaming from his eyes, he cried:

> "O Lord! I make my complaint unto Thee out of my feebleness and the vanity of my wishes. I am insignificant in the sight of men. O Thou Most Merciful! Lord of the weak! Thou art my Lord. Do not forsake me. Leave me not a prey to strangers, nor to mine enemies. If thou art not offended, I am safe. I seek refuge in the light of Thy countenance, by which all darkness is dispersed, and peace comes here and hereafter. Let not Thy anger descend on me; solve my difficulties as it pleaseth Thee. There is no power, no help, but in Thee."

Mohammed returned to Mecca, sorely stricken in heart. He lived there for some time, retired from his people, preaching occasionally, but confining his efforts mainly of strangers congregated in Mecca, and its vicinity, during the season of the annual pilgrimage; hoping, as Tabari expresses it, to find among them some who would believe in him, and carry the truth to their people.

One day, whilst thus sadly and sorrowfully, but yet hopefully working among these half-traders, half-pilgrims, he came upon a group of six men, from the distant city of Yathreb, conversing together. He asked them to sit down and listen to him; and they sat down, and listened. Struck by his earnestness, and the truth of his words they became his proselytes, (620A.C.); and, returning to their city, they spread the news, with lightning-rapidity, that a Prophet had risen among the Arabs, who was to call them to God, and put an end to their dissensions which had lasted for centuries.

Next year these Yathrebites returned, and brought six more of their fellow-citizens as deputies from the two principal tribes who occupied that city.

On the self-same spot which had witnessed the conversion of the former six, the new-comers gave in their adhesion to Mohammed. This is called the first Pledge of Akaba, from the name of the hill on which the conference was held .

The Pledge they took was as follows:—

> "We will not associate anything with God; we will not steal; nor commit adultery, nor fornication; we will not kill our children; we will abstain from calumny and slander; we will obey the Prophet in everything that is right; and we will be faithful to him in weal and in sorrow"

After the Pledge, they returned home with a disciple of Mohammed to teach them the fundamental doctrines of the new religion, which rapidly spread among the inhabitants of Yathreb.

The interval which elapsed between the first and second Pledge is remarkable, as, one of the most critical periods of Mohammed's mission. The sublime trust of Mohammed in God, and the grandeur of his character never stand forth more prominently than at this period. He was sad at the sight of his people so sternly wedded to idolatry; but his sorrow was assuaged by the hope that the truth would in the end prevail. He might not live to see it; but as surely as darkness flies before the rays of the sun, so surely falsehood would vanish before truth. Regarding this epoch, a few words of unconscious admiration escape even the lips of Muir: "Mahomet, thus holding his people at bay; waiting, in the still expectation of victory, to outward appearance defenceless, and with his little hand as it were in the lion's mouth; yet, trusting in His Almighty power, whose mesenger he believed himself to be, resolute and unmoved; —presents a spectacle of sublimity, paralleled only in the Sacred Records by such scenes as that of the Prophet of Israel, when he complained to his Master, 'I, even I only, am left."

This period is also remarkable for that notable vision of the ascension, which has furnished worlds of golden dreams for the imaginative genius of poets and traditionists. They have woven beautiful and gorgeous legends round the simple words of the Koran: "Praise be to Him who carried His servant "by night from the sacred temple to the temple that is more remote, whose precincts we have blessed, that we might show him some of our signs! For He is the Hearer, the Seer." And again: "And remember we said to thee, verily, thy Lord is round about mankind; we ordained the vision which we showed thee." "All that Mohammedans must believe respecting the Meraj is, that the Prophet saw himself, in a vision," transported from Mecca to Jerusalem", and that in such vision he really beheld some of the greatest signs of his Lord. It must be evident to the reader that the visions also of a prophet are a mode of divine inspiration."

The following year (622 B.C.) the Yathrebites, who had adopted the new religion, repaired to Mecca, to the number of seventy-five, in company with their idolatrous brethren, to invite the Prophet to their city;- but the idolaters had no knowledge of the intention of their companions.

The Pillars

In the stillness of night, when all hostile elements appeared slumbering, these pioneers of the new faith met tunder the hill which had witnessed the first Pledge. Mohammed appeared among them, accompanied by his uncle Abbas, who, though not a convert, yet took a warm interest in the progress of Islam. He opened the conference and vividly described to the Yathrebites the risks they incurred by adopting Islam, and inviting its teacher to their city. They replied with one voice they adopted the religion though conscious of the dangers that surrounded them. "Speak, O Prophet of God," said they, "and exact any pledge for thyself and thy

"Lord." The Prophet began, as was his wont, by reciting several passages of the Koran; he then invited all present to the service of God, and dwelt upon the blessings of the new dispensation. The former Pledge was repeated, that they would worship none but God—that they would observe the precepts of Islam—that they would obey Mohammed in all that was right, and defend him and his even as they would their women and children. "And," said they, "if we die in the cause of God, what shall "be our return?" "Happiness hereafter," was the reply. "But," said they, "thou will not leave us in the hour of prosperity, to return to thy people?" The Prophet smiled and said: "Nay, never; your blood is my blood; I am yours, you are mine" "Give us then thy hand;" and each one, placing his hand on the Prophet's hand, swore allegiance to him and his God. Scarcely had the compact been concluded, when the voice of a Meccan, who had been watching this scene from a distance, came floating on the night air, striking a sudden panic into the self-denying hearts there assembled. The firm words of Mohammed restored their presence of mind.

The Allegiance

Mohammed then selected twelve men from among them,—men of position, pointed out to him by the voice of the people, as his delegates (Nakibas).Thus was concluded the second Pledge of Akaba.

The Meccan spy had already spread the news of this conference through the city. Astounded at the temerity of Mohammed and his followers, the Koreish proceeded in a body to the caravan of the Yathrebites, to demand the men who had entered into the Pledge with him. Finding no clue, however, as to the persons who had taken part at the meeting, they allowed the caravan to depart unmolested. But this apparent moderation on the part of the Koreish formed only a prelude to a furious persecution of Mohammed and his disciples. The position of the latter became every day more and more perilous. The Prophet, fearing a general massacre, advised his followers to seek immediate safety at Yathreb; whereupon, about one hundred families. silently disappeared by twos and threes from Mecca, and proceeded to Yathreb, where they were received with enthusiasm. Entire quarters of the city thus became deserted; and Otba, the son of Rabia, at the sight of these vacant abodes, once so full of life, "sighed heavily," and recited the old verse: "Every dwelling-place, even if it has been blessed ever so long, will one day become a prey to unhappiness and bitter wind." "And" he sorrowfully added, "all this is the work of the son of our brother, who has scattered our assemblies, ruined our affairs, and created dissension amongst us."

As it was with Jesus, so it was with Mohammed; only with this difference, that in one case the Teacher himself says: "Think not that I came to send peace on earth; I came not to send peace, but a sword: for I am come to set a man at variance against his father, and the daughter against her mother, and the daughter-in-law against her mother-in law." In Mohammed's case it is one of his most persevering opponents who accuse him of creating dissension in families.

But throughout this period, when the storm was at its height and might at any moment burst over his head, Mohammed never quailed. All his disciples had left for Yathreb; alone he remained, bravely at his post, with the devoted Ali and the venerable Abu Bakr.

Meanwhile the clouds were gathering fast. Fearful of the escape of the Prophet, an assembly of the Koreish met in all dispatch in the town-hall (*Dar-un-Nedwa*), and some chiefs of other clans were invited to attend. The matter had become one of life and death. Stormy was the meeting, for fear had entered their hearts. Imprisonment for life, expulsion from the city, each was debated in turn. Assassination was then proposed; but assassination by one man would have exposed him and his family to the vengeance of blood. The difficulty was at last solved by Abu Jahl, who suggested that a number of courageous men, chosen from different families should sheathe their swords simultaneously in Mohammed's bosom, in order that the responsibility of the deed might rest upon all, and the relations of Mohammed might consequently be unable to avenge it. This proposal was accepted, and a number of noble youths were selected for the sanguinary deed. As the night advanced, the assassins posted themselves round the Prophet's house. Thus they watched all night long, waiting to kill him when he should leave his house early in the dawn, peeping now and then through a hole in the door to make sure that he still lay on his bed. But, meanwhile, the instinct of self-preseivation, the instinct which had often led the great Prophet of Nazareth to evade his enemies, had warned Mohammed of the danger. In order to keep the attention of the assassins fixed upon the bed, he put his own green garment upon the devoted and faithful Ali, bade him lie on his bed, "and escaped, as David had escaped, through the window." He repaired, to the house of Abu Bakr; and they fled together, unobserved, from the inhospitable city of their birth. They lay hidden for several days in a cavern of Mount Thour, a hill to the south of Mecca.

The fury of the Koreish was now unbounded. The news that the assassins had returned unsuccessful, and Mohammed had escaped, aroused their whole energy. Horsemen scoured the country. A price was set upon Mohammed's head. Once or twice the danger approached so near that the heart of old Abu Bakr quaked with fear. "We are but two," said he. "Nay, "said Mohammed, "we are three; God is with us."And he was with them. After three days the Koreish slackened their efforts. All this time Mohammed and his companion were sustained by food brought to them at night by the daughter of Abu Bakr. On the evening of the third day the fugitives left the cavern, and, procuring with great difficulty two camels, endeavoured to reach Yathreb by unfrequented paths. But even here the way was full of danger. The heavy price set upon Mohammed's head had brought out many horsemen from Mecca, and they were still diligently seeking for the helpless wanderer. One, a wild and fierce warrior, actually caught sight of the fugitives and pursued them. Again the heart of

Abu Bakr misgave him, and he cried, "We are lost;" "Be not afraid," said the Prophet, "God will protect us." As the idolater overtook Mohammed, his horse reared and fell. Struck with awe, he entreated the forgiveness of the man whom he was pursuing, and asked for an attestation of his pardon. This was given to him on a piece of bone by Abu Bakr.

The fugitives continued their journey without further molestation, and soon they reached the territories of Yathreb. It was a hot day in June 622, of the Christian era, when Mohammed alighted from his camel upon the soil which was thenceforth to become his home and his refuge. A Jew watching on a tower first espied him, and thus were the words of the Koran fulfilled, "They to whom the Scriptures have been given, recognise him as they do their own children. Mohammed and his companion rested for a few days at a village called Koba, situated only two miles to the south of Yathreb, and remarkable for its beauty and fertility. Here he was joined by Ali, who had been severely maltreated by the Idolaters after their disappointment at Mohammeds's escape. Ali fled from Mecca, and journeyed on foot, hiding himself in the daytime, and travelling only at night, lest he should fall into the hands of the Koreish.

The Bani-Amr-ben-Auf, to whom the village belonged requested Mohammed to prolong his stay amongst them. But the duty of the Prophet lay before him; and he proceeded towards Yathreb, attended by a numerous body of his disciples. He entered the city on the morning of a Friday, 16th of Rabi I corresponding (according to M. Caussin de Perceval) with the 2nd of July, 622.

Thus was accomplished the Hijrat, called in European annals, "The Flight of Mohammed," from which dates the Mohammedan calendar.

4

The Fundamentals

The Belief

For the conservation of a true religious spirit,—a spirit frequently wanting in other creeds, Mohammed attached to his religion certain practical duties, of which the following are the principal:

- Namaz (Prayer)
- Saum (Fasting)
- Zakat (Almsgiving)
- Haj (Pilgrimage).

The Prayers

Man's consciousness of supreme, all-seeing, all pervading Power; his helplessness in the eternal conflict of nature, his sense of benefaction; all lead him to pour out the over flowing sentiments of his heart, in words of gratitude and love, or repentance and solicitation to one who is ever-wakeful and merciful. Prayers are only the utterances of the sentiments which fill the human heart. All these emotions, however, are the results of a superior development. The savage, if supplications do not answer his purpose, resorts to the castigation of his fetish. But all religious systems, with any organic element in them, have recognised, in some shape or other, the efficacy of prayer. In most, however, the urgic character predominates over the moral; in some the moral idea is entirely wanting.

The Mago-Zoroastrian and the Sabean lived in an atmosphere of prayer. The Zoroastrian prayed when he sneezed, when he cut his nails or hair, while preparing meals, day and night, at the lighting of lamps, etc. Ormuzd was first invoked, and then not only heaven, earth, the elements and stars, but trees, especially the moon-plant,and beasts. The formulae were often to be repeated, as many as twelve hundred times. The moral idea, however pure in some cases, would be perfectly eliminated from the minds, was in many cases monopolised by the ministers of religion. The barriers of special holiness which divided the priesthood from the laity, shut out the latter, more or less, from all spiritual enjoyments of a nobler type. The Magians, like the Ophici, had two forms of worship, or rather two modes of understanding the objects of worship; one esoteric, especially reserved for the priestly classes, the other exoteric, in which alone the vulgar could participate.

The Mosaic law contained no ordinances respecting prayers; only on the payment of tithes to the priest and the domestic solemnity of the presentation of the firstlings, was there a prescribed formula of prayer and acknowledgment, when the father of the house, on the strength of his having obediently performed the behests of the law, supplicated blessings from Jehovah on Israel, "even, as he had sworn unto their fathers." But with the rise of a more spiritual idea of the Deity, among the people and the teachers, and the decline of an uncompromising anthropomorphism, the real nature of prayer, as the medium of intercommunication between God and man, began to be understood. Tradition and custom, in default of any express regulation by the law, made the Jews at last, as Dollinger says, a people of prayer. Three hours daily were consecrated to devotional exercises, viz. nine, twelve, and three o'clock. The necessity, however, for the service of priests, combined with the absence of any positive precedent coming down from the Lawgiver himself, tended to make prayer, in the majority of cases, merely mechanical. Phylacteries were in use in the time of Jesus, and the Koran reproaches the Jews in bitter terms for "selling the signs of God."

The teachings of Jesus, representing a later development of the religious faculty in man, recognised the true character of prayer. He consecrated the practice by his own example. The early disciples, in the true spirit of their Master, laid great stress on the habit of devotion and thanksgiving to God. But the want of some definite rule for the guidance of the masses in process of time left them completely adrift in all that regarded the practice of devotion, and under subjection to the priests, who monopolised the office of regulating the number, length, and the terminology of prayers. Hence missals, liturgies, councils and convocations to settle articles of faith and matters of conscience; hence also the mechanical worship of droning monks, and the hebdomadal flocking into churches and chapels on one day in the week, to make up for the deficiency of spiritual food during the other six; hence also the "presbyter," who, merely a "servant" at first, came to regard himself as "the lord of the spiritual heritage" bequeathed by Jesus.

All these evils had culminated to a point in the 7th century, when the Prophet of Arabia began to preach a reformed religion. In instituting prayers, Mohammed recognised the yearning of the human soul to pour out its love and gratitude to the God of Truth, and by making the practice of devotion periodic, he impressed that disciplinary character on the observance of prayer, which keeps the thought from wandering into the regions of the material. The formulae, consecrated by his example and practice, whilst sparing the Islamic world the evils of contests regarding liturgies, leave to the individual worshipper the amplest scope for the most heartfelt outpouring of devotion and humility before the Almighty Presence.

The value of prayer, as the means of moral elevation, and the purification of the heart, has been clearly set forth by the Koran:—

"Rehearse that which hath been revealed unto thee of the Book, and be constant at prayer, for prayer preserveth from crimes; and from that which is blameable; and the remembering of God is surely a most sacred duty."

The forms of the supplicatory hymns, consecrated by the example of Mohammed, evince the beauty of the moral element in the teachings of Islam:—

"O Lord! I supplicate Thee for firmness in faith, and direction towards rectitude; and to assist me in being grateful to Thee; and in adoring Thee in every good way; and I supplicate Thee for an innocent heart, which shall not incline to wickedness; and I supplicate Thee for a true tongue; and for that virtue which Thou knowest; and I pray Thee to defend me from that vice, which Thou knowest; and for forgiveness of those faults, which Thou knowest. O my Defender! assist me in remembering Thee and being grateful to Thee, and in worshipping Thee with the excess of my strength. O Lord! I have injured my own soul; and no one can pardon the faults of Thy servants but Thou; forgive me out of Thy loving kindness, and have mercy on me; for verily Thou art the Forgiver of offences and the Bestower of blessings on Thy servants."

Another traditional prayer, called the prayer of David, runs thus:—

"O Lord, grant to me the love of Thee; grant that I may love those that love Thee;grant that I may do the deeds that may win Thy love; make Thy love to be dearer to me than myself, my family, than wealth, and even than cool water."

"It is one of the glories of Islam," says an English writer, "that its temples are not made with hands, and that its ceremonies can be performed anywhere upon God's earth or under His heaven." Every place in which the Almighty is faithfully worshipped is equally pure. The Moslem, whether he be at home or abroad when the hour of prayer arrives, pours forth his soul in a brief but earnest supplicatory address; his attention is not wearied by the length of his prayers, the theme of which is always self humiliation, the glorification of the Giver of all good, and reliance on His mercy. The intensity of the devotional spirit embalmed in the church of Mohammed has hardly been realised by Christendom. Tradition, that faithful chronicler of the past amongst the Moslems, with its hundred corroborative witnesses, records how the Prophet wept during his prayers with the fervour of his emotions; how his noble cousin and son-in-law became so absorbed in his devotions, that his corporeal frame grew benumbed.

Certain ceremonies are prescribed for the due observance of the rites of prayer; but, as it has been said by the Imam-al-Ghazzali, it is to the devotional state of the mind the Searcher of the spirit looks:

> "It is not the flesh or the blood of that which ye sacrifice which is acceptable to God; it is your piety which is acceptable to the Lord." "It is not righteousness," continues the Koran, "that ye turn your faces in prayer towards the east or the west; but righteousness is of him who believeth in God;.. who giveth money for God's sake unto his kindred, and unto orphans, and the needy, and the stranger, and those who ask, and for the redemption of captives; who is constant at prayers and giveth alms; and of those who perform their covenant, when they have convenanted; and who behave themselves patiently in adversity, and hardships, and in times of violence; these are they who are true..."

The practice of baptism in the Christain Church, even the lustrations which the Egyptians, the Jews, or the hierophants of the heathen religions in the East and the West required, as preliminary to the performance of devotional or religious exercises, show the peculiar sanctity which was attached to external purifications. Mohammed conserved and consecrated this ancient and beneficent custom. He required frequent ablutions as proper preliminaries to the worship and adoration of the Pure God. At the same time he especially in culcated that mere external or rather physical purity was not the essence of devotion. He distinctly laid down that the all-pervading Soul of the Universe can only be approached in purity and humility of spirit. The celebrated Imam-al-Ghazzali expressly says, as against those who are only solicitous about external purifications, and have their hearts full of pride and hypocrisy—that the Prophet of God declared that the most important purification is the cleansing of the heart from all blameable inclinations and frailties, and the mind from all vicious ideas, and from all thoughts which distract the human attention from God.

In order to keep alive in the Moslem world the memory of the birthplace of Islam, Mohammed directed that during prayers the Moslem should turn his face towards Mecca as the glorious centre which saw the first glimmerings of the light of regenerated truth. But that this rule is not an essential requisite for devotion is evident from the passage of the Koran quoted above,

The Fasts

The institution of fasting has existed more or less among all nations. But it may be said, that throughout the ancient world the idea attached to it was, without exception, more of penitence than of abstinence. Even in Judaism, the notion of fasting as an exercise of self-castigation or self-abnegation was of later growth. The Essenians, (from their connexion with the Pythagoreans, and through them with the asceticism of the further East), were the first among the Jews to grasp this moral element in the principle of fasting. And Jesus probably derived this idea, like other conceptions, from them.

The example of Jesus consecrated the custom in the Church. But the predominating idea in Christianity, with respect to fasts generally, is one of penitence or expiation; and partially, of precedent. Voluntary corporeal mortifications have been as frequent in the Christian Church as in other churches; but the tendency of such mortifications has invariably been the destruction of mental and bodily energies and the fostering of a morbid asceticism. The institution of fasting in Islam, on the contrary, has the legitimate object of restraining the passions, by diurnal abstinence, for a limited and definite period, from all the gratifications of the senses, and of directing the overflow of the animal spirits into a healthy channel. Mohammed's religion, as a religion of humanity, strictly excluded all notions of ascetic mortificatios of the senses.

The wisdom, however, of the Koranic laws is more apparent in the prohibitory rules than even in the positive enactments. The following conditions were required to make fasting obligatory, and show how wonderfully adapted this regulation is for the restraint of the animal propensities of our being, which develop themselves under special circumstances. These conditions are, (Istly) maturity; (2ndly) healthiness of mind; (3rdly) healthiness of body; (4thly) the condition of being at one's home, or what is equivalent to it; and for women, freedom from all ailments. Mark the wisdom of the rule, as given in the Koran:

> "O that have believed, a "fast is ordained to you,.... that ye may practise piety; a fast of a computed number of days. But he, among you, who shall be ailing or on a journey (shall fast) an equal number of other days; and they that are able to keep it (and do not) shall make atonement by maintaining a poor man... .But if ye fast, it will be better for you, if ye comprehend; God willeth that which is easy for you."

This rule of abstinence is restricted to the day; in the night, in the intervals of prayer and devotion, the Moslem is allowed, perhaps indeed is bound, to refresh the system by partaking in moderation of food and drink, and otherwise enjoying himself lawfully. In the true spirit of the Teacher, the legists invariably laid down the rule that, during the fasts, abstinence of mind from all base thoughts is as incumbent as the abstinence of the body.

The Alms

No religion of the world, prior to Islam, had consecrated charity, the support of the widow, the orphan, and the helpless poor—by enrolling its principles among the positive enactments of the system.

The Agapae or feasts of charity, among the early Christians, depended on the will of individuals; their influence, therefore, could only be irregular and spasmodic. It is a matter of history that this very irregularity led to the suppression of the "feasts of charity, or love-feasts," only a short time after their introduction.

By the laws of Islam, every individual is bound to contribute a certain part of this substance towards the help and assistance of his poorer neighbours. This portion is usually one part in forty, or 2½ percent on the value of all goods, chattels, emblements, on profits of trade, mercantile business, etc. But Zakat (alms) are due only when the property amounts to a certain value, and has been in the possession of a person for one whole year; nor are any due from cattle employed in agriculture or in the carrying of burdens. Besides, at the end of the month of Ramadhan (the month of fasting), and on the day of the id-ul-fitr, the festival which celebrates the close of the Moslem Lent, each head of a family has to give away in Fitra (alms), for himself and for every member of his household, and for each guest who breaks his fast and sleeps in his house during the month, a measure of wheat, barley, dates, raisins, rice, or any other grain, or the value of the same.

The rightful recipients of the Zakat (alms), as pointed out by the practice of Mohammed and his disciples, are (1) the poor and the indigent; (2) those who help in the collection and distribution of Zakat (the obligatory alms); (3) Slaves, who wish to buy their freedom and have not the means for so doing; (4) debtors, who cannot pay their debts; (5) travellers and strangers". General charity is inculcated to the Moslem by the Koran in the most forcible terms. But the glory of Islam consists in having embodied the beautiful sentiment of Jesus into definite laws.

The Pilgrimage

The wisdom which incorporated into Islam the time-honoured Arabian custom of annual pilgrimage to Mecca and to the shrine of the Kaaba, has breathed into Mohammed's religion a freemasonry and brotherhood of faith, in spite of sectarian divisions. The eyes of the whole Moslem world fixed on that central spot keep alive in the bosom of each spark of the celestial fire, which lighted up the earth in that century of darkness. Here again, the wisdom of the inspired Lawgiver shines forth in the negative part of the enactments, in the conditions necessary to make the enactment obligatory:—(1) The ripeness of intelligence and discernment; (2) perfect freedom and liberty; (3) possession of the means of transport and subsistence during the journey; (4) possession of means sufficient to support the pilgrim's family during his absence; (5) the possibility and practicability of the voyage.

Such are the institutions of Mohammed with reference to the practical duties of religion.

"Faith and charity," to use the words of the Christian historian, "are not incompatible with external rites and positive institutions, which indeed are necessary in this imperfect state, to keep alive a sense of religion in the common mass." And accordingly Mohammed had attached a few rites to his teachings in order to give a more tangible conception to the generality of mankind. Jesus himself had instituted two rites—Baptism and the Holy Supper. Probably had he lived longer, he would have added more. But one thing is certain, that had a longer career been vouchsafed to him, he would have placed his teachings on a more systematic basis. This fundamental defect in Christianity has been, in fact, the real cause of the assembling of Councils and Convocations for the establishment of articles and dogmas, which snap asunder at every slight tension of Reason and Free thought. The work of Jesus was left unfinished. It was reserved for another Teacher to systematize the laws of morality. Thus Mohammeds' teachings are in no way opposed to those of Jesus; they are simply complementary to them.

Inner Feelings

Our relations with our Creator are matters of conscience; our relations with our fellow beings must be matters of positive rules; and what higher sanction—to use a legal expression—can be attached for the enforcement of the relative duties of man to man, than the sanction of religion. Religion is not to be regarded merely as a subject for punctuous declamations by "select preachers," or as some strange theory for the peculiar gratification of dreamy minds. Religion ought to mean the rule of life; its chief object ought to be the elevation of Humanity towards that perfection which is the end of our existence. The religion, therefore, which places on a systematic basis the fundamental principles of morality, regulating social obligations, and human duties, which brings us nearer and nearer by its compatibility with the highest development of intellect, to the All Perfect—that religion, we say, has the greatest claim to our consideration and respect. It is the distinctive characteristic of Islam that it combines within itself the grandest and the most prominent features in all ethnic and catholic religions, compatible with the reason and moral intuition of man. It is not merely a system of positive moral rules, based, on a true conception of Human Progress, but it is also "the establishment of certain principles, the enforcement of certain dispositions, the cultivation of a certain temper of mind, which the conscience is to apply to the ever-varying exigencies of time and place." The Teacher of Islam, preached in a thousand varied ways, universal love and brotherhood, as the emblem of the love borne towards the Primal Cause of All.

> "Do you wish to approach the Lord, love his creatures, love for them what you love yourself, reject for them what you reject for yourself, do unto them what you wish to be done unto you." The wonderful adaptability of the Islamic precepts for all ages and nations; their entire concordance with the light of Reason; the absence of all mysterious doctrines to cast a shade of sentimental ignorance round the primal truths implanted in the human breast—all prove that Islam represents the latest development of the religious faculties of our

being. Those who have ignored the historic significance of some of its precepts, have deemed that their seeming harshness or unadaptability to present modes of thought, ought to exclude it from every claim to universality. But a little inquiry into the historic value of laws and precepts, a little more fairness in the examination of facts, would evince the temporary character of such rules as may appear scarcely consonant with the requirements or prejudices of modem times. The catholicity of Islam, its expansiveness, and its charity towards all moral creeds have been utterly mistaken, perverted, or wilfully concealed by the bigotry of rival religions.

"Verily," says the Koran, "those who believe (the Moslems), and those who are Jews, Christians or Sabeans, whoever hath faith in God and the last day (future existence); and worketh that which is right and good, for them shall be the reward with their Lord; there will come no fear on them; neither shall they be grieved.'

The same sentiment is repeated in similar words in the fifth Sura (chapter of the Koran); and a hundred other passages, prove that Islam does not confine "salvation" to the followers of Mohammed alone:—To every one have We given a Law and a Way... And if God had pleased. He would have made you all (all mankind) one people (people of one religion). But He hath done otherwise, that He might try you in that which He hath severally given unto you, wherefore press forward in good works. Unto God shall ye return, and He will tell you that concerning which ye disagree."

There are certain ages," says the historian of European Rationalism, "in which the sense of virtue has been the mainspring of religion; there are other ages, in which this position is occupied by the sense of sin." In the one case, a consciousness of human dignity furnishes the motive power to our action; in the other, a sense of the utter sinfulness of man. The philosophies of ancient Greece and Rome embalmed the first principle; Christianity the latter.

Of all systems of religion, Islam alone combines both of these two conceptions. The belief that man will be judged by his works solely, throws the Moslem on the practice of self-denial and universal charity; the belief in Divine Providence, in the mercy, love, and omnipotence of God leads him to self-humiliation before the Sovereign of the universe, and to the practice of those heroic virtues which have given rise to the charge that "the virtues of Islam are stoical" patience, resignation, and firmness in the trials of life. It leads him (to use once more Lecky's phraseology), to interrogate his conscience with nervous anxiety, to study with scrupulous care the motives that actuate him, to distrust his own strength, and to rely upon the assistance of an almighty and all-loving power, in the conflict between Good and Evil.

Various Concepts

Thus Islam combines all the highest principles which have actuated humanity from the time it saw light on earth.

In some religions, the precepts which inculcated duties have been so utterly deviod of practicability, so completely wanting in a knowledge of human nature and partaking so much of the dreamy vagueness of enthusiasts, as to become in the real battles of life simply useless. The practical character of a religion, its abiding influence in the common relations of mankind—in the affairs of every-day life, its power on the masses—are the true criteria for judging of its universality. We do not look to exceptional minds to recognize the nature of a religion. We search among the masses to understand its true character. Does it exercise deep power over them? does it elevate them? does it regulate their conception of rights and duties? Does it, if carried to the South Sea Islander, or preached to the Caffrarians, improve or degrade them?—are the questions we naturally ask ourselves. In Islam is joined a lofty idealism with the most rationalistic practicality. It did not ignore human nature; it never entangled itself in the tortuous pathways which lie outside the domains of the actual and the real. Its object, like that of other systems, was the elevation of humanity towards the absolute Ideal of Perfection; but it attained, or tries to attain, this object by grasping the truth that the nature of man is, in this existence, imperfect. If it did not say, "If thy other also to him" if it allowed the punishment of the wanton wrongdoer to the extent of the injury he had done—it also taught in fervid words and ten thousand varied strains, the practice of forgiveness and benevolence, and the return of good for evil:—"Who speaketh better," says the Koran, than he who inviteth unto God, and worketh good….. good and evil shall not be held equal. Turn away evil with that which is better." And again, speaking of paradise, it says:—"It is prepared for the godly; who give alms in prosperity and adversity; who bridle their anger and forgive men; for God loveth the beneficent."

The practice of these noble precepts does not lie enshrined in the limbo of false sentimentalism. With the Moslem, they form the active principles of life. History has preserved, for the admiration of wondering posterity, many examples of patience under suffering exhibited by the followers of other creeds. But the practice of the virtues of patient forgiveness is easier in adversity, when we have no power to punish the evil doer, than in prosperity. It is related of Hussain, that noble martyr of Kerbela, that a slave, having once thrown the contents of a scalding dish over him as he sat at dinner, fell on his knees and repeated the verse of the Koran:— "Paradise is for those who bridle their anger"—"I am not angry," answered Hussain; the slave proceeded, and for those who forgive men:" "I forgive you. "The slave, however, finished the verse, adding, "for God loveth the beneficent:" "I give you your liberty and four hundred pieces of silver," replied Hussain.

The author of the Kasshafthus sums up the essence of the Islamic teachings:—"Seek again him who drives you away; give to him who takes away from you; pardon him who injures you; for God loveth that you should cast into the depth of your souls, the roots of His Perfections."

We shall conclude this chapter with the following passage from the Koran:—

The servants of the Merciful are they that walk upon the earth softly; and when the ignorant speak unto them, they reply. Peace! They that spend the night worshipping their Lord, prostrate and standing:—

"And that say,—Oh, our Lord! turn away from us the torment of Hell; verily, from the torment there of, there is no release. Surely it is an evil abode and resting-place! Those that when they spend are neither profuse nor niggardly, but take a middle course:— Those that invoke not with God; and slay not a soul that God hath forbidden, otherwise than by right; and commit not fornication; for he who doeth that is involved in sin,—His torment shall be doubled in the day of judgment: therein ignominously shall he remain for ever;—excepting him that shall repent and believe and perform righteous works; as for them. God shall change their evil things into good; and God is forgiving and merciful. And whoever repenteth and doeth good works, verily, he tumeth unto God with a true repentance. They who bear not witness to that which is false; and when they pass by vain sport, they pass it by with dignity:—they who, when admonished by the revelations of the Lord, thereupon fall not down as if deaf and blind; who say, Oh, our Lord, grant us of our wives and children such as shall be a comfort unto us, and make us examples unto the pious—These shall be rewarded with lofty mansions [in paradise], for that they persevered; and they shall be accosted therein with welcome and salutation:—For ever therein;—a fair Abode and Resting-place!

5

Holy Prophet as Role Model

The study of the Holy Prophet's Life Provides briefly an idea of the difficulties and hardships he (PBUH) had to face in the procla-mation of his prophethood, propagation of his teachings and pro-tection of all those taking to his teachings.

In a country where there was no government and law and order. Where murder and blood shed was in the days work, whose citizens might be resembling ravenous beasts and worse than cattle in ignorance and total absence of discernment and rationality, putting up a claim, queer to the entire country, and fomenting trouble and opposition among all the tribes, was not so easy. Again, this claim gaining favour under conditions of the unlimited opposi-tion of millions of people, bent on wiping it out with all their might, hearts and minds, and means at their disposal, persistently for years together, is certainly a vivid proof of the Divine Aid.

In connection with the events related earlier, the morals, excellence, attributes and laudable deeds outshine like pure gold in sand and dirt. And it is these events that bring to light the fact that in the totally opposite conditions of oppression and helpless-ness and power and majesty, existence with the same simplicity can be the accomplishment of one whose heart has been totally possessed by the Divine Law. When it has been purged of the worldly involvements.

The blessed events of the Prophet's (PBUH) life are a model and an example for every country, every class, both for individuals and groups and parties.

Instead of the perfections of the prophethood and characteristics of the Prophet, only those simple natural good habits, good disposition, amiability and extremely good manners shall be taken up which a fortunate person of a docile nature can take as a model of moral perfection:

Ye have indeed in the Messenger of Allah an excellent example. Al Quran XXXIII: 21

Our leader, Muhammad (PBUH) was unlettered. And upto the time of his being raised a Prophet, had not had the company of any learned person.

Archery, horsemanship, use of lance in fighting, poetry, panegyric or laudative poetry, geneology were those arts and skills of that period which every young man of a noble family did pick up for the sake of fame and prestige, and without which no one had any chance of coming to a position of honour or distinction in his community. The Prophet had not learnt or picked up any of these from any body as a student. Nor did he ever shown any interest in learning them.

French Professor Cideo writes about the Prophet (PBUH):

"He had a smiling countenance, sociable, mostly quiet (a man of few words), remembering God most of the time, far removed from absurdity, abhorring frivolity and had the most appropriate opinion and wisest (among those around him)."

"In the matter of doing justice, he never made any distinction between the far and near (close to him or present before him and a stranger or one absent). He loved the indigent and was happy among the poverty stricken. He never meted out a degrading treatment to a poor person because of his lack of means. He captivated the hearts of his associates and patiently put up with the uncouthness or objectionable conduct of the ignorant. He never parted with any one talking to him until he himself left him. He loved his companions most. He had no hesitation in sitting on the ground if nothing to cover it was available. He himself repaired his own shoes and put patches on his clothes. Met even his enemies and unbelievers with a cheerful countenance."

Hujjah-al-Islam Ghazali writes:

The Prophet offered green fodder to the cattle himself, tied the camels, cleaned the house, milked the goat, took his food with his servant or slave, gave a helping hand to the servant in his work, went to the market for purchase of the necessities of life and himself brought these things home. He was always the first to greet (say salam) to every one young or old, high or low (never allowing them precedence over himself). Whoever accompanied him, he walked hand in hand with him.

He never made distinction between master and man, Abyssinian and a Turk. He had the same attire for the day and night wear. However lowly a person invited him to dine with him, he accepted without reserve. And whatever was offered to him, he took it cheerfully. He was not given to saving for the morning from the night's rituals, nor from the day's food for the night contentment and real trust in Allah. He was good natured, of a generous disposition and cheerful countenance (smiling face) but never laughed (loudly). He was mostly full of anxiety for one reason or another but not ill-tempered. He was meek but without meanness. He was awe-inspiring but not a harsh countenance. He was generous but not prodigal. He was merciful to one and all but expected nothing from anyone. He mostly kept him head bent.

Shah Wali-al-Allah writes:

Whoever happened to confront him suddenly he became awe-inspired and whoever sat with him for a while became devoted follower and admirer.

He was particularly kind to his kinsmen and those serving him. Anas (R) served him for ten years but never heard even 'ugh!' or hunh'! from him. Never a foul word or abuse befouled his pure clean tongue, nor he ever cursed any one. He showed remarkable patience in face of distress from others. He showed profound mercy to the people in general. None ever suffered at his hand or by his tongue. Reform of his family and the community received his first attention. He was aware of every body and everything. His attention was focused on the Kingdom of Heaven.

In Sahih Bukhari it has been said:

The Prophet (PBUH) gave glad tidings to the obedient and warned the disobedient and transgressor. Allah's servant and His Messenger offered asylum to the uninformed. Leaving everything to Allah (after doing what was his own due). Neither harsh in behaviour nor in speech. Never raised his voice in speaking, nor tit for tat in dealings. Those seeking forgiveness, he readily forgave (if it was not a transgression against God). He forgave the sinner also. His mission was to correct the crookedness in religions. His teachings gave eyes to the blind, ears to the deaf and lifted the curtains from the hearts of the negligent. The Prophet's (PBUH) character was decorated with every excellence and qualified with all the finest attributes. Peace and tranquillity was attire and doing good his distinctive sign, taqwa, (piety), his conscience, wisdom his speech, justice his conduct, His Shari'ah wholly uprightness and his millat (Belief and Faith). Guidance in his guide. He removes misguidance, elevating the position of the lowly and making the little known outstanding, changing minority into majority and the want or destitution into richness.

Oral and Silent Expressions

The Prophet as a matter of habit remained silent never speaking needlessly. The Prophet (PBUH) was extremely sweet spoken and eloquent. His speech was not at all affected. His words were so captivating that they went to the listener's heart and soul. This quality of his speech was such as compelled even the adversaries to admit it. And again, it was this marvel of his speech which the ignorant attributed to sorcery.

The continuity of his speech was such that, in word or purport, there was no fault. He used words with such precision and order that if the listener liked, he could count them.

Good Actions

The Prophet never laughed loudly, nor did he burst into laughter on his own. His laughter was limited to a serene smile. However, in the pre-down prayer (Tahajjud) he burst into tears at times.

At other times, the death of a sincere associate (companion) or kinsman his eyes welled up with tears.

His infant son, Ibrahim, had died while yet a suckling. When he was put into the grave, it was too much for a loving father and mercy for mankind and brought tears to his eyes. He said:

"The eyes manifest grief, the heart is grieved too, but we say only what our Lord and Sustainer loves to hear from us: O Ibrahim thou in thy parting caused us grief.

On another occasion he happened to lift on to his lap his grand daughter, Zainab's (R) dying daughter. His love for the child and in death pangs, proved too much for him and it brought tears to his eyes. Sa'd (R) asked him about this phenomenon and was told that it was due to those tender chords in the human heart that are touched. It is God-given mercy. And Allah too will be merciful only to those of his servant that are kind-hearted and show mercy to fellow-beings.

Once Abdullah Ibn Mas'ood (R) was reciting Quran before the Prophet (at his bidding). When he came to the verse:

> How then if we brought from each people a witness and we brought thee as a witness against these people. (Q.IV: 41)

He said to him: "That's enough." Ibn Masood (R) lifting his eyes saw tears running down the Prophet's (PBUH) eyes.

Ideal Food

The Prophet (PBUH) advised people not to go to sleep on a hungry stomach (missing the night meal) and pointed to it as a sign of senility. He also advised them against going to sleep immediately after supper.

He used to persuade people to be sparing or at least moderate in eating. He used to say to them that they should keep one third of the stomach for food, another one third for water and the last one third for the stomach itself (meaning that the stomach should not be fully stuffed to cause it pain or at least inconvenience and hardship).

He used to take fruits and vegetable with their correctives.

To be cautious against certain diseases and the healthy to be careful were his orders.

Sick persons were advised by him to get treated by a physician clever at his job and also stressed abstention. He forbade a novice and a quack to practise medicine and held him responsible for damage to people's health.

He also forbade use of prohibited things as medicines and said: "Allah has not kept healing properties in the prohibited things for you."

Courtesy Calls

Whoever among the companions fell ill, he used to visit him. He used to sit very close to the sick person and tried to console him. He used to encourage him saying: "Allah willing you shall be all right, there is no cause for worry." He also asked the patient if he desired anything, and if it was not harmful to him, he would arrange it for him. A Jewish boy who used to wait on him, fell ill and the Prophet visited him in his sick bed and it is reported also asked him to embrace Islam and after approval of his father, he did.

When suffering from any ailment, he himself used medicine and advised others also to do the same saying:

"O ye servants of Allah! Do take medicine, since Allah has appointed a cure for every malady, save one disease. People asked him which is that? He said: "It is extreme old age (decrepitude). (When the body reaction to inherent deterioration as well as foreign invaders becomes minimum or totally absent).

He used to harangue people standing on the floor or from a pulpit or on camels back, beginning from bearing witness to the unity of Allah and concluded with asking Allah for forgiveness. Something from the Quran was a must as part of it and the Islamic principles were taught (preached) in it.

"All those things were explained in the speeches (of the Prophet) which were the need of the hour for the Muslim community and according to the time and its demand everything was covered in them. (Zad-al-Ma'ad Vol. I, P. 49)

These harangues were not limited to Friday congregations, but whenever he felt there was need for it he would speak with the Word of God to support his own.

At the time of speaking, he held in his hand a club, a bow on which, if need be, he would temporarily support himself. But there is no instance of his ever holding a sword in his hand when speaking to an audience nor he ever used it as a body support.

Allamah Ibn-al-Qayyim says: "The ignorant are often heard saying that the Prophet (PBUH) took the pulpit sword in hand, pointing to the (most erroneous) belief that Islam was propagated at the point of sword." The 'Allamah goes on to say, (is of the opinion) that this common belief of the ignorant masses is totally wrong.

1. Supporting himself on a sword has no proof.

2. Harangues started in Medina and had been conquered with the force of the Quran and not the might of the sword. Again, the

Allamah also goes on to add that the Islamic Faith was established with the Heavenly revelation.

Charitable Acts

He never used anything coming as Sadaqah (charity). However, he had no objection to accept gifts.

The gifts from sincere companions (R) as well as Christians and Jews were accepted and in turn gifts were sent to them. But those from the polytheists were rejected outright.

He rode the mule sent by Maquqas, the king of Egypt, and in the battle of Hunain that same mule was under him. But he rejected outright the horse sent by 'Amir bin Malik and plainly stated, "We do not accept gifts from a polytheist."

The precious gifts coming to the Prophet (PBUH) were usually given to his companions.

The Praiseworthy

Any such laudation of his that would bring any other prophet lower, he disapproved, and used to say:

Never resort to a mode in relation to the prophet's attributes which lowers one than any other.

He attended a marriage ceremony where girls of a very tender age were singing the songs of laudable deeds of their encounters. They also sang in praise of the Prophet (PBUH) that they had among them a Prophet who can tell you today of the happenings of tommorrow. The Prophet stopped them from saying those words and asked them to continue with their songs of ancestors.

Reforming Acts

Death occurred of the Prophet's son Ibrahim. And that also happened to be the day of solar eclipse. People started talking. The sun too is mourning the death of Ibrahim. It is eclipsed. The Prophet addressed those present there: Solar and Lunar eclipses are not due to anybody's death.

When the Quraysh renovated Ka'bah during the pre-Islamic period it was not raised on the old foundation. They left out some covered area outside, with a plinth so high that ladder was needed to enter the enclosure and with only one door. The Prophet one day commented on it addressing 'Ayeshah (R).

"Your community (Quraysh) have embraced Islam only lately, otherwise I would have demolished their structure and made certain necessary alterations. Ka'bah needs two doors, one for entry and another for departure."

When the mischievous activities of the hypocrites crossed all limits of decency and humanity, 'Umar Faruq (R) suggested that they should be put to the sword. The Prophet said to him: "No. People will adversely comment: "Mohammad has started killing his friends."

Holy Status

The Prophet always tried to show his commands emanating from him as an Apostle separate from those he issued as a human being:

1. Once he said: "I am after all human and conflicts and quarrels are put up before me. Someone of you can express himself and put up his case better than the other which gives a notion of his truth, and I decide the case in his favour. So if a Muslim gets anything from his Muslim brothers share, he should clearly understand that it is a part of fire, it is up to him to take it or leave it."

2. He pleaded the case of Mughith and intercessed with Baridah a slave girl, his, (Mughith's) wife. She had had separation from him after freedom. Baridah asked the Prophet (PBUH): Is that your command to me?" The Prophet replied:? No. It is my intercession on his behalf." To this she said: "I have no need of Mughith."

The Madinites, on the basis of experience used to sprinkle the pollen dust of male date palm trees on the female tree's flowers. The Prophet once casually remarked: "Where is the need of this operation?" The owners of date palm groves gave up the practice, with the result that due to scanty pollination by natural agencies like wind alone, fruit that year was scanty too. The date palm growers brought this phenomenon to the Prophet's (PBUH) notice. He owned it without reserve that they knew their worldly affairs better than he did. "Follow me unstintedly with certainty only in those things I order you relating to your Faith," he concluded.

Love for All

Passing by the children on his way, he greeted them initially with the Islamic salutation (As-Salam-u-Alaikum, peace be on you). He placed his hand on their heads and at times lifted one on to his lap.

After the conquest of Mecca, Abu Bakr Siddiq (R) brought his old decrepit blind father to the Prophet (PBUH) for Baiah (oath of fealty). The Prophet (PBUH) said to Abu Bakr, "Why did you give all this trouble to an old man (in this state of disabilities)? I would have myself visited him."

Sa'd bin Mu'az (R) who (came by a severed artery of the arm at Uhud which could not be sealed and ultimately caused his death), had been named by the Banu Quraiza Jews to pronounce his decision in their case (of high treason) and called to the scene of action. When he had come to the mosque, the Prophet (PBUH) asked his companions of Aus tribe to pay their respects to him by advancing to receive him, saying "Greet and receive your leader." And his tribesmen (Aus) did the Prophet's bidding.

> Hassan bin Thabit composed couplets lauding Islam and most effective retorts to the adversaries. As a recognition of his services to Islam, a pulpit was laid in the mosque for his recital.

Pious People

Anas bin Malik (R) served the Prophet for ten years in Medina. During this long period he never took him to task. One day he prayed for him: "O Allah! confer on him plentiful wealth and progeny and also bless them for him."

1. The Prophet never sat with extended feet (legs) in company.

2. Whoever met him on the way, he had precedence in greeting him.

3. He also had precedence in shake-hand.

4. He called his companions by their patronymic appellations. (This was the mode of calling people honourably in Arabia)

5. He never interrupted anybody talking.

6. If he was offering supererogatory prayer and somebody happened to come to see him, he would shorten it and after meeting his need continued the prayer.

7. He was smiling most of the time.

8. One of the she camels (dromedaries) of the Prophet (PBUH) was called 'Asba. It was swift footed and never allowed any camel to get and advance over her. A bedouin Arab coming along on his mount surpassed 'Asba and the Muslims so to say, took it ill, but the Prophet said:

   The sunnah of Allah in this world is that if He exalts any, He also brings him low.

9. There came a person who called the Prophet (PBUH) the best (superior most) of the created beings. The Prophet (PBUH) said to him: "That title befits only the Prophet Ibrahim (PBUH)."

10. Somebody came to see the Prophet (PBUH) and was awe-inspired. He, however, reassured him saying: "Be at ease. I am not a king. I am the son of a poor woman of Quraysh who used to take dried meat."

'Ayeshah Siddiqah (R) says:

1. Nobody in sweet nature and politeness came close to the Prophet (PBUH). Whether a companion called him

or a member of his own house his usual answer was "I am here."

2. Supererogatory devotional acts were always performed in seclusion so that the Ummah may not be overburdened in his pursuit.

3. When there appeared two alternatives before him, he would resort to the simpler or easier one.

4. He entered a contract with his Lord that whomsoever he called a bad name or cursed, Allah should make it an atonement for his sins and a means of His Mercy, forgiveness and closeness.

5. He had instructed that they should not talk about one another in my presence. I want to leave this world without any ill opinion about any one.

6. Once on the occasion of solar eclipse, in the special congregation, he wept and prayed like this:

   O my Lord and Cherisher! Thou hast promised me that my ummah shall not be the recipient of any visitation from Thee,

   (a) So long I am Here with them, and

   (b) As long as they are beseeching Thee for their forgiveness.

   And at present My Lord, I am among them and they are all seeking Thy forgiveness.

For every prophet, there was a specific prayer and they invoked that and it was blessed with response. As for the specific one for me, I have kept it for the Last Day.

If two persons fell out of each other he meted out justice to them. If however, he had a personal complaint against anybody he would always forgive.

1. A respectable lady of Quraysh, Fatimah bint-Mazan, was found guilty of theft. The tribe wanted to save her from the prescribed punishment of this crime, chopping of the hand. So as an "effective" measure they made Osamah bin Zaid a favourite of the Prophet (PBUH), her intercessor at the court of the Shari'ah. The Prophet (PBUH), in spite of his indulgence, disapproved Osamah's involving himself in the case, saying: "Dare you intercess in a limit set by Allah? Listen to me, If Fatimah bint Muhammad committed theft, I would have her hand chopped off."

2. Sawad bin 'Umar relates that one day he went to the Prophet (PBUH) gaudily dressed. The Prophet (PBUH) disapproved of it and patted my abdomen with the stick he had in his hand. I said to the Prophet (PBUH): "I shall avenge myself." The Prophet bared his abdomen, said to him: "You are welcome to it." (But all that he did was kissing the seal of prophethood).

Treating Foes

1. A severe famine struck Mecca, until the starving lot was compelled to subsist on carrion and bones. Abu Sufyan (one of the arch enemies of Islam and Muslims) came to the Prophet (PBUH) and addressed him thus: "Muhammad! You preach kind treatment of kinsmen. Your community is at the doorstep of total annihilation. Kindly pray to God, which the Prophet most graciously did and in response brought heavy rains.

2. Thamamah bin Athal stopped supply of food grains to Mecca (after his embracing Islam) as a sign of goodwill to the Muslim community against their deadly enemies.

However, the Prophet (PBUH) prevented him from persisting with it.

3. In Hudaibiah, the Prophet was offering prayer with the Muslims when seventy or eighty persons quietly came down the Tan'im mount with the evil intent of taking a heavy toll of Muslim lives while they were engaged in prayers. But they could not succeed in their satanic design and were taken prisoners. But the Prophet granted them their freedom without any ransom or punishment.

4. He never turned away a beggar (anyone asking for help). Flat refusal was almost a taboo with him. If he was unable to do anything for him, he would put up an excuse as if he were requesting to be forgiven for a shrotcoming.

5. Somebody came to him asking for alms. The Prophet (PBUH) said to him that he had nothing to give him just then. He could, however, borrow in his name which he would meet later. 'Umar Faruq (R) said to him (the Prophet (PBUH)) that Allah had not compelled him to go beyond his means to help people. The Prophet kept quiet, evading his objection. An Ansari sitting close by spoke out: "O Apostle of Allah why not respond to him saying, Allah, the Master and Lord of the Throne is our Sustainer and as such there is no fear of poverty and destination." The Prophet smiled and his face was aglow with delight and he said: "You are right. I have these commandments from Him (My Master, Lord and Sustainer)."

6. Once he gave an indigent person half a 'wasaq' of grain borrowed from some one. The creditor turned up later for recovery of his loan. The Prophet ordered payment of full one wasaq of grains to this creditor, half that he had loaned and an additional half from us as a gesture

of generosity and reward for a good deed (helping a destitute).

7. He used to say and had almost declared it as a matter of policy that the assets of the dead is the share of the inheritors and the debts the liability of the Islamic state if he died a destitute.

Modesty and Bashfulness

1. Abu Sa'eed Khudri (R) says that the Prophet (PBUH) was more modest than a purdah observing bashful girl. Whenever something disgusting came before him in people's mutual talk, his face showed that disgust from his facial expression.

2. 'Ayeshah Tayyibah (R) has stated that if the Prophet did not like any deed or word of any person, he did not object to and forbid it pointedly but in a general way showed his disapproval of that word or deed (to avoid embarrassment of the guilty.)

3. In day-to-day affairs and dealings, he would take upon himself the greatest burden but would not order anyone else to undertake it or offer a helping hand, out of modesty.

4. Whenever some repentant person begged to be excused, the Prophet (instead of scolding or lecturing him from a superior stand according to the way of people) modestly hung his head.

5. 'Ayeshah Tayyibah (R) reports that she never saw him naked.

It is better for you to leave your inheritors independent rather than leaving them penniless beggars.

Woman is like a rib (curved normally) which can be broken in an attempt to straighten it out. But it is possible to make use of it curved as it is. (Cleverly handling a woman in as much as letting her have her own way according to her particular bent of mind, harmlessly, she can cooperate and help a lot in running a household and bringing up children nicely).

Status of Women

A woman is the ruler in her husband's house and over her offspring.

Study of the Holy Book

A person who has gone deep into the Quran pondering (over) its words, meanings, the background and the broad principles about the nature of this scripture, will be with the revered chosen and virtuous messengers (angels).

Almighty's Pleasure

These are just two words so dear to Rahman, easy to pronounce but heavy on the scales (evaluating men's deeds):

Glory to Allah and Praise for Him, Glory to Allah (who is free from all faults they ascribe to Him), (Allah), the supreme (in Glory).

Divine World

If a learned person were to write about the life of the Prophet (PBUH) the chosen of Allah, in great detail, he will have to discuss the Quran, revealed to him. But even if somebody, like me writing in a simple and brief manner his biography, he too will find himself compelled to present a sample of the Quranic teachings, though leaving out the finer point demanding detailed discussions. To my mind, the life history of the Apostle of Allah without any mention of the Quran with samples, is incomplete, sadly tacking in this most important aspect. Somebody had asked 'Ayeshah Siddiqah (R) about the morals of the Prophet (PBUH), she had replied: "The Quran is his (sublime) morals."

It is our sacred belief that every word of the glorious Quran is the word of Allah. (It is known by the name of the Word of God). But it was the Apostle of Allah (PBUH) who introduced this word of Allah to the world.

It was revealed to Muhammad, the Apostle of Allah (PBUH) in twenty three years. It exists in those very words in which he recited it and gave to the world. It has been preserved intact by Allah and shall remain so to the end of days. It is in our hearts and minds pervading them and on our tongues having the marvel of memorization, seen nowhere else in the world with any other scripture existing today.

This pure and clean Word of God exist every where in the world, even the remotest corners which Muslims have found access or non Muslims have embraced Islam. Millions of men all over the world recite different portions of it in their five times daily prayers.

Since its revelation its propagation has been on the increase. From the moment, the mother of the believer, Khadijah Al Kubra (R) heard from the Prophet (PBUH) the first ever revelation in Hira cave, day-by-day, rather every moment the number of its votaries is on the increase. No country, no particular period customs and manners, the favourable or adverse condition of its followers or antagonists, can become an inpediment in its progression.

In many countries and languages faulty translations to misguide the world were put forth and its true and clear teachings were confused with misleading explanatory foot notes, but none of these satanic devices could bring down its greater and greater publication and distribution with the time.

Unlike other scriptures, the Holy Quran is extant in the language it was revealed and the world has access to it everywhere.

Not an iota got changed during a millenium and a half. But the other holy books like Torah (the old Testament) and Injil (The Gospels) and the epistles of the saints, Vedas and Zand and Pazand can not claim to be the original versions and free from tampering, so much so that it becomes difficult to believe that their greater part could be the revealed scriptures. In fact no religious book save the Quran could escape perversion. Even the languages in which they are said to have been revealed exist today nor any copy of the original to be seen. The earliest Gospel is the Greek version of Injil and not the original Aramic.

Since the Quran itself relates all those objections levelled against it or the false accusations brought forth against the Prophet about the origin of Quran, it is its own true history, showing both sides of the picture clearly. The Glorious Quran due to its truth and unassailable position has demonstrated that boldness which no other scripture in the world can claim for itself (and for obvious reasons).

The Quranic teachings have that undeniable truth in them that those religious communities and nations that did not acknowledge it openly, yet claimed that their religious books too had those truth in them, which either preceded the Quran or followed it. How true is the word of Allah:

> No falsehood can approach it from before or behind it. It is sent down by one Full of Wisdom. (Q. XLI: 42)

What have put forth as claim in the above lines will become manifest to you, reader, when you will study the conditions extant in the pre-Qu'ranic period of Judaism, Christianity, Zoroastrianism, Buddhism, and Sanatan or Aryah Dharm of Hinduism (their social and political orders) and then come to study their progress in all walks of life to date, considering at the same time that long before this revolution in this country, the teachings of the Quran were in usage in most spheres of life if not all.

Now whether any religious or ethnic group acknowledges the blessings and bounties of the Glorious Quran, as do the founders of Brahmo Samaj, or Martin Luther, the rebel of the Roman Catholic Church as he stands accused of his strong learnings to be derivations from the Quran, by the orthodox Catholics, or those who find it repugnant to acknowledge even that much remotely derived benefit as many religious sects that have definitely though stealthily borrowed Quranic teachings, are going on borrowing as problems arise which Quran alone has solved. (Some of them openly praise Islamic laws minus the courage of adoption, like our prime minister who recently lauded the Muslim Divorce Laws beside other things that appeal to him and many others of that bilk from time to time). (There is a big flow in this type of thinking of people like Gandhiji. He held the rule of Abu Bakr (R) and 'Umar Faruq (R) as his ideal but was either ignorant of or deliberately over lacking the very common principle that laws divorced from an ideology, the driving force of action, are not effective at all or very little).

The Glorious Quran is the only scripture with the glad tidings:

> This day have I perfected your religion for you completed my favour upon you.
> —Al Quran V: 3

Discernment of the Divine Entity

1. In the name of Allah, the Beneficent, Most Merciful.

2. No vision can grasp Him. But His grasp is over all vision. (Q. 6: 103)

3. There is nothing whatsoever like unto Him. But He is the One that hears and sees. —Al Quran XLII: 11

4. Allah is the Protector of those who have faith: from the depths of darkness He leads them forth into light. (Q. II: 257)

5. Allah! There is no god but He—the Living, the Self-Subsisting, Supporter of all, no slumber can seize Him, nor sleep. His are all things in the heavens and earth. Who is there can intercede in His Presence except as He permitteth? He knoweth what (appeareth to His creatures as) Before or After or Behind them. Nor shall they compass aught of His knowledge except as He willeth. His Throne doth extend over the heavens and the earth, and He feeleth no fatigue in guarding and preserving them, for, He is the Most High, the Supreme in Glory. —Al Quran II: 255

6. He hath inscribed for Himself (the rule of) Mercy.Q. VI: 12

7. Say: He is Allah, the One, Allah, the Eternal, Absolute, He begetteth not, nor is He begotten; and there is none like unto Him. —Al Quran CXII: 1-4

The Definition of True Faith

1. The nature in which Allah has made mankind. No change (there is) in the work (wrought) by Allah: that is the true Religion, but most among mankind know not. (Q. XXX: 30)

2. (Our religion) takes its true from Allah and who can give a better true than Allah. —Al Quran II: 138

3. The same religion has he established for you as that which He enjoined on Noah—the which We have sent by inspiration to thee—and that which we enjoined on Abraham Moses and Jesus, namely that you should remain steadfast in Religion, and make no divisions therein: —Al Quran XLII: 13

What for Does Allah Want Good Deeds From Man

It is not their meat, their blood, that reaches Him:
(Q. XXII: 37)

Shari'ah was Meant to Perfect Man's Humanity

1. Allah doth not wish to place you in difficulty, but to make you clean, and to complete His favour to you, that ye may be grateful. —Al Quran V: 6

2. For, prayer restrains from shameful and evil deeds; and remembrance of Allah is the greatest (thing in life) without doubts. —Al Quran: XXIX: 45

The Duties of the Prophet

1. A similar (favour have ye already received) in that We have sent among you a Messenger of your own, rehearsing to you Our Signs, purifying you and introducing you in scripture and wisdom, and in new knowledge. (Q H: 151)

2. For he commands them what is just and forbids them what is evil; he allows them as lawful what is good (and pure) and prohibits them from what is bad (and impure); he releases them from heavy burdens and from the yokes that are upon them. (Q. VII: 157)

Retribution both Here and Hereafter

1. If the people of the towns had but believed and feared Allah, we should indeed have opened out to them (all kinds of) blessings from heaven and earth, but they rejected (the truth) and We brought them to book for their misdeeds. —Al Quran VII: 96

2. If only they had stood fast by the Torah, the Gospel, and all the revelation that was sent to them from their Lord, they would have eaten both from above them and from below their feet. —Al Quran V: 66

3. Whatever misfortune happens to you is because of the things your hands have wrought, and for many (a sin) He grants forgiveness. —Al Quran XLII: 30

4. Now no person knows what delights of the eye are kept hidden (in reserve) for them —as a reward for their (good) deeds.

The Divine Sunnah Alters Not

1. No change will thou find in Allah's Way (of dealing).

2. No turning off will thou find in Allah's Way (of dealing). —Al Quran XXXV: 43

3. He Who created the seven heavens one above another. No want of proportion will thou see in the creation of the Most Glorious. So turn thy vision again, seest thou any flaw. Again turn they vision a second time: (thy) vision will come back to thee dull and discomfited, in a state worn out. —Al Quran LXVIL3-4

Only Personal Effort can be Fruitful

1. That man can have nothing but what he strives for; Q. LIII: 39

2. Verily this (the bounties in Heaven) is a reward for you. (from Allah) and your Endeavour is accepted and recognized. —Al Quran LXXVI: 22

3. That was a people that hath passed away. They shall reap the fruit of what they did and ye of what ye do! —Al Quran 141

The Lofty Position of Patience and Piety

1. If ye persevere patiently and guard against evil, then that indeed is a matter of great resolution.
—Al Quran III: 186

The Position of Wisdom

1. And he to whom wisdom is granted receive indeed a benefit over-whelming. —Al Quran 32: 24

The Fruit of Patience:

1. And We appointed from among them, leaders giving guidance under Our command, so long as they persevered with patience. —Al Quran 32: 24

Cutting Oneself off from Greed

1. Nor strain thy eyes in longing for the things We have given for enjoyment to parties of them. (Q. XX: 131)

Not to Consign to Oblivion the Hereafter in the Luxuriance of Life Here

1. Nor forget thy position in the world but do thou good.

Guard against Self Destruction

1. And spend of your substance in the cause of Allah, and make not your own hands contribute to (your) destruction. —Al Quran II: 195

Forging Falsehood is Inimical to Belief

1. It is those who believe not in the Signs of Allah, it is they who forge falsehood. It is they who lie.
—Al Quran XVI: 105

Absolutely Prohibited Things

1. Say: The things that my Lord hath indeed forbidden are: indecent deeds whether open or secret: sins and trespasses against truth or reason, assigning of partners to Allah for which he hath given no authority: and saying things about Allah of which ye have no knowledge.
—Al Quran VII: 33

Worship of Allah is Divine Baptism

1. (Our religion) takes its true from Allah and who can give a better hue than Allah. It is He Whom we worship.
—Al Quran II: 138

Pen and Writing Praise Worthy

1. Nun. By the Pen and by the (Record) which men write.
—Al Quran LXVIII: 1

Signs of Allah for the Wise

1. Behold! In the creation of the heavens and the earth, in the alternation of the Night and the Day, in the sailing of ships through the ocean, for the profit of mankind, in the rain which Allah sends down from the skies, and the life which He gives there with, to an earth that is dead; in the beasts of all kinds that he scatters through the earth; in the change of winds and the clouds which they trail like their slaves between the sky and the earth. (Here) indeed are Signs for a people that are Wiser.
—Al Quran II: 164

Swearing Prohibited

1. Obey not every mean swearer. —Al Quran LXVIII: 10

2. And make not Allah's (name) an excuse for your oaths.
(Q. II: 224)

3. Keep to your oaths. —Al Quran V: 89

Call to Total Peace (Islam the Religion of Peace)

1. O ye who believe! Enter into Islam whole heartedly; and follow not the footsteps of the satan, for he is to you an avowed enemy. —Al Quran 11: 208

Mutual Reform

1. Make peace between persons. —Al Quran II: 224

2. And keep relations straight between yourselves.

Teaching Forgiveness and Overlooking Faults

1. Let them forgive and overlook. Do you not wish that Allah should forgive you? For Allah is Oft-Forgiving, Most Merciful. —Al Quran XXIV: 22

True Teachings Manifest Themselves

1. Soon will We show them in the (furthest) regions (of the earth), and in their own souls, until it becomes manifest to them that this is the Truth.

—Al Quran XLI: 53

Rules of Administration

Judges Must be Learned

And remember David and Solomon when they gave judgement in the matter of the field into which the steep of certain people had strayed by might: We did witness their judgement. To Solomon, We inspired the right understanding of the matter to each (of them).

—Al Quran XXI: 78-79

Mischief Prohibited

> Do not mischief on the earth, after it hath been set in order.
> —Al Quran VII: 56

Iniquity Brings Destruction

> How many were the towns We utterly destroyed because of their iniquities and setting up in their places other peoples.
> —Al Quran XXI: 11

Righteousness Gives Stability

> Nor would thy Lord be the One to destroy the towns unjustly while their people are righteous. (Q. XI: 117)

To Avoid War Preparedness is the Only Way

> Against them make ready your strength to the utmost of your power, including steeds of war, to strike terror (into the hearts of) the enemies of Allah and your enemies.
> —Al Quran VIII: 60

To Conduct the Affairs of the State Consultation is a Must

1. And consult them in affairs (of moment). Then when thou hast taken a decision, put thy trust in Allah.

2. Who (conduct) their affairs by mutual consultation:
—(Quran XLII:.38)

3. She said: "Ye chiefs! Advise me in (this) my affair: no affair have I decided except in your presence."
(Q. XXVII:32)

The Scholarship

Listening to Wisdom, Pondering over Them and Adopting the Best

> So announce the Good News to My servants — those who listen to the Word, and follow the best of it: those are the ones whom Allah has guided, and those are the ones endued with understanding.
>
> —Al Quran XXXIX: 17-18

Acquiring Knowledge from Aliens

> Say: 'Have you any certain knowledge? If so produce it before us. —Al Quran VI: 148

Establishment of a Party Calling to Faith a Must

> Let there arise out of you a band of people to all that is good, enjoining what is right, and forbidding what is wrong: they are the ones to attain felicity. (Q. III: 104)

Selected Few from Neo-muslim Groups Should Visit the Centre of Faith and Religious Learning and Go Back to Teach the Ignorant Lot

> It is not for the believers to go forth together: if a contingent from every expedition goes forth to devote themselves to studies in religion and admonish the people when they return to them. —that thus they may learn to guard themselves (against evil). (Q. IX: 122)

Characteristics of the Finer Sex (Frailties of Women)

> Is then one brought up among trinkets, and unable to give a clear account in a dispute (to be associated with Allah). —Al Quran XLIII: 18

The Intimate Relationship of Husband and Wife

> They are your garments and ye are their garments.
> (Q. II: 187)

His garments save man from inclemency of weather, improves his appearance. It is also a measure of the cultural level of any people. Besides decoration it secretes many defects (physical). Similarly should be the intimate relations of husband and wife and not only physically close but culturally also and guarding secrets mutually.

> He created for you mates from among yourselves, that ye may dwell in tranquillity with them, and He has put love and Mercy between your hearts.
> —Al Quran XXX: 21

Mutual Obligations of Husband and Wife

1. Men are the protectors and maintainers of women.
   —Al Quran IV: 34

2. And women shall have rights similar to the rights against them, according to what is equitable; But men have a degree over them. —Al Quran II: 228

Love of Allah in the Highest Degree, the Demand of Belief

> But those of Faith are overflowing in their love for Allah.
> —Al Quran II: 165

Faith and Knowledge Raise and in the Sight of Allah

> Allah will raise up to (suitable) ranks (and degree), those of you who believe and have been granted knowledge.
> —Al Quran LVIII: 11

Man Specially Favoured by Allah

> We have honoured the sons of Adam, provided them transport on land and sea, given them for sustenance things good and pure, and centered on them special favours, above a great part of our creation. (Q. XVII: 70)

Superiority of Man Demands Unitarianism (Total Rejection of Ascribing Partners to Allah)

> He (Moses) said: "Shall I seek for you a god other than Allah, when it is He Who hath favoured you above (all) creatures. (pickthall) —Al Quran VII: 140

Man Can Take a Lesson from Lowly Creatures

> "Woe is me!" said he; "Was I not even above to be even as this raven and to hide the naked body of my brother?" Then he became full of regards
>
> — (Al Quran V: 31)

Signs Every Where for Those with Seeing Eyes

> And how many signs in the heavens and the earth do they pass by? Yet they turn (their faces) away from them!
>
> —Al Quran XII: 105

Hearts and Minds Learn Wisdom Through Travel and Also Eyes See Better and Ears Hear Better

> Do they not travel through the land, so that their hearts (and minds) may thus learn wisdom and their ear may thus learn to hear? Truly, it is not the eyes that are blind but the hearts which are in their breasts.
>
> —Al Quran XXII: 46

Forbidden Things not Clean and Pure and Clean and Pure Things not Forbidden

O ye people! Eat of what is on earth lawful and good; and do not follow the footsteps of Satan, for he is to you an avowed enemy. —Al Quran II: 168

And to Give up Clean and Pure Things is a Satanic Act

And therefore, to give up pure and clean things would be to follow in the footsteps of Satan. (Q.II: 168)

Insight and Guidance Only in the Life Term Granted as Trial and not on its Closure

But those who were blind in this world, will be blind in the Hereafter, and most astray from the Path. (Q. XVII: 72)

Only Those True in Faith Can Attain High Position

So lose not heart nor fall into despair, for you must gain mastery if ye are true in Faith. (Q. III : 139)

Animals and Birds have Communities Like those of Human Beings, Ultimately to be Gathered to Their Lord

There is not an animal (that lives) on the earth, nor a being that flies on its wings but (forms part of) communities like you. Nothing have We omitted from the book and they (all) shall be gathered to their Lord in the end. —Al Quran VI: 38

Every Thing Here on Earth has Been Created for the Benefit of Mankind

It is He Who has created for you all things that are on earth, then He turned to the heaven and made them into seven heavens (firmaments). (Q. II: 29)

Every One Acts According to His Innate Nature

1. Every one acts according to his own disposition. But your Lord knows best who it is best guided on the Way. (Q. XVIII: 84)

2. Seest thou not that to Allah protstrate all things that are in the heavens or on earth, the sun, the moon, the stars, the hills, the trees, the animals and a great number among mankind? But a great number are (also) such as unto whom the chastisement is justly due. (Q. XXII: 18)

3. So, he who gives (in charity) and fears (Allah) and (in all sincerity) testifies to the best, we will indeed make smooth for him the Path to Ease. But he who is a greedy miser and thinks himself self-sufficient and gives the lie to the Best. We will indeed make smooth for him the Path to Misery. —Al Quran XCII: 5-10

Different Classes of People of Various Grades Needed to Run a Political Set Up as Part of the Trial, the Purpose of Creation

It is He Who has made you the inheritors of the earth. He hath raised you in ranks, some above others, that He may try you in the gifts. He hath given you. For thy Lord is quick in punishment: yet He is indeed Oft-Forgiving Most Merciful. —Al Quran VI: 165

Emphasis on Equality in Rights and Equity

And He has set up the Balance (of Justice) in order that ye may not transgress (due) balance. So establish weight with due justice and fail not short in the balance.

The Muslim Ummah is the Well Wisher of Humanity

Ye are the best of people, evolved for mankind, enjoining what is right, forbidding what is wrong, and believing in Allah. —Al Quran III: 110

The Basis of Muslim Fraternity

> The Believers are but a single brotherhood. So make peace and reconciliation between your two (contending) brothers, and fear Allah that ye may receive Mercy.
>
> (Q. XLIX: 10)

Those Incapable of it Should Not be Entrusted with Their Property (Which is Really National Wealth).

> To those (orphans) weak of understanding give not your (national) property which Allah has assigned to you to manage but feed and clothe them therewith and speak to them kindly and justly. —Al Quran IV: 5

Fear of Impoverishment Satanic Suggestion and Should not Prevent Us From Generous Deeds

> Satan threatens you with poverty and bids you to conduct unseenly. Allah promiseth you His Forgiveness and Bounties. And Allah careth for all and knoweth all things. —Al Quran II: 268

Covetous Selfishness is Not Good for Us

> And those saved from the covetousness of their own souls—they are the one that achieve prosperity.
>
> (Q. LXIV: 16)

The Servants of Rahman are Neither Stingy Nor Yet Extravagant

> Those who, when they spend, are not extravagant and not niggardly either, but hold a just (balance) between these (extremes) —Al Quran XXV: 67

Sea-borne Trade More Profitable to Man

In the sailing of Ships through the ocean for the profit of mankind (are also signs of Allah). —Al Quran II: 164

For Whom the Abiding Bounties of Allah

Whatever ye are given here is (but) the enjoyment of this life: but that which is with Allah is better and more lasting: it is for those who believe and put their trust in their Lord. Those who avoid the greater sins and indecencies, and when they are angry even then forgive; Those who respond to their Lord, and establish regular prayer, who (conduct) their affair by mutual consultation; who spend out of what We bestow on them for sustenance: and those who, when an oppressive wrong is inflicted on them are not cowed but help and defend themselves. The recompense for an injury is an injury equal there to (in degree): but if a person forgives and makes reconciliation, his reward is due from Allah: for, Allah loveth not those who do wrong. But indeed any do help and defend himself after a wrong (done) to him, against such there is no cause of blame. The blame is only against those who oppress men with wrong-doing and insolently transgress beyond bounds through the land defying right and justice: For such there will be a chastisement grievous. But indeed if they show patience and forgive, that would truly be an affair of great Resolution. —Al Quran XLII: 36-43

6

Spread of Faith

Deputations arrival, return and meeting different communities and tribes at every stage of their journey and conveying the voice of Islam reached one and all. They came across—how beautifully all this was conducted.

The defensive battles that the Prophet (PBUH) fought under compulsion were limited to a small area. But when we look at these deputations we find that they were coming from every part of the country.

Guidance to the Right Path and Islam are the two streams that the Prophet (PBUH) made to gush forth in the dry land without a blade of grass to which rushed all those thirsting for them from every corner of the country.

The other argument in favour of a general call to Faith by him is the coming of these deputations to him. The following are the tribes whose deputations came to the Prophet (PBUH). Those coming to him for political or personal ends have not been included in this list:

Dans, Sada', Thaqif, Abd-al-Qays, Bani Hanifah, Tay, Ash'arin, Azd, Farvah Jazami, "Amdan, Tariq bin Abd-Allah, Najib, Bani Sa'd Huzaim, Banu Asad, Bahra, Azra, Khaulan, Maharib, Ghassan, Bani-al-Harith, Bani Eish, Chamid, Bani Fazarah, Salaman, Najran, Nakh's.

Now we shall take up briefly the account of the above deputations.

Tufail bin 'Amr Dausi's account of entering the fold of Islam has come for mention earlier. When departing for home, he had made a request to the Prophet that he should pray that his community too, may enter the fold of Islam. The Prophet prayed for it: "O Allah! Make Tufail a sign." When Tufail got home, his old father came to see him. Tufail said to him: "My dear father! now neither I am yours nor you are mine." The old man asked him: "Why so?" Tufail told him: I have taken to Islam, the Faith of Muhammad." The old man said to him: "My dear son! Whichever is your faith, the same is mine." Tufail said: "That is very good. Now, please get up, take bath, put on clean clothes and come to me so that I may impart teachings of Islam to you." Then came his wife and with her too came up the same topic of talk and she also embraced Islam. After these successes, he started with general call for Islam to his people, but they did not pay any attention to his call.

Tufail once more went to see the Prophet and confided to him that his community was given to fornication and adultery very much. Since Islam strictly forbids it, my people do not subscribe to Islam. He requested the Prophet to pray for it too. He prayed as requested: "O Allah! Show Daus the Straight Path." Then he said to Tufail to go home.

Essential Guidance

Call men to the Religion of Allah, treat them kindly. This time, Tufail scored better success. In the 5th year of Hijrah, he had converted 80 persons to Islam, with whom he visited Medina. On learning that the Prophet had gone to Khaiber, he too made it his destination and it was there that all these companions of his saw the Prophet. Ja'far (R) the cousin of the Prophet (PBUH) also reached Khaibar from Abyssinia with all those Abyssinian converts, after a long stay there since his migration from Mecca with others.

Ja'far's reaching Khaibar with his Abyssinian converts and Tufail with his own community's Muslim families was in a way a warning to the Jews that whereas the Islamic teachings had succeeded in winning over men from such far-off places as Yemen and Abyssinia, they persisted with their reliance on their forts of stone and bricks in opposing Islam.

Invitation to Islam

This deputation had come to the Prophet in B.A.H. First of all a person of this community, Ziyad bin Harith Sada'i came to the Prophet. On a second visit by the same, Ziyad came with 15 persons of his community. Sa'd bin 'Ubadah was detailed to look after their needs. After his return to his people. They responded to the call of Islam and so many became Muslims.

Ziyad submitted to the Prophet (PBUH) that had only one well to draw water from in their tribal habitations. During winters there was no difficulty but in summers it dried up. The tribe get dispersed to tide over the summer somehow. And they have recently taken to Islam. They need to be taught and trained in the Islamic system. Kindly pray for us that the well may not dry up in summer season.

The Prophet asked him to bring seven pebbles to him which Ziyad readily did. The Prophet kept them in his hand and returned them to him. He instructed him to drop them one by one into the well saying Allah every time a pebble was dropped. Ziyad is reported to have stated later that after the dropping of pebbles, the well remained filled with ample water for their needs.

The first person of Thaqif tribe who came to learn the teachings of Islam, to the Prophet (PBUH) was Urwah bin Mas'ood Thaqafi. He was the chief of his tribe. On the occasion of the treaty of Hudaibiyah, he had come to the Prophet as the advocate (representative) of the Makkan pagan. After the battle of Hawazin and Thaqif with the Grace of Allah, he came to Medina and embraced Islam. 'Urwah had ten wives. The Prophet directed him to retain four of them and divorce the rest. He complied with the orders.

When 'Urwah (R) had learnt Islamic teachings, he requested the Prophet to permit him to go and call people to Islam. The Prophet said to him that his community will murder him. 'Urwah submitted that his people loved him just as a lover has love and regard for his beloved. He came back to his people and started preaching. One day while he was offering prayer in the upper story of his house, some wretch shot an arrow which martyred him.

Although 'Urwah could not survive, the voice that he had raised, the call that he had given to his community did not fail to melt their hardened hearts. Soon after, the nation sent their representatives to the Prophet so that they may acquire adequate knowledge about Islam.

This deputation had come to the Prophet (PBUH) in 9 A.H. The leader of the deputation was 'Abd Yaleel to convey the Message to whom the Prophet had gone to Ta'if in the tenth year of his raising and he had not only refused to listen to him but had set the street urchin, and vagabonds to vex and disgrace the Prophet, and at whose encouragement stones were rained on him and dirt and filth was flung on him.

The Apostle of Allah had declared that he would not curse them. For, if they themselves do not come to believe in Islam, Allah will grace their progeny with Belief and Faith. And now the same enemies of Islam had found a place for Islam in their hearts and had come to the Prophet with longing hearts.

Mughirah bin Shaibah submitted to the Apostle of Allah that the Thaqifites were the people of his community. "Shall I take them with me as my guests and entertain them" he sought permission of the Prophet.

The Prophet said in reply: I do not disallow you to honour your own community. But let them stay at a place where they are within hearing distance of the recitation of the Quran.

So their tents were set on the open space of the mosque, where they could listen to the recitation of the Quran and watch people praying. This device was helpful in impressing upon their minds the truth of Islam and they entered Islam through Bai'ah at the hands of the Apostle of Allah. Before Bai'ah, they sought exemption from prayer. The Prophet pointed out to them: "There is no goodness in any religion without prayer. Then they requested him not to be called for Jihad and Zakat should not be realized from them. The Prophet accepted this request and explained to the companions that under the impact of Islam they would automatically observe both elements.

'Abd Yaleel, their leader, at different times, discussed the following issues as well with the Messenger of Allah:

Fornication is Strictly Prohibited in Islam

O Apostle of Allah! What is your opinion about fornication? The people of our station are so often away from their homes and the irresistible sexual urge of many makes fornication inevitable. The Apostle of Allah (PBUH) said: "Fornication is strictly prohibited and Allah has ordained in His book, the Quran:

> Nor come nigh to adultery: for it is an indecent (deed) and an evil way. —Al Quran XVII: 32

Usury (Taking Interest on Things Lent) is Also Strictly Prohibited

The second question that he put to the Prophet was as to his opinion (edict) about interest. This is virtually our own goods. The Apostle of Allah (PBUH) said: "You can take your principal (actual amount lent). Just think over, Allah has warned thus:

> "O ye who believe! Fear Allah and give up what remains of your demand for usury, if ye are indeed believers."
> (Q. II: 278)

Liquor is Also Strictly Prohibited

The third question that he brought up was about taking liquor: "O Apostle of Allah! What do you say about liquor. It is after all our own country's juice and we cannot live without it."

The Prophet told him: "Allah has ordained its prohibition. Just listen what He has declared in the Quran:

> "O ye who believe! Intoxicants and gambling: sacrificing to stones, and (divination by arrows are an abomination. Eschew such (abomination) that ye may prosper."
> (Q. V: 90)

Next day, he came and submitted: "Very well, we shall abide by what you have ordained. But what is to be done to rabbahs this rabbah is the feminine of Rab (Lord and Sustainer or cherisher). The goddess they worshipped was called 'rabbah.' The Prophet replied: "Demolish it."

The deputationists cried out: "Ah! If 'rabbah' got news of it that you are bent upon its demolition, she is sure to destroy us."

'Umar bin Khattab (R) said to him: "Alas Ibn 'Abd Yaleel! You do not realize that it is nothing but a piece of stone."

Ibn Abd yaleel said to him peevishly: "Umar! We have not come here to talk to you." Then addressing the Prophet he submitted: "Kindly take the responsibility of getting it felled by your own men." The Prophet said in reply: "All right: I shall send somebody to do it for you."

One of them submitted, adding: "Send the man undertaking demolition after we have left. He will not accompany us."

In short, all the deputationists returned home as believers.

Departing they requested the Prophet to appoint an Imam (the leader of the congregational prayer) for them.

One of the deputationists was 'Uthman bin Abu-al-'As, who happened to be the youngest of the lot. He had been covertly learning the Quran and the laws of the Islamic Shari'ah. He learnt all that from the Prophet (PBUH) and Abu Bakr (R) by turns. So the Prophet appointed him as their Imam.

The deputation on their way home by common consent decided that keeping our Islam secret let us disappoint our community. When they got home, the people of their community asked them: "How did you fare in your journey to Medina?"

The members of the deputation said to them: "We had to deal with a person very harsh in speech who commands us to take to things impossible to undertake, for example demolition of Lat and 'Uzza, giving up the interest on money, regarding higher and fornication they are strictly forbidden. Their community declared on oath that they would never undertake them.

The deputation said to them: "In that case, get ready with your arms in perfect trim, make preparations for a war, with repairs of you forts."

For two days, the Thaqifites remained firm on this resolve. But the third day, they themselves softened to declare:

"How can we fight against Muhammad, the entire Arabia is at his feet." Then addressing the members of the deputation they confided to them: "Accept whatever he ordains or demands of us as Muslims."

The deputationists said to them: "Now we shall disclose the whole truth. We found Muhammad superior most in taqwa (piety), fidelity and sincerity, mercy and truth. You and we were all very much benefited by this journey of ours."

Their community said to them by way of reproach: "Why did you then keep it hidden from us and cause such grief and anxiety to us?"

The deputation explained: "Our aim in this device was simply this that you may get rid of your satanic pride in your hearts. After this, they one and all entered the fold of Islam.

After a few days, the party of men sent to Ta'if under the command of Khalid bin Waleed, intended to fell the idol Lat. The Thaqifites had imagined it to be a very difficult task. The purdah observing ladies and children had also rushed to the scene of the occasion. Mughirah bin Sha'bah shot an arrow to fell it but his zealous effort was too much for him to maintain body equilibrium and he fell forward. Allah reproved Mughirah and 'rabbah' killed him. And in their gleeful mood called out: "However hard you may try but you cannot demolish."

Mughirah bin Sha'bah said in an angry tone: "You Thaqifites! you are very simple folk indeed. What can this piece of stone do?. O ye men! Take to the obedience of Allah, and worship Him alone. Then he entered the small temple and closing the door, he smashed the idol and then got up the temple walls and started demolishing them. Then other Muslims too got up and took part in demolition work until not a stone was left on another stone of that building.

The priest of the temple said to the audience: "The foundation of the temple must prove their undoing." Mughirah on hearing this superstitious exclamation of his set to work and pulled out the base as well, thus strengthening the foundation of Islam in the hearts of these people.

The deputation of the tribe of 'Abd-al-Qais came to the Prophet (PBUH). He asked them: To which community do you belong? "From the Rabi'ah community," they submitted. The Prophet welcomed them.

They said: Between you and us the pagan tribe Madar is a great obstacle, a great danger and we can present ourselves only in the Prohibited Months (Ze Qa'dah, Zu-al-Hijjah, Muharram — Haj pilgrimage, and Rajab-Umrah, prohibiting violence). Therefore, we would like to clearly understand Islam and its teachings which may become our routine in life and also that of the rest of our community.

The Prophet in reply to this request of deputation said:

I command you to act on four teachings of Islam and to desist from the other four things to Adhere to

1. To believe in one and only god, Allah which alludes to bear witness to in practical form of the epitome of Islam, the Kalimah: "There is no god but Allah (and) Muhammad is His Messenger."

2. Prayer

3. Zakat

4. Fasting in the month of Ramadan and taking out a fifth of the booty for the cause of Islam

And the four prohibited things are the following:

1. Tauba (tauba- a hollow gourd to brew wine or to keep it in).

2. Hantam-basins made of lac (a dark red coloured resin) or coaled with lac.

3. Naqeer- a kind of liquor or a wooden utensil to contain it.

4. Mazaft- a vessel polluted with 'qeer' a kind of liquor

The deputationists asked the Prophet: "O Apostle of Allah how do you know what is Naqeer? He said, I know. A date palm tree is tapped for serum, rather thick milky exudate collected in a vessel and dates are put into it and water added which ferments the fluid and when brewed, it is taken as an intoxicant. It is possible that one intoxicated with it may murder his cousin. How amazing that one of these deputationists had murdered his cousin while intoxicated with this particular wine 'Naqeer.'

They then asked him: "O Apostle of Allahi In which type of vessel we should keep water and drink it from?" The Prophet told them: use small leather bags for this purpose whose mouths can be tied with a string to close them." They informed the Prophet (PBUH) that theirs was a rat infested area and leather bags can not last long. He insisted on them, intact or damaged by rats, they have to be used.

Jarud bin-al-'Ula had come with this deputation. He was a Christian. He said to the Prophet (PBUH): "O Apostle of Allah (PBUH)! I already subscribe to a religion. If we discard our own and adopt yours, can you guarantee our safety (salvation)? The Prophet (PBUH) assured him of such a guarantee from himself, since the religion he was calling him to was superior to the one he believed in at that time.

A deputation of Banu Hanifah came to the Prophet (PBUH). Through the efforts of Thamamah bin Aihal, Islam had been introduced to the residents of this region. This deputation embraced Islam in Medina. Musailamah 'Kazzab' (the false claimant to prophethood) was also with this deputation. When in Medina he went on saying to Madinites that if Muhammad (PBUH) agreed to make him his successor, he would embrace Islam at his hands." The Prophet came to know about it, he said, "I do not want to take his pledge even at the cost of this branch of date palm in my hand. If he does not pledge his loyalty to Islam, Allah will destroy him. Allah has shown me his evil end. I saw in a dream that I had golden bracelets on my wrists. They appeared disgusting to me. Revelation in the dream directed me to blow them off. I blew at them and they disappeared. I think that they represented Musailamah the ruler of Yamamah and 'Anasi ruler of Su'aa.

Although claimant to prophethood, Musailamah recognized the Prophet (PBUH) also as the Apostle of Allah. What he probably meant by this double dealing was to keep the people of these lands in good humour.

In the 10th year of Hijrah, the following correspondence also took place between Musailamah and the Prophet (PBUH):

From Musailamah the 'Apostle of Allah' to Muhammad the Apostle of Allah. It should be quite evident that half the earth belongs to us and the remaining half to the Quraish. But the Quraish are not inclined to justice and fairplay. Peace be upon you.

The Prophet replied:

In the name of Allah, the Beneficent, Most Merciful

From Muhammad the Apostle of Allah to Musailamah, the damned liar (the false claimant to prophethood). It should be evident the earth belongs to Allah and He makes its inheritor whomsoever He is pleased and the prosperity of the Hereafter is the share of God-fearing. Peace be on those taking to the straight Path.

The letter of the Prophet (PBUH) had been delivered to Musailamah by Habib bin Zaid bin 'Asin and Kazzab had both of his hands and feet chopped off.

The deputation of the Tay tribe under the leadership of Zaid-al-Khail came to the Prophet (PBUH). The Apostle of Allah remarked: "Whoever of the tribes of Arabia was extolled in my presence, proved much less on experience. But Zaid-al-Khalid is an exception. Then his name was changed to Zaid-al-Khair. All the members of the deputation embraced Islam.

The Ash'ariyah tribe of Yemen came to the Prophet (PBUH). On their arrival, the Prophet (PBUH) had said:

The Yemenites came to me whose hearts are gentle and are easily moved. When entering Medina they were chanting the following couplet:

Tomorrow we are going to meet our friends (meaning Muhammad (PBUH) and his companions).

This deputation comprised seven persons. When they came to the Prophet (PBUH) he approved of their condition, manners and conduct. "Who are you," he asked then. They replied: We are believers. The Prophet said to them: "Every utterance has a reality behind it. Tell me what is the reality of your utterance about your belief?"

They said: "We have fifteen characteristics, habits and customary practices. The first five are those we were instructed to repose belief in other by your preachers: Belief in Allah, His angels. His revealed Books, His Messengers and Resurrection. And the other five to act upon and live upto are:

To declare one's creed saying there is no god save Allah and establishing five times daily regular prayers, paying Zakat, fasting during the month of Ramadan and pilgrimage to the House of Allah in case of having the requisite means.

And the remaining five that we had known earlier also: To thank Allah in times of prosperity and plenty, to persevere patiently in distress, to be resigned to the decree of Allah, to stand firm on Truth in moments of trial, not to gloat over the misfortune of our opponents.

The Prophet said to them: Those who taught you the last five were really wise and learned men, and their prudence shows that (so to say) they were prophets. I would like to add five more to these fifteen to take the number to twenty.

(a) Do not store those things which you do not eat.

(b) Do not make a house you do not have to live in.

(c) Do not compete in things you love to abandon tomorrow.

(d) Be God fearing, for to have to return and present yourself to render account. Create an affinity for those things that will stand you in good stead in the Hereafter or life eternal.

These people followed the stressed advice of the Prophet (PBUH).

Farwah bin 'Amr was the governor of the northern territory of Arabia under the control of the eastern wing of the Roman empire. The capital of his territory was Mu'an. The adjacent region of Palestine was also under his control.

The Prophet had sent him the letter conveying the message of Islam. Farwah (R) had embraced Islam and had sent a costly white mule to the Prophet as a gift.

When the king of Constantinople came to know of his Islam, he called him back to himself.

He persuaded him to discard Islam. When he refused to oblige he was incarcerated. Finally, it was decided to crucify him and he was crucified at 'Ifre tank in Palestine. When he was taken to the cross, he recited some couplets denoting the cross and crucification in the form of a riddle.

This tribe came from Yemen. Khalid bin Waleed (R) had been detailed to preach Islam to them. He stayed there long enough but without success. The Prophet then sent 'Ali Murtaza (R) for propagation of Islam there. Through his graceful efforts, the entire tribe got converted to Islam.

When the Prophet heard from Ali about his success, he fell in prostration as a token of thanks to Allah and pronounced: "Peace be on Hamdan."

This deputation consisted of men who had earlier pledged their fealty to Islam at the hands of 'Ali (R) and had come now to see the Prophet (PBUH).

Tariq bin Abd-Allah had stated that he was standing one day in the market place of Suq-al-Majaz in Mecca when there came a person who was giving a clarion call:

"O ye people utter "there is no god but Allah" and you will prosper."

Another person came after him who threw pebbles at him and said: "O ye people! Do not believe in what he says. He is a liar."

I enquired as to the identity of those two persons.

They explained to me: This is a person from Bani Hashim who deems himself the Apostle of Allàh. And this second person following him is his uncle Abd-al-'Uzza (Abu Lahab's real name).

Tariq says that many years passed after this incident and the Prophet (PBUH) migrated and settled in Medina. About this time, some of our people including myself went to Medina to purchase dates. When we were approaching the town, we decided to bathe and change the travel-sodden clothes before entering the town.

On this occasion, there came a person with two old sheets on him. After greetings, he enquired of us: "Where from and where to?" We said in reply: "We hail from Rabza and this (Medina) is our destination. He further enquired about the purpose of our visits. We told him that we had come for purchasing dates.

We had a red camel with a nose string. He asked us whether we would like to sell that camel to him. We assented adding: "In exchange for dates worth this animal." On hearing our terms we were surprised that he did not utter a word about reduction in price (bargaining) and holding the nose string of the camel he went into the town. When hc had disappeared from our sight we started reproaching ourselves for we had done unwillingly. We have sold our camels to a person who was a total stranger to us and there was apparently no way of realizing the price of the camel.

We had with us a lady in a litter on the camel's back. She spoke out: "I had seen the face of the person luminous like the bright side of the moon. If a person like him does not pay you, I will."

We were engaged in this discussion when a person came to us and said that the Prophet (PBUH) had sent him with dates the price of the camel, and as a gift for them some more by way of their entertainment, requesting us to measure the dates for our satisfaction.

When we were refreshed after eating dates, we entered the town and saw the same person (who had come to us) in mosque preaching. We could catch the following words:

"O ye people! Give alms. It is better for you to give alms. The upper (generous) hand is superior to the lower (at the receiving end). Spend on your mother, father, sister, brother, the next of kin and then next to him."

Thirteen persons of the Najeeb tribe had come to Medina. They had come with the Zakat of their goods and animals. The Prophet (PBUH) said to them: Take it back to your own people and spend on the have-nots of the tribe. They explained that this is what has remained after meeting the local needs.

Abu Bakr Siddiq (R) submitted by way of approval that that was the best deputation upto that time.

The Prophet said: Guidance is in the hands of Allah, the Exalted. Whomsoever He wants to favour, he opens up his chest (heart or mind) for belief.

These deputationists had put some questions to the Prophet (PBUH) and he had got their answers written for them.

They were much inclined towards learning the teachings of the Quran and Sunnah of the Prophet (PBUH) so Bilal (R) was appointed to look after their needs in particulars.

These people appeared to be feeling uneasy in their stay and were looking longingly for seeking permission to leave Medina. The companions of the Prophet enquired as to why they were perturbed by delay in leaving for home.

They said: "What we gained in his blessed company and the beneficence and blessings we were the recipients of, from talking to him as also other advantages we derived in the most excellent company, all this we are very eager to convey to our community."

The Prophet honoured them with gifts and saw them off. Before parting, he had asked them if there was any one left behind while you have been here. They replied that they had left behind a young boy to keep a watch over their goods. The Prophet asked them to send him also. When he came he said to the Prophet (PBUH): "O Apostle of Allah! you have been so kind and merciful to my people here. Let me also seek some favour from you."

The Prophet (PBUH) asked him: "What do you want?"

He submitted that his aim was different from those of his party. Although I know that the love of Islam has brought them here and they had also brought the sadaqat with them.

The Prophet asked him: "Then what do you want in particular?"

The young boy said: "I came from my house for the sole purpose of making an humble request to you to pray for me that Allah may forgive me, have mercy on me and make me independent of worldly goods."

The Prophet prayed for him as he wished. In the 10th year of Hijrah, when the Apostle of Allah went to Mecca for Hajj pilgrimage, the men of this tribe again saw the Prophet (PBUH). He asked them about that young boy. They submitted: "O Apostle of Allah! A person like him has never been seen. A contended person like him was never heard of. If the wealth of the entire world were being distributed before him he would not cast a glance at it."

This tribe was an offshoot of Quza'ah, when they entered the mosque of the Prophet (PBUH) they found him leading the funeral prayer.

They agreed together that before seeing the Prophet (PBUH) they should do nothing. So they sat aside doing nothing, (not joining even the funeral prayer). When the Prophet (PBUH) was free, he called them and enquired if they were Muslims? And when they replied in the affirmative, he put another question: Why did you not then join the prayer for your (Muslim) brother?

They explained that they had taken it into their heads that it did not become them to do anything before taking pledge of alegiance to Islam at the hands of the Prophet. The Prophet however corrected them saying that they had become Muslims as soon as they embraced Islam (and subject to all the obligations of a Muslim).

Meanwhile, the person whom they had left in charge of their mounts, also came up to them. The deputationists said to the Prophet (PBUH): "O Apostle of Allah! Since he is the youngest among us, he is our servant." He said in reply: "Yes the youngest person of a community is their servant, servant of his elders. May Allah bless him for his services." It was the effect of this prayer that he became the Imam of the community and with the best knowledge of the Quran in the entire community.

When this deputation got home the entire tribe entered the fold of Islam.

It comprised ten persons including Wabisah bin Ma'bad and Talhah bin Khuwailad. The Prophet was in the mosque with his companions. One of the deputationist said: "O Apostle of Allah! We bear witness that Allah is One and Only, without any partners and you are His servant and Apostle. Just consider O Apostle of Allah! We are here of our own accord. You did not even send any person to us (to convey the Message of Islam). At this pretensious claim of theirs, the following Quranic verse was revealed:

> They impress on thee as a favour that they have embraced Islam. Say, Count not your Islam as a favour upon me. Nay, Allah has conferred a favour upon you.

> That he has guided you to the Faith, if ye be true and sincere. (Q. XLIX: 17)

Then they asked him about the permissibility of regarding the calls of birds and other auguries of auspicious and otherwise as omens and the Prophet forbade all that nonsense.

They further asked him about geomancy to which he gave only a conditional reply that some prophet had taught people as a science and those who know it as originally taught by him with certainty can adopt it otherwise not. (Doubtful is dangerous in Islam).

These people came to Medina and made their camels sit in front of the house of Miqdad (R) who said to his own family to prepare something for them and himself went out to meet them and welcoming them brought them to his house, entertaining them with Eish (a preparation with parched ground barley and dates cooked in butter or ghee or any other fat).

Miqdad (R) sent some of this delicacy to the Prophet also. The Prophet partaking of some of it returned the rest to him. Now made it a practice to place that utensil with the remainder of Eish returned by the Prophet (PBUH) morning and evening before them and they enjoyed it but could not finish it, (such being the blessing of the Prophet (PBUH) having taken a little from it). His guests were surprised and asked their host for an explanation, saying that they were under the impression that Madinites subsisted mostly on parched ground barley but he had been feeding them lavishly on food considered a delicacy and we cannot afford it daily. Besides, it is so delicious that we never ate before this.

Miqdad said to them: "Gentlemen! This is a blessing of the Apostle of Allah, since it has been touched by his fingers."

On hearing it they all said with one voice and refreshed their belief saying that undoubtedly he is the Apostle of Allah. They stayed in Medina for some time and after learning Quran and the Islamic Shariah, they returned home.

This deputation had come to Medina in 9th year of Hijrah and comprised 19 persons. Hamzah bin No'man was one of them. The Prophet asked him: "Who are you?" He replied: "We are Bani 'Azrah and brothers of Qusa'y (on the mother's side). We helped Qusa'y to progress and turned out Khuza'ah and Bani Bakr from Mecca. Therefore, we claim relationship as well as ancestry. The Prophet welcomed them, and also prophesied that Syria will be conquered in near future and Hereclitus shall flee from their region.

Then the Prophet prohibited to them putting questions to sooth sayers (regarding future events), and also stop all those sacrifices they have been accustomed to so far. Now only one sacrifice, that of Eid-al-Azha abides. They stayed in Medina for sometime and departed after receiving gifts and a general assessment.

These were ten people who had come to the Prophet (PBUH) in the month of Sha'ban 10 A.H. They submitted that they had come as representatives of the backward section of our Community. "We are believers in Allah and His Apostle (PBUH). We have come to you covering a long distance and we humbly affirm that we are under obligation to Allah and His Apostle (PBUH). Here we have presented ourselves to see you."

The Apostle of Allah (PBUH) said: "Whoever came to see me in Medina will be my neighbour (close to me) on the Day of Judgement." Then the Apostle of Allah asked them about 'Amm-e-Anas, (an idol this tribe worshipped). The deputationists replied: "We thank Allah that He has made your teachings a much better substitute for its worship. There are only a few old men and women who persist with its worship. God-willing, we shall demolish it on our return. For a long time we have been in dark and victims to a fraud and a mischief. The Prophet asked them to relate some incident connected with it.

The deputationist stated: "O Apostle of Allah! We collected once a hundred bulls and they were sacrificed to 'Amm-e-Anas in one day and left for the ravenous beasts when we ourselves stood in sure need of animals and their flesh."

They also stated that out of our animals and agricultural produce too he (the idol) had a share. Whenever somebody took to forming he would keep the central part of the cultivated land reserved for 'Amm-e-'Anas and on the border piece of land for God. If the crop failed due to a wind storm, the portion dedicated to God was transferred to 'Amm-e-Anas, but never the vice versa.

The Apostle of Allah taught them the obligatory Acts of the Faith and in particular the following:

1. Fulfilling the pledges.

2. Returning the Trust (intact).

3. Kind treatment of the neighbours.

4. Not to tyrannise anyone pointing out at the same time that injustice shall be darkness on the Day of Reckoning.

This deputation comprised ten persons who came to Medina in the 10th year of Hijrah as representatives of their community. Bilal (R) had been detailed for the hospitality to be offered to them. It was he who brought the day and the evening meals for them. One day, the Prophet (PBUH) devoted his time from Zuhr (midday prayer) to 'Asr (late afternoon prayer) for their instruction.

At one of them, the Prophet looked intently saying that he thought, he had seen him before that also.

This person spoke out: "By Allah! you had seen me and talked to me also and I had replied to you using most uncivil language, and rudely rejected your words. This incident is associated with 'Akaz market where you were preaching to people." The Prophet remembering, agreed.

That person said: "O Apostle of Allah! That day there was no other person opposing you and further from Islam than myself. All others save myself met their end professing their ancestral religion. Thank God, only I have survived by his Grace, and lucky enough to believe in you and obey you."

The Prophet (PBUH) said: "Our hearts are all in Allah's hands (and He alone guides, whom He likes, to the right Path)."

That person said: "O Apostle of Allah! Pray for my forgiveness of earlier transgression."

The Prophet (PBUH) told him: "Islam wipes out all that happened during the period of unbelief."

Three persons of Ghassan tribe came to the Prophet (PBUH) in Ramadan of 10th Hijrah and after embracing Islam went back home with the intent of the guidance of their community. It appears they could not succeed in the propagation of Islam. Two of them had died earlier and only one survivor lived when Syria was conquered by Abu 'Ubaidah bin Jarah during the caliphate of 'Umar Faruq (R).

This deputation came to the Prophet (PBUH) in Shawwal 10 A.H. Khalid bin Waleed (R) had been deputed to preach Islam to them and people had taken to Islam. Khalid bin Waleed sent the report of his mission to the Prophet (PBUH) and himself stayed there for their guidance and instruction. The Prophet wrote to him to come back, taking with him some of the local community. It was in this deputation that Qais bin -Al- Husain and 'Abd-Allah bin Farad and others had come to the Prophet (PBUH).

The Prophet (PBUH) put a question to them: "How is it that whoever fought against you during the period of Jahiliyah (ignorance or un-Islam) was vanquished?"

They submitted: "O Apostle of Allah! We never became aggressors to go and attack anyone. And once we have entered the battle array we do not allow it to be disarrayed. We never initiate injustice."

The Prophet said: "You are right. This is the reason of your success in confrontation with your opponents."

This deputation had come only four months before the Prophet's (PBUH) passing away. They were residents of Najran, and had come to the Prophet (PBUH) after embracing Islam. They submitted to him: "O Apostle of Allah! we have heard from the preachers of Islam as reporting your declaration:

"There is no Islam for those not undertaking migration."

"We have worldly goods and animals on which we subsist. So if without migration our Islam is not in order, how our wherewithal can avail us and what use are our cattle? So, would it not be better if we sell out every thing that we have there and come to you one and all."

The Prophet said to them: "Take to piety and persevere with it where you are living and nothing will be detracted from your deeds (the rewards thereof)."

In this answer to their query, the Prophet has made it clear that through their concentration in the Islamic centre, making it over populated and short of space due to over crowding is inappropriate. Muslims, on the other hand, should adopt it as their policy, to spread over the far flung lands and conveying Islam to them. Those who immigrate to Muslim countries in our own times, should call to mind that it is against the teaching of the Prophet, as also in direct contravention to the expediency of the Islamic Faith. The great majority of Muslims all over the world have become this-worldly in their approach to life problems and rum to green or pastures totally unmindful of their duties as Muslims in their own lands of birth first and love most what to say of other lands that need them if they cannot lift them to great heights of pelf and pomp. Moreover, they utterly lack in both the passion for it and capability. They and their children take, without a qualm of conscience to the ancient and modern Jahiliyah in their strife for a better position in life.

This deputation with ten persons on it had come in 10 A.H. They stopped short of Medina and camped there. Leaving behind a young boy to look after their goods and animals. They came to the Prophet (PBUH), who informed them that after they had left him, the boy went to sleep and a person came and ran away with your provisions of the journey. Finding them mentally disturbed. The Prophet informed them: There is no cause for grief and panic. The boy woke up in time and running after the thief not only caught him but recovered intact every thing stolen and carried away.

When they reached their camp after seeing the Prophet (PBUH) asking the boy found every thing exactly as they were told by the Prophet (PBUH) This incident alone brought them to the fold of Islam. The Prophet appointed Uba'i Ibn Ka'b to teach them the Quran, teaching as well the Islamic Shariah. When departing, they were given some instruction regarding the Islamic Shar'iah in writing also.

When the Prophet (PBUH) returned from Tabuk, a deputation of Bani Fazarah comprising ten to fifteen persons came to him. They had faith in Islam. Their mounts were emaciated and weak. The Prophet (PBUH) asked them about the conditions in their localities.

One of them said: "O Apostle of Allah! Our land is famine-stricken. Animals died (of starvation) and groves have been destroyed by drought and our families are starving. Kindly pray to Allah that He may have mercy on us. Recommend us to Allah and Allah may recommend us to you."

The Apostle of Allah said: "Allah is free from such things (acts) Woe to you! I shall certainly recommend you to Allah but whom Allah is going to recommend to? He alone is worthy of worship noneelse. He is most exalted and grand. His rule extends over things, the earth and the skies. He prayed for them to be blessed with rains in the following words:

"O Allah! Refresh your servants and animals and extend your Mercy to them and revive your dead lands. O Allah! let the merciful rains, the relieving, providing comfort come early, without delay— with benefit and not harm. Refresh us, O Allah! refresh us with your Mercy bountiful rains and not as a visitation devastation, drowning and not being right. O Allah! Refresh and revive us with rains and give us victory over our foes.

They were 17 persons that came to the Prophet (PBUH) and embraced Islam. Habib bin 'Amr was one of them. They had enquired which is the best deed of man in the sight of Allah. And the Prophet (PBUH) had said: "Offering prayers in time."

These people then requested him to pray for rainfall in their region as there had been no rains. The Prophet (PBUH) said the following words without formally raising his hands in prayer.

"O Allah! Refresh by sending rains to their lands."

Habib submitted: "O Apostle of Allah, kindly raise your hands and pray for us." The Prophet (PBUH) smiled and raising his hands prayed again for them. When this deputation returned home, they came to know that it had rained there the same day when the Prophet (PBUH) had prayed for the rains.

A careful consideration of all those traditions found in the various compilations of Hadith, it appears that two reliable representatives of the Christians had came to the Prophet (PBUH). Therefore, it has been taken up in this serial order.

It has been reported that the Prophet had addressed the Christians of Najran to invite them to the Islamic Faith. When their bishop read the letter, his body began to shiver. He called at once Sharjeel bin Dawa'ah who belonged to Hamdan tribe. No important decisions were taken without consulting him.

The bishop gave him the letter and when he had read, the Bishop said: Kindly let us know your opinion, O Abu Maryam.

Sharjeel said to him: "You know very well that Allah has promised Abraham that in the lineage of Isma'il also there is going to be Prophethood. May be the sender of this letter is that person, a prophet in the line of Isma'il. But what can my humble opinion about prophethood be worth? Had it been some worldly affair I would certainly have considered it fully, and expressed my opinion on it. The bishop asked him to remain seated. He then called another person Abd-Allah bin Sharjeel, and showing him the letter asked him for his opinion. He too gave the same answer which Sharjeel bin Dawa'ah had given. The bishop then called Hubar bin Qais showed him the letter and asked for his opinion on it. He too was of a similar opinion.

The bishop finally called a general meeting of his neighbourhood and in that grand assembly of Christians it was decided that Sharjeel, Abd-Allah and Hubar should be sent to the Prophet (PBUH) and they should tell us in detail about the situation.

These persons reached Medina and met the Prophet (PBUH), spending a few days with him. They discussed the identity and personality of 'Isa (Jesus son of Mary) with him. The following Quranic verses were revealed about this discussion:

> The similitude of Jesus before Allah is as that of Adam; He created him from dust, then said to him: be and He was. The truth comes from thy Lord alone. So be not of those who doubt-If any one disputes in the matter with thee, now after full knowledge hath come to thee, Say:

> come let us gather together, our sons and your sons, our women and your women, ourselves and yourselves: Then let us earnestly pray and invoke the curse of Allah on those who lie. — Al Quran III: 59-61

After revelation of these verses, the Prophet called Hasan, Husain and their blessed mother Fatimah (Allah be pleased with all of them).

These Christians talked together in solitude. Sharjeel said to his companions: "It is not easy to come to a final opinion about this person (the Prophet (PBUH)), since in the entire Arabian peninsula, we alone shall be his target. And if he is a Messenger sent by Allah, his curse shall be our undoing. So in my opinion it would be better to agree to live with him under a pledge of loyalty to the Islam in state and protection guaranteed by Allah and His Apostle, paying a nominal amount as Jizyah to the state in lieu of military service. Let us also leave the per head amount of Jizyah to him, since as far as I have experienced he is not harsh in dealings and general behaviour. Both of them agreed on this proposal and going to the Prophet (PBUH) they put it up before him saying: "Better than invoking the curse of Allah on the liar would be living as loyal subjects of the Islamic state under a pledge and paying Jizyah. So kindly let us know by tomorrow morning its annual amount that you decide upon in our case."

Next day, the Prophet fixed the amount of Jizyah and an agreement or pledge written by a companion, Mughirah (R) and signed over to them. A particular section granting them privileges, leave and favours over and above rights is relevant of his generosity with regard to Christians. It may almost be called his indulgence (if that may not be unbecoming) in view of the Quranic view of the Christian community of that age:

> And nearest among them in love to the Believers will thou find those who say, "We are Christians"
> — Al Quran V: 82

"The residents of Najran shall be under protection of Allah and His Apostle Muhammad, concerning life, religion and land and property, all those present or absent, tribes men or their followers, shall enjoy rights and no changes shall be made in them and conditions of living. And whatever more or less they have in their possession shall not be changed. On account of doubts or contentions relating to murders no charges shall be made and no suits filed against them. They will not be called for forced labour (without wages). No armies shall cross their territory."

On getting a copy of the pact, they went back to Najran. The bishop and other elite came out to greet and receive them at a long distance on the road from their residences. The deputation put up the edict (agreement) before the bishop, who started reading it at once. His brother was with him and became so engrossed in reading the edict that he lost his balance and fell down from his mount. He attributed his fall to the agreement and to another whom he cursed. The bishop tried to stop him saying that the author is a true prophet (PBUH). But he despite efforts to stop him from going to Medina failed. He got there and embracing Islam stayed there and finally got martyred.

A monk also hearing about all this went to Medina with some gifts, acquired knowledge of Islam and returned to Najran with Prophet's (PBUH) permission.

After sometime, another deputation of 60 persons arrived in Medina and was allowed to say their prayer in the Prophet's mosque in spite of objections. At the time of its departure, comprising mostly clergy, was honoured with an edict granting rights and privileges to the Christians and the priestly class. And also at their request for a trustworthy person to pay Jizyah to, Abu 'Ubaidah bin Jarali (R) as the most trustworthy person of the ummah was sent with them.

This was the last deputation and visited the Prophet (PBUH) about the middle of Muharram 11 A.H. It comprised two hundred persons and entering the fold of Islam at the hands of Mu'az bin Jabal (R), had come to Medina. They stayed at the Guest House and entertained.

One of them, Zararah bin 'Amr said to the Prophet that he had had some dreams which related to him and heard revealing interpretation from the Prophet (PBUH).

Messages of Almighty

A remarkable characteristic of the Da'wah (call to Faith) of the Prophet (PBUH), not met with in those of other prophets, is the presentation of Islam as a universal Faith which actually it is, and has been the Faith of all the prophets of Allah from Adam, Noah to 'Isa Ibn Maryam and they one and all preached it with this denomination as brought out by the Quran in clear terms:

1. He has chosen you and imposed no difficulties on you in religion, it is the religion of your father Abraham. It is he who has named ye Muslim, —Al Quran XXII: 78

2. The religion before Allah is Islam (submission to His Will). Nor did the People of the Book dissent therefrom except through envy of each other, after knowledge had come to them. —Al Quran III: 19

3. If any one denies a religion other than Islam (submission to Allah) never will it be accepted of him, and in the Hereafter he will be in the ranks of those who have lost (ruined themselves). —Al Quran III: 85

And it was for this reason that from those early days when even the Makkans had not become well-acquainted with Islam, the Prophet (PBUH) had started propagating it among other nations and followers of other religions. Bilal (R) of Abyssinia, Suhaib Rumi, Salman Farsi, Addas of Nineveh are some of those who had entered the Fold of the religion of Allah as the prime representatives of Abyssinia, Greece, Iran and Central Asia.

That he was commissioned for the guidance of entire humanity (directly and indirectly) is supported by the Quran:

1. We have not sent thee but as a (Messenger) to all mankind, giving them Glad tidings, and warning them (against sin), but most men know not.

— Al Quran XXXIV: 28

2. It is He Who has sent His Messenger with Guidance and the Religion of Truth, to make it prevail over all religion, and enough is Allah for a witness.

—Al Quran XLVIII: 28 and LXI: 9

3. We sent thee not but as a mercy for all creatures.

— Al Quran XXI: 107

4. Say: "O men! I am sent unto you all as the Messenger of Allah to Whom belongeth the dominion of the heavens and the earth. There is no god but He. It is He that giveth both life and death. So believe in Allah and His Messenger. The unlettered Prophet, who believeth in Allah and His Word. follow Him that (so) ye may be guided.

—Al Quran VII: 158

It was to follow these Quranic verses that the Prophet (PBUH) had sent letters conveying the message of Islam to those managing the affairs of various nations and religions. And in these letters, he had written also this to each one of them that in case of rejection of Islam, you will come to grief not only because in your personal capacity you have deprived yourself of the greatest bounty of God but as a result of it your nation too shall stop short at your instance and you shall be held responsible for their misguidance and resulting ruination and shall pay for it, since in this edict you have not been addressed in your individual capacity but as their ruler, patron, leader and guide.

In connection with the propagation of Islam this measure adopted by the Messenger of Allah (PBUH) is unparalleled in the history of the religions of the world and lives of religious leaders.

Since they did not resort to it, we can take it for granted that they themselves regarded their faith as limited in scope and meant only for a particular nation in which they were raised. (Time was not ripe for a universal religion, man had not come of age and means of communication at his disposal in that distant past were not developed enough to bear the strain of this heavy service).

Now, if their followers digress from the prescribed path and go beyond the allowed limits, it is their own concern. It cannot become an authority from the religious point of view.

On 1st Muharram 7 A.H., the Prophet (PBUH) sent out his ambassadors with letters conveying the message of Islam to the rulers of kingdoms, petty chiefs of even principalities. Only that person was chosen as ambassador for any country who knew the language both spoken and written, so that he may worthily discharge the duty of propagation of Islam in that country.

So far, the Prophet had not used a seal of his name and identity. Now that the situation demanded that to make the letters (edicts) reliable with his seal on them, he had to get it made. Made of silver, it had three words one above the other.

Assertion on Prophethood

In looking at these edicts (some have been preserved and can be seen even today in museums and elsewhere) addressed to the Christian kings had in them invariably the following Quranic verse:

> Say: O People of the Book! Come to common terms as between us and you that we worship none but Allah. That we associate no partners with Him, that we erect

not from among ourselves, lords and patrons other than Allah.

Now we shall briefly take up these ambassadorial performances and their reactions one by one:

To Asham bin Abjaz, the Christian king of Abyssinia the edict of the Prophet (PBUH) had been taken by 'Amr bin Umayyah Al-Dauri:

In the name of Allah, Gracious, Most Merciful

This is a letter from Muhammad, the Apostle of Allah (PBUH) to Najashi Asham the king of Abyssinia. May thou rest in peace. I make a beginning with the praise of Allah Who is the Sovereign, the Holy One, the source of Peace (and Perfection), the Guardian of Faith, the preserver of Safety, the Exalted in Might, the irresistible, the Justly Proud. And I make it manifest to you that 'Isa Ibn Maryam is the created being and Allah's Command, which was sent towards Maryam, virgin (Mary), pure and chaste, causing her to conceive 'Isa. Allah created Adam with His Hand and Breath. Now I call you to belief in Allah Who is One and the Only without any partner and spend thy life in obedience to Him alone. And follow me and affirm my teachings sincerely, since I am the Messenger of Allah.

Before this, I have sent a paternal cousin of mine, Ja'far at the head of a party of Muslims. Let them rest in peace with you. Najashi, shed pride since I have called you to Allah the Most Exalted in Might. Lo! I have conveyed to you the command of Allah and explained to you everything clearly. It is now in the fitness of things that you listen to my adivce. And Peace be on him who takes to the Path of Guidance.

Najashi on perusal of this edict embraced Islam, and wrote back this letter to the Prophet (PBUH).

In the name of Allah, Beneficent, Most Merciful

To Muhammad, the Messenger of Allah, from Najashi Al-Asham bin Abjaz. O Prophet of Allah, Allah's Peace, Mercy and Blessings on you. Allah save Whom there is no one worthy of worship, and Who has guided me to the Straight Path of Islam. Now I must submit that your edict honoured me greatly. Whatever you have said about 'Isa, by Allah, the Creator and Lord of the earth and the sky, he ('Isa) is not a whit more than that. His position is only that you have stated in your edict. We have learnt your teachings. Your cousin and other Muslims are quite comfortable here with me. I affirm that you are the Messenger of Allah, true yourself and bringing out the truth of other people. I enter bai'ah (take oath of loyalty) with you. I have already performed the ceremonial bai'ah at the hand of your cousin and sworn obedience to Allah and I am sending my son Arha' to you. I am only the master of myself and if you order me, I shall present myself there, at your service, since it is my firm conviction that whatever you say is True."

"O Messenger of Allah may peace be on you."

Munzar bin Sawi was the king of Bahrain, paying tribute to the Emperor of Iran. Ala' bin Al Hadrani had taken the Prophet's edict to him. He too embraced Islam and so did the major part of his subjects. In reply to the edict, he had written to the Prophet that some people have manifested great liking for Islam, while others have shown their aversion to it, some others have even opposed it. My land abounds in Jews and Magi. I may deal with them as you direct me." The Prophet wrote back to him:

(1) He who is exhorted does so for his own good.

(2) He who sticks to his Judaism or Muzdaism should pay Jizyah.

(3) The letter to Jaffar and Abd sons of Jolandi of 'Oman had been sent with 'Amr bin 'As (R).

'Amr says that when I reached Oman, I met 'Abd, a chief and gentle and more polite than his brother. I told him that I was an ambassador of the Prophet (PBUH) and had come to him and his brother.

'Abd said in reply: "My brother is older than I am and also the ruler of this land. I shall take you to him. But please let me know what do you call us to?"

'Amr bin 'As said: "We call you to Allah, the One and only. God, Allah Who has no partners. Also to bear witness that Muhammad (PBUH) is His servant and Messenger."

'Abd said to 'Amr: "You are the son of the chief of his community.

Tell me what did your father do, for we can take him as a model."

'Amr bin 'As replied: He died and had not believed in the Prophet. If only he had believed and affirmed the uprightness of the Apostle of Allah.

"I too was in agreement with my father until Allah guided me to Islam."

'Abd: "When did you come to follow Muhammad?" 'Amr bin 'As: "Recently". 'Abd: "Where was it."

'Amr bin 'As: "At Najashi's court. And Najashi too embraced Islam."

Abd: And what did his subjects do to Najashi?"

'Amr bin 'As: "They let him remain a Muslim. And they too embraced Islam."

'Abd: (Amazed) And Bishop and other clergy too?" 'Amr bin 'As: "Yes."

'Abd: "Mind your tongue. Nothing more degrading for man than lying."

'Amr bin 'As: "I did not tell a lie. Islam does not permit it."

Abd: "What was the reaction of Heraclitus? Does he know about Najashi's Islam?"

'Amr bin 'As: Najashi used to pay tribute to Heraclitus. But from the time he has embraced Islam, he has declared that he would not pay him anything."

Heraclitus came to know about it. His brother, Binaq said to him: "Najashi, this humble servant of your majesty has the insolence to deny payment of tribute to you. And he has discarded your faith also." Heraclitus said to him: "What is wrong with it if he has chosen a new Faith for himself and entered its fold also?" What is that to me (how does it concern me)? By God, if this exalted position of emperorship had not stood in my way, I too most readily would have followed Najashi."

'Abd: "Just think over what you are saying?"

'Amr bin 'As: "By God, I am telling the truth."

'Abd: "Alright. Tell me what are those things that he enjoins and what forbids."

'Amr bin 'As: "He commands you to obey Allah, the Exalted and Glorious, and forbids transgression against Him. He also forbids fornication, use of liquor and worship of stone idols and the cross."

'Abd: "How excellent are the commands he invites us to."

How I wish my brother agreed with me and both of us embraced Islam at his hands! It is my considered opinion that if my brother rejected this message and remained inclined to this worldliness, he will prove deleterious to his own country as well.

"Amr bin 'As: "If he embraces Islam, the Prophet will let him rule his country. He will do only that much in your system realising sadaqat. Your haves will distribute them among the have nots in your kingdom."

'Abd: "This is very nice. But what do you mean by sadaqat?"

'Amr bin 'As explained to him the rules of Zakat. But when he told him that Zakat has also to be paid from Camels (depending on the number of animals and the period of possession, 'Abd said to him: "Would they demand sadaqah from our animals also?" A camel takes care of itself by feeding on tree leaves and can go out to quench its thirst."

'Amr bin 'As said: "Yes sadaqah is realized from your camels also."

'Abd: "I do not know what is going to be the reaction of my community men in connection with this item. They are in large numbers and dispersed over a large areas. I have my doubts in this behalf."

In short, 'Amr bin 'As stayed there for a while and during this period 'Abd used to communicate to his brother whatever passed here between his and 'Amr. One day 'Amr bin 'As was called to the presence of the king. The mace bearers (ushers) presented him to the king holding his arms on either side. The king ordered release of his arms. And when 'Amr intended to take a seat, they again stopped him. The king asked him: What is your name? 'Amr handed over the letter of the Prophet (PBUH) to him.

Jaffar broke the seal, read it and gave it to his brother. He too read it. 'Amr noticed that the younger brother was really gentle. The king asked him: "How it goes with Quraysh (where do they stand) 'Amr bin' As told him that they had, one and all, (somehow) willy nilly submitted to his (the Prophet (PBUH)) authority. The king asked him: Who are his companions? 'Amr bin As: They are those who came to embrace Islam willingly, and cutting themselves off from other involvements remain attached to him, having judged and tested him in the light of thoughtful consideration, intellect and experience. The king said to him: "Do see me tomorrow."

'Amr bin 'As next day saw the king's brother first. He said to him: "If no hazard to our kingdom threatens us, the king will embrace Islam."

'Amr bin 'As then went to see the king, who said to him: "I have given serious thought to this affair. If I submit to a person whose armies have not yet entered my country, I shall be regarded the weakest person (monarch) in Arabia, whereas (I am not weak) and if his armies really come here, I can give them such a tough fight you might have never experienced before that."

'Amr bin 'As said: "Very well, I shall be going back tomorrow." The king said to him: "No, stay tomorrow also."

Next day, the king called him and both the brothers (Jaffar and 'Abd) embraced Islam at his hands, and the major portion of his subjects followed suit.

Munzar bin Harith bin Abu Shimar was the ruler of Damascus and governor of Syria. Shuja' bin Wahab-al-Asadi went to him as ambassador.

On reading the letter he at once flew into a rage and said to the ambassador that he would himself invade Medina. But finally at parting he honoured him which was his due. He did not, however, embrace Islam.

Hanzah bin Ali, ruler of Yamanah was a Christian. Saleet bin 'Amr had taken the blessed letter to him. His arrogant reply to the ambassador was that if to help the Islamic territories his claim to rule is agreed upon, I can become a Muslim. Shortly after this ignorance and arrogance he died.

Juraih bin Mati, entitled Maquqas, ruler of Alexandria and Egypt was a Christian. Hatib bin Abi Balta'ah went to him as the Prophet's (PBUH) ambassador. He had added to his letter the warning that if he rejected the call to Islam, he would be held responsible for the deprivation of all Egyptians (copt's) deprivation of this greatest bounty of Allah, Islam and liable to punishment for it in the Hereafter.

In addition to the delivery of the letter (edict), he had enlightened him in these words:

Since, there has been a person in this country before you who raised the land paganish slogan: "I am your most exalted Lord" before his courtiers and subjects in general, and Allah brought him down in disgrace here and worse still in the Hereafter. When Allah's wrath descended on them every thing was ruined. So it is imperative that he be warned and should take a lesson from others and not that others should take a lesson from you.

The king said to him (the ambassador) that he himself had subscribed to a religion and shall not discard it, before he come upon a better one.

Hatib said to him: I call you to the Islamic Faith which makes you independent of all other religions.

The Prophet has called all the communities, nations and religions to Islam. The Quraysh opposed it and the Judaic community showed animosity, but the Christians have been closest among all these in gentleness and love. By God, the way Moses gave the glad tidings of the coming of Jesus after him, so did Jesus convey Glad tidings of Muhammad (PBUH) to be raised after him the Messenger of Allah with the "Kingdom of Heaven Here and Hereafter" that Jesus had prophesied. We invite you to the Quran as you invite those holding Torah to the teachings of Injil (the revelation to 'Isa Ibn Maryam). Which ever prophet was raised in any community's existence, is his community or millat and the prophet was their prophet. Therefore, it is imperative that "you should believe in and obey the prophet (PBUH) you come upon in your lifetime. You should take it that we are calling you to the Faith of Masih (Jesus Christ the Messiah).

Maquqas said that he thought about your prophet (of Arabia) but he did not feel inclined to him in the least. Although he does not hold back from any thing desirable, I can perceive that he is neither a sorcerer doing danger, nor a lying soothsayer. Rather he manifests signs of prophethood. Anyway, I shall think over this issue a little longer. Then he put that letter in an ivory casket and sealing it sent it to his treasury for preservation. He sent gifts to the Prophet and in reply to his letter he wrote that he knew that a prophet was yet to arrive, but somehow he took it into his head that he would come in Syria. The well-known mule, 'Duldul' was sent by him as gift to the Prophet.

Heraclitus, the well-known ruler of the eastern wing of the Roman empire (because of which Syria, Iraq and adjoining territories came to be called Rome by the Arabs was a Christian. (Pagan Romans after persecution of Christian, for a long time had adopted Christianity but corrupted it thoroughly with their Greece-roman pagan tradition according to their own taste and poor Christians, their subjects were helpless). Dahya bin Khalifah Al-Kalbi had taken the Prophet's (PBUH) edict to him. He met the monarch at Bait-al-Maqdis. Heraclitus held a grand darbar in honour of the ambassador from the Prophet (PBUH) and enquired of him many things about him (the Prophet (PBUH)).

After that for further investigation from other independent sources, he ordered that if there is any citizen of Mecca present in the town, he should be brought to his presence.

As a matter of chance, Abu Sufyan with some other traders of Mecca had come to Syria for business: He was taken to bait- al-Maqdis with his companions and brought to the royal court. He said to his companions that during my interrogation of Abu Sufyan if he makes a false statement point it out to me at once.

Abu Sufyan was a sworn enemy of the Prophet these days. He is on record to have admitted that if he had no fear of being exposed by his own companions he would have said many things against fact, but under the circumstances he had no choice save sticking to truth.

The interrogation started like this:

Caesar: "Tell me about the family and ancestry of Muhammad."

Abu Sufyan: Traders, noble and great.

On hearing this answer from him Heraclitus said: "The prophets have always come of noble families so that none may fell degraded in obedience to them."

Caesar: "Has anyone claimed prophethood in his family before him?"

Abu Sufyan: "No"

At this statement of the Sufyan, Caesar remarked: "If it had been so I would have taken it to be emulation of the former claimant or following his tradition."

Caesar: "Was he used to tell lies before his claim to prophethood or was he ever accused of slander?"

Abu Sufyan: "No."

Remark of Heraclitus on this answer from Abu Sufyan was: "It is not possible that a person who does not tell lies relating to men, could have the audacity to tell lies pertaining to God."

Caesar: "Has anyone of his ancestors been a king?"

Abu Sufyan: "No."

Heraclitus' remark on this answer was: "If it had been so I would have attributed it to his clever device to create a kingdom for himself in continuity of ancestral tradition under cover of prophethood."

Caesar: "The majority of Muhammad's (PBUH) followers comprises the poor, the weak and the indigent or chiefs of tribes and the mighty?"

Abu Sufyan: "Meek and lowly."

Heraclitus on this answer of his gave the following remark:

"The early followers of every prophet have been the poor and the meek. (They are the first to seek support and justice honour and fraternity in society since they have long been oppressed and depressed).

Caesar: "Is the number of his followers on the increase or decreasing?"

Abu Sufyan: "It is going up day-by-day."

Heraclitus by way of explanation added: "Belief has this characteristic that it develops becoming firmer with the passage of time and attains perfection."

Caesar: "Has any one getting sick of his faith, ever become apostate?"

Abu Sufyan: "No."

Heraclitus said: "The taste and joy of Belief is always like that. Once it has gone down to the heart and the soul has been influenced by it, it does not part."

Caesar: "Has he ever been guilty of the breach of Trust."

Abu Sufyan: "No. But this year we have entered a pact with him. Nobody knows what may happen."

Abu Sufyan says that he could add only this small sentence to the true brief answer - "Any thing may happen." But Caesar did not pay any attention to it, and said: "Undoubtedly the prophets are not faithless to their plighted word. Only the worldly wise are guilty of breach of faith. And the Prophets never seek worldly gains."

Caesar: "Have you fought any battle with this person?"

Abu Sufyan: "Yes."

Caesar: "What was the out come of the battle?"

Abu Sufyan: "At times he was the victor as in Badr and at some other time we came out as victors."

Heraclitus said: "The Prophets of Allah's are like that. But finally the divine aid and victory are theirs."

Caesar: "What are his teachings?"

Abu Sufyan: "He enjoins worship of One and only God, abandoning the ways of the ancestors, idol worship, having recourse to modest and chastity and kind treatment of one's blood relations."

Heraclitus remarked: These are the signs of the Promised Messiah that have come down to us. I knew that "that Prophet" was about to be raised, but not that he will be raised in Arabia. Abu Sufyan! If you have been true in your answers, he will one day dominate the land where I am sitting (Syria and Bait-al-Maqdis (Jerusalem). How I long to be with him and take to washing his feet.

After this, the blessed letter of the Apostle of Allah was read out and listening to it incited the courtiers to raise their voices in protest and we were driven out of the darbar. From that day onward my own vileness and objectness was impressed on my heart and also the future greatness of the Prophet (PBUH).

Khuro Parvez was the emperor of half the eastern world, subscribing to Zorostrian religion. Abdullah bin Khudamah had taken the edict of the Apostle of Allah to him. It ran like this:

In the name of Allah, Beneficent, Most Merciful.

"From Muhammad (PBUH) the Messenger of Allah to the great Kisra of Iran. Peace be on him who takes to the right path and believes in Allah and His Apostle (PBUH) and bears witness that there is none worthy of worship save Allah and that Muhammad (PBUH) is His servant and Messenger of Allah. I have been sent to the entire progeny of Adam (PBUH), so that whoever is living in this age may be warned of the Divine Retribution and in case of those rejecting these truths the word of Allah may prove true. Embrace Islam and you will come to safety or else the fault of Magi (adherents of Mazdaism will become your accountability.)"

Khusro on looking at the blessed letter tore it to pieces in a rage and blurted out that a subject of mine writes a letter to me and in it his name precedes mine (a serious presumption indeed!).

After that Khusro sent orders to Bazam, his viceroy in Yemen and the entire Arabia was regarded to be under his authority and rule or at least under his political influence, that this person should be arrested and sent to him.

Bazam sent out a military contingent under the command of Khar Khusro. Accompanying them was an administrative officer, Banoyah with instruction to study the affairs of the Prophet (PBUH) and take him to Kisra. In case he refuses to go, he should come back and submit a report.

When this military detachment reached Ta'if, the Ta'ifians were overjoyed that Muhammad is now sure to come to harm since Kisra the emperor of Iran had ordered punishment for his insolence.

When these officers presented themselves to the Prophet (PBUH) at Medina, he asked them to come the next day. When they came to him the next day he said to them: "Last night your king has been killed by Allah. Go and make it certain to yourselves. On hearing the news they returned to Yemen. The viceroy had received this news officially, that Khusro had been murdered by his son and the claimant to the throne was 'Sheroyah, the murderer of his father.

Now after this incident, Bazam made thorough enquiries about the habits, morals, teachings and guidance of the Prophet (PBUH) and (duly satisfied) he entered the fold of Islam and so did the majority of his courtiers and the subjects also embraced Islam.

7

Holy Prophet's Commands–1

Hazrat Abdullah bin Umar (R.A.A.) reports:

"Once some Jews came to the Prophet of Allah (PBUH) and informed him that a man and woman from amongst them had committed adultery.

The Messenger of Allah asked them:

"What, according to Torah (Old Testament), is the legal punishment of illegal sexual intercourse?" "We announce their crime and lash them," the Jews replied.

"You are telling a lie; the Torah contains the order of "Rajm" (stoning), Abdullah bin Salam, a learned Jew turned Muslim said.

Thereupon, they brought the Torah and opening it placed their hand on the verse of "Rajm" and read the verses preceding and following it.

"Lift your hand," Abdullah bin Salam asked them.

When they lifted their hand, the Verse of "Rajm" was found written there.

"Muhammad (PBUH) has told the truth; certainly, the Torah has the Verse of 'Rajm'.

Thereafter, the Holy Prophet (PBUH) issued order that the convicted should be stoned to death.

The order was implemented without loss of time. Abdullah bin Umar (R.A.A.) said:

> "I saw the man leaning over the woman to shelter her from the stones." (Bukhari).

Hazrat Bara bin Azib (R.A.A.) reports:

"A certain companion of the Holy Prophet (PBUH) recited Surah Kahaf in his prayer. A riding animal in the house got frightened and started jumping.

The person, while finishing his prayer, found something like cloud or mist hovering over him. When he informed the Apostle of Allah of the occurrence, the Apostle said:

> "O so–and–so it (cloud or mist) was sign of peace descending for the recitation of Quran." (Bukhari).

Hazrat Abu Sayeed Khudri (R.A.A.) reports:

"On a journey with the Holy Prophet (PBUH), we reached 'Usfan and passed some nights there. Some of us uttered that their stay there served no purpose, and their children were left unnoticed and unsafe. When the Messenger of Allah heard, he told:

> "I swear by Him in whose hand my soul is that there is no ravine or mountain pass in Madina which does not have two angels on guard till your return to Madina.

The Prophet of Allah then asked us to set out and we came back to Madina. Then, by Him in whose name oaths are taken, we had not yet unloaded our beasts after entering Madina that we were attacked by Banu Ghatfan.

Hazrat Abu Ayub Ansari (R.A.A.) reports:

"Once on hearing a loud sound, the Holy Prophet (PBUH) came out; while the sun had already sat and he told us:

"The Jews are being punished in their graves."
(Bukhari, Muslim)

Asim bin Kulaib reports from his father on the authority of an Ansar:

"Once we accompanied the Holy Prophet (PBUH) to a funeral. On coming back from the graveyard, someone invited the Apostle on behalf of a widow. He accepted the invitation and we went for the feast alongwith him.

Food was served. We, alongwith the Messenger of Allah, put morsels of food in our mouths. We noticed that the Apostle of Allah was moving a morsel round in his mouth. Then he said:

"This flesh of a sheep has been taken without the permission of its owner."

When informed, the woman sent her messenger to the Apostle who explained the matter on her behalf:

"Messenger of Allah:I sent to "an–Naqi" (a place where sheep were sold) to bring a sheep for the feast. But no sheep was available there. Thereafter, I sent a neighbour of mine to bring the sheep he had purchased for him and charge the price from me. But he did not turn up with the sheep. Later on, I sent another man to his wife who sent the sheep to me."

Hearing this, the Messenger of Allah said:

> "Give this food to the prisoners."
>
> (Abu Dawud; Baihaqi).

True Dreams

Hazrat Abu Musa Ash'ari (R.A.A.) reports the Holy Prophet (PBUH) to have said:

> "Once in a dream I saw migrating from Makkah to a place having plenty of date–palms. I thought that to be either Yamawa or Hajar. But it was Madina (Yathrib). In the same dream I saw myself brandishing a sword and its blade got broken. It only symbolised our defeat in the Battle of Uhud. When I moved the sword again, it became normal as before and symbolised our final victory in the same battle." (Bukhari).

Hazrat Abdullah Ibn Abbas (R.A.A.) reports:

Once Musailma al–Kazzab (i.e. liar) came to Madina with his followers and said:

> "If Muhammad (PBUH) appoint me his successor, I am ready to follow him."

The Messenger of Allah went to him with Thabit bin Qais bin Shams. He then had a leaf of date–palm in his hand. Standing before Musailma and his followers, the Holy Prophet (PBUH) said:

"If you ask me even this piece of a leaf, I would not give it to you. And you can not save yourself from the wrath of Allah, the Almighty. If you reject Islam, Allah will destroy you. I think you are most probably the same person I have seen in my dream."

Later on, Hadrat Abu Hurairah (R.A.A.) narrated to me that the Messenger of Allah told him:

"Once I was sleeping that I saw (in dream) two gold bracelets round my arm. I was too much worried at the sight. In the meantime, I was divinely instructed that I should blow them off. I did according to the instruction, and both of them flew away.

Now I interpret the two bracelets as symbols of two liars who will claim prophethood after me."

This prophecy came true as Al–Ansi and Musailma Kaz'zab claimed prophethood.

Jarir (R.A.A.) narrates:

"Once the Holy Prophet (PBUH) said to me:

"Why do you not give me rest from Dhul Khalasa?" I replied him:

"I could certainly do it but I am unable to keep from falling off a horse's back.

Thereupon, the Messenger of Allah gave me such a blow on my chest that I could see the mark of his hand on it and said:

"O Allah, make him sit firm and guide him to lead it (the horse) right."

Thereafter, I never fell off from my horse. And following this event, he left with one hundred and fifty horsemen and got victory.

Hazrat Anas (R.A.A.) reports:

"Once there occurred a great alarm in Madina so that the Companions of the Holy Prophet (PBUH) got embarrassed. When the Messenger of Allah heard it, he came out at once, took a horse and left to enquire about the matter. The horse belonged to Abu Talha. It was a slow horse and took short steps.

Having returned, the Prophet of Allah said:

"I found this horse of yours running like a great river."

> Thereafter, no horse could compete with it in speed and no horse could ever outstrip it." (Bukhari).

Hazrat Jabir (R.A.A.) reports:

"Once I accompanied the Holy Prophet (PBUH) to an expedition on a camel which was used for drawing water. It had grown weak and weary and could hardly go on. The Messenger of Allah came near me and asked what was the trouble with my camel. Thereupon, the Prophet of Allah came behind my camel and urged it to go on fast and made supplication for the speed. The camel speeded up and outstripped all other camels. The Messenger of Allah (PBUH) asked me again how I found my camel:"It is fine now due to your blessing," I said to him.

"Would you sell it to me for an 'Uqiya'?" the Apostle asked me.

> I agreed on condition that I might ride it till we come back to Madina. When we came back to Madina, I took the camel and appeared before the Prophet of Allah early next morning. He gave me the price of the camel fixed by him and then returned my camel to me too. (Bukhari; Muslim).

Sa'sa'a reports Abu Saeed Al–Khudri (R.A.A.) to have said:

"I see that you love sheep and you keep them. Hence keep them well and take care of their food; for I have heard the Holy Prophet (PBUH) say:

> "A time will come in the life of the Muslims that their best property will be their sheep. They will take this property of theirs to the tops of mountains and to the

> places of rainfalls in order to save their religion from afflictions." (Bukhari).

Urwah (R.A.A.) reports:

> "Once the Holy Prophet (PBUH) gave me one 'dinar' to buy a sheep for him. I brought two sheep for him with the money. Then I sold one of the two sheep for one dinar and brought one dinar and a sheep to the Messenger of Allah (PBUH). Thereupon, the Prophet of Allah blessed me in my deals. From that day on, I would gain even if I dealt in dust." (Bukhari).

Hazrat Abu Hurairah (R.A.A.) reports the Holy Prophet (PBUH) to have said:

"A horse may be kept for one of the three purposes: for one it may be a source of reward; for another it may be a means of living; and for a third one it may be a burden.

As for the man for whom the horse is a source of reward, he is the one who keeps his horse for the sake of 'Jihad'. In Allah's cause; he ties it with a long rope in a pasture or in a garden. So whatever its rope allows it to graze, will become rewardable (for its owner).

A horse is an honest means of providing a livelihood which is right, legal and honest.

> But the horse is a burden for those who use it for committing sins and earning illegal living. Moreover, if such a horse is kept for showing pride and for harming the Believers, it is a burden." (Bukhari).

Hazrat Abu Hurairah (R.A.A.) reports:

"My mother was a polytheist and I used to ask her to accept Islam. Once I invited her to profess Islam, but she uttered such words for the Holy Prophet (PBUH) that I can not dare repeat them. However, I went weeping to the Messenger of Allah and requested him to supplicate Almighty Allah to guide my mother. "O Allah, guide Abu Hurairah's mother," the Apostle said.

I rushed back home very cheerfully. When I reached my house I found the door shut. Having heard the sound of my feet, my mother said:

"Stay where you are, Abu Hurairah." I did accordingly. In the meantime, I heard splashing of water and thought she was taking bath. My notion was true. She finished her bath, put on her chemise and hurriedly opened the door to take me in.

As I came face to face with my mother, she spoke out with great zeal:

"I testify Abu Hurairah, that none has the right to be worshipped but Allah and I testify that Muhammad (PBUH) is His servant and Messenger."

> In a fit of joy I turned back running to the Prophet of Allah with the good news of my mother accepting Islam, the Apostle praised Almighty Allah and uttered some good words." (Muslim).

Hazrat Abu Hurairah (R.A.A.) narrates:

"You generally say that Abu Hurairah reports much more from the Holy Prophet (PBUH), but Allah, the Almighty knows the truth very well. My brethren among the Emigrants (Muhajirin) would remain occupied with their business in the markets; and the Helpers (Ansar) are engaged with the affairs of their property. But I, being a poor man, had no other business other than keeping myself close to the Messenger of Allah (PBUH) and filling my stomach with what is available.

One day, the Prophet of Allah rose to address us and said in the beginning:"No one among you who spreads his garment and keeps it so till I finish my address will ever forget to what I say."

> Having heard the Apostle saying so, I spread my wollen garment till the Messenger of Allah finished his address. Thereafter, I gathered the garment and embraced it; and I swear by Him who sent him (the Apostle) with Truth that until this day I retain each word of his address.
> (Bukhari; Muslim)

Holy Treatment

Hazrat Ya'la bin Murra Thaqafi (R.A.A.) reports:

Three things I have seen relating to the Holy Prophet (PBUH): Once we were travelling with the Messenger of Islam that we passed a camel which on seeing the Apostle rumbled and kept its neck down. The Apostle of Allah stopped near it and asked about the owner of the camel. When he turned up, the Apostle asked him:

"Will you sell it to me?"

"No, I shall give it to you, Messenger of Allah" he said, and added, "It belongs to a family which has no other means of livelihood."

The Holy Prophet (PBUH) said:

"Since you have mentioned all this, note that it has complained to me of too much work and a very small amount of fodder; so treat it well and fear Allah, the Almighty."

Thereafter, we proceeded till we came to a state that we needed rest. The Prophet of Allah lay down to have a sleep. All of a sudden, a tree rushed towards the Prophet of Allah cleaving the earth till it overshadowed him and then it went back to its former place.

As the Apostle of Allah awoke, I mentioned the matter to him.

Thereupon, the Apostle said:

"It is a tree which asked its Lord's permission to give me its salutation and He allowed it to do so."

We then travelled on till we passed a watering–place and there a woman brought her son who was possessed. The Prophet of Allah (PBUH) seized the nostril of the boy and said:

"Come out, for I am Muhammad, the Messenger of Allah."

On the return journey when we passed the watering–place, the Apostle asked the woman about her son and she said:

> "I swear by Him who appointed you with the Truth that no disturbing sign appeared since you left the place." (Sharh as–sunna).

Hazrat Abdullah ibn Abbas (R.A.A.) reports:

"A woman brought her son to the Holy Prophet (PBUH) and said:

O Messenger of Allah, my son is possessed, and it seizes him at morning and evening meals."

> Hearing this the Prophet of Allah gave a blow to his breast and made a supplication and the possessed boy vomited some puppy–like object and got recovered. (Darimi).

Junaid bin Abdur Rahman reports:

"I saw Sa'ib bin Yazid when he was ninety–four years old. He was then quite straight and strong. On enquiry he revealed:"I know that I am enjoying good health, eye sight and auditory power only because of the invocation of the Messenger of Allah. Once my aunt took me to him and entreated:

> "O Prophet of Allah! my nephew is sick, so please invoke Allah for him. The Apostle of .Allah, the Almighty, invoked and the result is before you." (Bukhari).

Hazrat Abdullah bin Abbas (R.A.A.) reports:

"When the Holy Prophet (PBUH) visited a patient, he would console by saying:

"No harm will befall you! May Allah cure you! May Allah cure you!"

Once the Messenger of Allah visited a sick Bedouin and uttered the same words. Thereupon, the Bedouin said:

"You say, may Allah cure me. But it is fever which boils in an old man."

"Then may it be so as you say." (Bukhari)

Against Evil Doers

Hazrat Salama bin Akwa (R.A.A.) reports:

"Once a man was eating with his left hand. When the Holy Prophet (PBUH) saw he said:

Eat with your right hand.

"I am not able to do so," he replied with pride.

"May you not be able!" the Messenger of Allah said.

The man narrated that he could not raise his hand up to mouth from day that on.

(Muslim).

Hazrat Anas (R.A.A.) reports:

A Christian embraced Islam and would recite Surah al–Baqara and Ali–Imran. He also used to write the revelation for the Holy Prophet (PBUH).

Later on, he reverted to Christianity and started saying:

"Muhammad (PBUH) knows nothing but what I have written for him." Then he died and was buried. But in the morning they found his body out of the grave. At this, they blamed that this was done by Muhammad and his Companions. They have opened the grave of our companion and took out the body, because he had renounced their religion.

Hence, they again dug a grave and got him buried in it. But the next morning they found to their wonder that the earth had thrown the body out. They again blamed Muhammad (PBUH) and his Companion for this. Thereafter, they dug a third grave as deep as they could and buried the body in it. But they found that the earth had once again thrown the body out.

Now they had to believe that the act was not performed by any man and hence they left the body unburied.
(Bukhari).

Wonderful Acts

Hazrat Anas (R.A.A.) reports:

"Once, in a very dark night, Usaid bin Hudhari and Abbad bin Bishr was talking with the Holy Prophet (PBUH) till late. They took leave at the dead of night. The night was so dark that there was nothing visible. Both of them had a staff each in their hands.

As they proceeded on, the staff of one of them gave light enough to make the way quite visible. They went on without any hinderence.

When their ways parted, the staff of the next one also produced light. Thus, both of them reached their houses safe and sound.

Jabir (R.A.A.) reports:

"Before the Battle of Uhud my father called me during the night and said:

"I feel that I shall be among the first of the Prophet's Companions to be killed, and after the Holy Prophet (PBUH), I love you most. I owe a debt; so pay it after I am no more and take care of your sisters."

The next morning he joined the battle and he was the first to be killed, and I buried him in a grave alongwith others.

Hazrat A 'isha (R.A.A.) reports:

"When Negus (Najashi), the king of Habsha (Abyssinia) died, they saw a light over his grave." (Abu Dawud).

Hazrat A'isha (R.A.A.) reports:

After the final departure of the Holy Prophet (PBUH), when the people wanted to wash his body a confusion arose over the manner of washing. They could not decide whether to strip the Apostle of his clothes as it is done with others or to wash with his clothes on. When they could not agree, Allah, the Almighty cast sleep on them, so that everybody's chin was on his breast. Then someone whose identity could not be known, addressed them from the comer of the house saying:

"Wash the Prophet with his clothes on."

> So they got up at once and washed the Messenger of Allah with his clothes on: pouring water over the shirt and rubbing the body with the shirt. (Baihaqi).

Ibn al–Munkadir (R.A.A.) reports:

Once Safina, the client of the Holy Prophet (PBUH) missed the Islamic army in the land of the Byzantines. He was anxiously running from pillar to post in search of the army. On his way, he came across a lion and addressing it he said:

"I am the client of the Messenger of Allah and I am now victim of such and such circumstances."

> Thereupon, the lion came forward wagging its tail and guided me along the way till I joined the army. The lion then went back. (Sharh Sunna).

Abu Khaleda (R.A.A.) reports:

Once I asked Abu Aliya whether he had heard anything from Anas about the saying of the Holy Prophet (PBUH) and he (Anas) said:

"I served the Messenger of Allah for ten years without a break and had his utmost blessings all these days. My garden would produce two crops of fruit every year; and a basin in the garden would give off odour of 'musk'.

Urwa bin Zubair reports:

Arwa, the daughter of Aus brought a dispute against Saeed bin Zaid bin Amr bin Naufal before Marwan bin Hakam. She claimed that he had grabbed a piece of her land. Saeed said:

"Would I take any piece of land belonging to her after what I heard from the Holy Prophet (PBUH)?"

"What have you heard from the Prophet of Allah?" he was asked. Thereupon, he said that he had heard the Apostle say:

"If anybody grabs a piece of land, it will be tied round his neck like a necklace."

"I shall ask you nothing after what you said," Marwan told Saeed.

"O' Allah! If she is lying, make her blind and kill her in her land," Saeed cursed her.

> She lost her eyesight and died falling into a hole in her land." (Bukhari, Muslim).

Hazrat Abdullah bin Umar (R.A.A.) reports:

Hazrat Umar bin Khattab (R.A.A.) appointed a man named Sariya as commander of the Islamic army.

After some days, Hazrat Umar (R.A.A.) was addressing the Believers from the pulpit of the Mosque of the Prophet. All of a sudden he shouted at the top of his voice:

"O Sariya! keep near the mountain!"

A messenger from the army came later to Madina and told the Caliphh of Islam with wonder:

"O Commander of the Faithful! We met our enemy and they were about to rout us that someone cautioned us by shouting loudly:

"Keep near the mountain, Sariya!"

> Hearing that call, we set our back to the mountain and routed the invading army." (Baihaqi).

Uqba bin Amir (R.A.A.) reports:

The Holy Prophet (PBUH) prayed for the martyrs of the Battle of Uhud eight years after the battle. He prayed in a manner as if he were bidding farewell to the living and the dead. He then mounted the pulpit and said:

> "I am one to go before you and I shall be a witness against you. Your appointed place is the Pond (of Kauthar) I am looking for. I do not fear that you will turn polytheists after I am gone, but I am afraid you will plunge into worldly comforts and perish like your predecessors." (Bukhari, Muslim)

Hazrat A'isha (R.A.A.) reports:

One of Allah's favours to me was that the Messenger of Allah passed away in my house and that he joined his saliva with that of mine when he died.

During his last hours, my brother, Abdur Rahman bin Abu Bakr, came in with a tooth–stick in his hand. The Holy Prophet (PBUH) looked at it. I knew that he liked to brush his teeth with it. When I asked him if he wanted to have it, he nodded his assent. I gave it to him. 'But it proved too hard for him. So, I asked him if I could soften it, and he nodded his assent. I softened by chewing it and then he moved it over his teeth. There was a jug of water in front of him and he began to put his hands into the water and wipe his face with them, saying meanwhile:"None has the right to be worshipped but Allah. Death has pang." Then he raised his hand and said:

> "(Put me) with the Highest Companion!" till his hands dropped. (Bukhari).

Hazrat A 'isha (R.A.A.) reports:

I heard the Holy Prophet (PBUH) say:

"No Prophet suffers from any illness unless he is given a choice between this world and the next one."

The Messenger of Allah, during his last illness, suffered from severe hoarseness, and I heard him say:

> "(Keep me) with those of Prophets, upright, martyrs and pious ones to whom you have shown your favour. Now one may infer from these words that the Last Prophet (PBUH) was also given a choice." (Bukhari, Muslim).

Hazrat Anas (R.A.A.) reports:

"When the Holy Prophet (PBUH) fell ill, he was found anxious. Thereupon, Fatima (R.A.A.) expressed her grief by saying:

"Alas for the anxiety, my father!"

"Your father will have no anxiety after today," the Apostle said.

"O my father! You have responded to a Lord who summoned you. O my father! Your destination is the Garden of Paradise."

When the Messenger of Allah was laid to rest and Hazrat Anas (R.A.A.) came back, Fatima (R.A.A.) said addressing him:

> "Anas, have you people found it an easy task to scatter dust over the Prophet of Allah?" (Bukhari).

Hazrat Anas (R.A.A.) reports:

When the Holy Prophet (PBUH) came to Madina, there was alround happiness. The Abyssinians played with their spears of joy. Abu Dawud transmitted it.

Darimi transmits him saying:I have never seen a brighter day than the day the Apostle of Allah arrived in Madina; and I have never seen a darker day than the day on which Allah's Messenger passed away.

Hazrat A 'isha (R.A.A.) reports:

When the Holy Prophet (PBUH) passed away, there was difference of opinion among the Companions regarding his place of burial. Thereupon, Abu Bakr (R.A.A.) said:

> "A Prophet is laid to rest at a place he passes away." Thereupon, the Messenger of Allah was buried at the place he passed away. (Tirmidhi).

Hazrat A'isha (R.A.A.) reports:

The Holy Prophet (PBUH) used to say, when he was well and good, that no Prophet leaves this world unless his resting–place in paradise is shown to him, and a choice is given to him.

She further narrates:

When death approached the Messenger of Allah, he had his head on my thigh and he fainted. When he regained his consciousness, he stared at the ceiling and uttered:

> "O Allah! (put me) with the Highest Companion." (Bukhari, Muslim).

Hazrat A'isha (R.A.A.) reports:

During his last illness, the Holy Prophet (PBUH) said:

> "A'isha, I still feel the pain from the food I ate at Khaibar." (Bukhari).

Hazrat Abdullah Ibn Abbas (R.A.A.) reports:

When the last moments of life drew near, the Holy Prophet (PBUH) asked those present to bring pen and paper and write a document so that they would not deviate from the right path after he was gone."

Umar Ibn Khattab (R.A.A.) who was also present there, stopped people from doing so as the pain was supposed to have overpowered the Apostle. He further said that the Book of Allah (Quran) was enough for them.

But the people in the house got divided and a section rose in favour of getting document written by the Messenger of Allah.

But when clamour and confusion prevailed, the Prophet of Allah said to the people.

"Get up and leave me." Ubaidullah reports Abbas to have said:

"It was a terrible calamity which intervened to prevent the Messenger of Allah from writing a document for us owing to disagreement and clamour."

Sufyan reports from Sulaiman to have heard from Abbas:

The prophet of Allah later gave three commands:

"Expel the polytheists from Arabia and keep rewarding the deputations."

As to the third command he reports:

> "The Apostle of Allah either did not mention it or I had forgotten it." (Bukhari; Muslim).

Hazrat Anas (R.A.A.) reports:

After the demise of the Prophet (PBUH), Hazrat Abu Bakr (R.A.A.) said to Hazrat Umar (R.A.A.):

"Come and let us visit Umm Aiman (R.A.A.) as the Messenger of Allah would do."

When the two great Companions of the Apostle came to her, she burst into tears."

"What makes you weep," they asked.

"I am not weeping because of the final departure of the Prophet of Allah; for what lies with Allah, the Almighty, is better for the Apostle of Allah. I am, rather, weeping that the process of Revelation has now ceased."

> This statement of Umm Aiman (R.A.A.) stirred the visitors and they also joined her in shedding tears." (Muslim).

Hazrat A 'isha (R.A.A.) reports:

Once I said, "O my head!" The Holy Prophet (PBUH) heard and said "If you were to die while I am alive I would ask forgiveness for you and make supplication on your behalf." Thereupon, I said:

"Alas! I swear by Allah that I think you want me to die; and if that happened you would spend that night with one of your wives."

> Following this, the Messenger of Allah smiled, and thereafter, the pain that caused death to the Apostle began to be felt. (Bukhari; Darimi).

Hazrat Abu Musa Ash'ari (R.A.A.) reports:

Once the Holy Prophet (PBUH) said:

> "When Allah, the Almighty, means mercy to a people He causes the Prophet of the time to die and makes him (the Prophet) a forerunner who goes before them. But when He means death and destruction to a people causes it during the very lifetime of the Prophet so that the Prophet gets comforted and satisfied that the disbelievers are suitably punished." (Muslim).

Hazrat Abu Hurairah (R.A.A.) reports:

Once the Holy Prophet (PBUH) said:

> "Even if the 'Deen' (religion) would be found hanging with the 'Suraiyya' (cluster of seven brilliant stars in Taurus), some people of Persia would get it."
> (Sahihain).

This saying of the Holy Prophet (PBUH) refers to men of wisdom and learning like Hazrat Imam Abu Haneefa and Hazrat Imam Bukhari and many others who served Islam at all levels.

Once the Holy Prophet (PBUH) said:

> "Very soon people will make long journey in search of knowledge, but none will be found greater than the scholar of Madina." (Hakim).

According to Sufyan bin Ayyiah, the scholar of Madina referred to by the Messenger of Allah was Hazrat Imam Malik.

Hazrat Abdullah Ibn Mas 'ood (R.A.A.) reports:

Once the Holy Prophet (PBUH) said:

> "A great scholar will be born among the Quraish and will fill the earth with the treasures of knowledge." (Abu Dawud).

The above saying of the Messenger of Allah has also been reported by Hazrat Ali (R.A.A.) and Hazrat Abdullah Ibn Abbas (R.A.A.) and is quoted in Baihaqui.

This prediction came true in the form of Hazrat Imam Shafai who was born among the Quraish and was the greatest scholar ever born among them. He was among the offsprings of Muttalib Ibn Abd Munaf.

Imam Ahmed and Abu Dawud quote from Hazrat Abdullah bin Umar (R.A.A.).

Once the Holy Prophet (PBUH) said:

> "A section of my Ummah will be called Qadriya and it will be like a Magi (a fire–worshipper)."

This saying of the Messenger of Allah is also being quoted by Tabrani from Hazrat Anas (R.A.A.).

> Qadriya is a sect which believes that all power rests with men and God has no business to interfere with. Thus God is helpless and worthless and men are powerful in all spheres of life.

Imam Mustaghfari reports from an authentic narrator in 'Dalail–e–Nabviya.'

The narrator puts:

"We three persons were going to Yemen. A man from Kufa was with us. He was reproaching Hazrat Abu Bakr and Hazrat

Umar. We tried to stop him and ask him not to use filthy language against the great Companions of the Messenger of Allah. But he did not pay any heed to our advice. Now it was night. We lay down to sleep at a place near Yemen. At dawn, we performed ablutions and awakened that person too. Having awakened from sleep, he said regretfully that alas, he would not be able to accompany them any further. It is because I saw in dream that the Apostle of Allah was standing at the head of my bedstead and saying:

"O transgressor! Your face will get deformed just over here."

However, we asked the 'Kufi' to get up and wash his face. But when he rolled his legs together, his fingers showed sign of changes. In a short while both his legs looked monkey–like and gradually the whole body turned into a monkey.

At last, we tied him with our camel and left. We reached a forest before sunset. There were a few monkeys in the forest. When the' Kufi monkey' saw them he broke the string and mixed up with them.

Imam Mustaghfari narrates:

"A virtuous man reported that a man from Kufa accompanied me in journey. He used to reproach Hazrat Abu Bakr and Hazrat Umar (R.A.A.). We tried our best to prevent him from doing so, but he did not pay any heed. At last, we excluded him from our company and left.

On our return journey, we met his slave and enquired about his master and told him to tell him to accompany us home.

The slave informed us that his master had undergone a wonderful change; both of his hands have turned like a pig.

Hearing this, we went to the 'Kufi' and asked him to accompany us home. Thereupon, he replied that he has suffered something very precarious. Saying this, he took out his hands which resembled like a pig. In the way, there was a group of pigs. The Kufi could not resist his temptation and jumped down from the mount and mixed up with them."

Abu Dawud, Tirmidhi and Hakim report the Holy Prophet (PBUH) to have said:

"In near future my Ummah will be divided into 73 sects, and all but one, will go to Hell."

Thereupon the Companions of the Holy Prophet (PBUH) asked.

"Which are the people that are destined to enter Paradise?"

"Those who will follow me and my Companions," the Messenger of Allah said.

The prophecy made by the Prophet of Allah in this saying has already come true. After the pious Caliphates, the people differed with respect to creeds and Rawafiz, Khawarij, Muntazila, Jabriya, etc. came into existence. Their number at last, reached 73. And among them there is only one to go to Heaven because they follow the path of the Holy Prophet (PBUH) and his Companions.

Hazrat Asma bint Abu Bakr (R.A.A.) reports the Holy Prophet (PBUH) to have said:

"Banu Thaqeef will produce one beast and one liar." (Muslim). The above prophecy came true. The blood–shedder born to Banu Thaqeef was Hajjaj bin Yusuf. His blood–thirstiness knew no bounds and volumes had been written on his love for shedding blood. Tirmidhi reports on the authority of Hisham bin Hibban that he got killed one lakh twenty thousand persons without any considerable fault.

> Another man belonging to Banu Thaqeef who was declared as liar by the Messenger of Allah was Mukhtar Thaqafi. He was a great liar and imposter. He claimed to be the successor of Imam Muhammad Hanafiah; earned name and fame by circulating his claim to avenge the martyrdom of Imam Husain; and at last claimed his own prophethood. (Muslim).

Hakim, Baihaqi and Abu Naeem report the Holy Prophet (PBUH) to have said about Thabit bin Qais (R.A.A.):

"O Thabit! you will remain alive commendably and you will die as a martyr."

The above prophecy came true as Hazrat Thabit (R.A.A.) was killed in the battle of Yamama fighting Musailma Kaz'zab during the Caliphate of Hazrat Abu Bakr (R.A.A.).

Hazrat Abu Zar (R.A.A.) reports the Holy Prophet (PBUH) to have said addressing him:

"Once Madina will see carnage on such a large scale that blood will stick to the black stones and will not remain visible."

This prophecy came true when the Madinites refrained from Yazeed after the martyrdom of Imam Husain. Yazeed sent a bloody expedition to Madina under the charge of Musrif bin Uqba. A bloody fight took place at Harra where black stones were lying. Hundreds of the Companions of the Holy Prophet (PBUH) and their offsprings were killed and black stones were covered with human blood.

Hazrat Raji bin Khadeej (R.A.A.) reports the Holy prophet (PBUH) to have said in an assembly:

"In this assembly of yours, there is one whose tooth–jaw will be like that of Uhud mountain in the Hell."

Hazrat Abu Hurairah (R.A.A.) narrates that all those present in that assembly, except two, passed away. That I am one of the two; and the next one was Killed in the battle of Yamama.

Thus, the prophecy of the Prophet of Allah regarding a man in that assembly came true.

Baihaqui reports:

"When the death period of Hazrat Abu Zar (R.A.A.) drew near, his wife began to weep because her husband was dying at Rabza where there was nothing except forests. There was none to get him shrouded and buried.

Hazrat Abu Zar (R.A.A.) asked his wife not to shed tears as the Messenger of Allah had told an assembly, and I was also present there, that one of you will die at a place where there will be no population; and a band of Muslims will arrive at the spot. I think I am the person who was referred to here."

Thereafter, he asked his wife to go out and wait on the way.

She narrates:

"When I went out I saw some persons approaching. I narrated to them all about Abu-Zar (R.A.A.). Hearing this, they came to Abu Zar (R.A.A.). He told them:

"Provide for me a shroud belonging neither to a Government official nor of a wealthy person."

Hearing this a young man advanced and said:

"My uncle! I give you my trousers–string and two pieces of cloth for shroud. These articles have been woven by the yarns spun by my mother."

Abu Zar (R.A.A.) accepted the shroud and when he died he was washed and buried after prayer was led for him. Thus, the prophecy of the Apostle came true.

Tabarani and Baihaqui report from Ibn Hakeem Ghabti:

"When Abu Hurairah (R.A.A.) would meet me he would ask about the well–being of Hazrat Sumra bin Jundab (R.A.A.). When I would say.

"Sumra is well and good," Abu Hurairah would express his joy.

One day I asked Abu Hurairah (R.A.A.):

"Why do you ask about the well–being of Sumra every now and then?"

Abu Hurairah (R.A.A.) replied:

"Once we ten persons were assembled in a house. On that occasion, the Holy Prophet (PBUH) said:

"Among you ten men the one who dies last will be in the fire."

Thereafter, Abu Hurairah (R.A.A.) added:

"Eight out of ten persons have already died. Now only Sumra and I are alive. Thus, if Sumara dies before me, I shall be left for the fire."

Abu Hurairah (R.A.A.) was frightened that even if someone would tell him out of joke that Sumra had died, he would get fainted. At last, he died before Sumra.

But the fear of Abu Hurairah (R.A.A.) was based on a misunderstanding.

Ibn Asakar reports from Ibn Sirin that Sumra had a disease which caused biting cold. Hence he would sit on a cauldron containing boiling water in it, for getting himself warmed. One day, while doing the same exercise he fell down into the cauldron and died.

By the Prophecy, the Messenger of Allah did not mean Fire of Hell; what he meant was the fire of this world only. Thus, his prophecy came true.

Hazrat Bukhari and Muslim report from Abu Saeed Khudri (R.A.A.) that the Holy Prophet (PBUH) said:

"You will follow in the footsteps of those who have passed before you." The Companions asked:

"Do you mean the Jews and Christians from our predecessors?" "Yes, who else then," the Apostle replied.

Now the Prophecy of the Messenger of Allah for the Muslims has come true as they have started aping the Jews and the Christians in traits and character, manners and conduct. Jealousy; hiding the truth; interpreting the verses wrongly for worldly gains, etc. were the ways of the Jews. While the Christians used to raise their Prophet and saints to the Divinity.

Each of the traits mentioned above is found among the Muslims of the present age.

Tabarani, Darqitni and Baihaqui report that addressing Hazrat Abdullah bin Zubair (R.A.A.), the Holy Prophet (PBUH) said:

"You will suffer from others and others from you."

This prophecy of the Messenger of Allah came true. Hazrat Abdullah bin Zubair (R.A.A.) bacame Caliph in 64 A.H. after the martyrdom of Imam Husain. All Islamic countries except Syria recognised his Caliphate.

In 73 A.H. Abdul Malik bin Marwan sent a large expedition against Hazrat Abdullah bin Zubair (R.A.A.). The army surrounded Makkah and killed Abdullah bin Zubair. Thus, the Caliph suffered. And since the followers of the Caliph were killed in large number, Kabah was stoned because of the house of the Caliph lying in the vicinity of the Ka'abah. Moreover, his killers were liable to be thrown into the Hell.

Baihaqui and Ibn Adi report the Holy Prophet (PBUH) to have said about Zaid bin Sujan:

"One of his organs will reach the Heaven before all others."

This prophecy came true as some historians had written that his left hand was cut off from his body in the battle of Nahawand.

Baihaqui and Hakim report from Hasan bin Muhammad that the Holy Prophet (PBUH) said to Hazrat Umar (R.A.A.):

"I hope Suhail bin Amr will do something to make you feel gratified."

It is said that when the sad news at the demise of the Messenger of Allah reached Makkah, the followers of the Apostle felt extremely disturbed and they might deviate from the path of Islam. But the fiery speeches of Suhail bin Amr kept them away from leaving the path of Islam. Thus, the prophecy made by the Prophet of Allah came true.

Imam Ahmed from Abdullah bin Abbas (R.A.A.) and Hakim and Baihaqui report from Hazrat A'isha (R.A.A.) that Abbas bin Abdul Muttalib was captured in the Battle of Badr and brought to Madina. On that occasion, a particular amount was fixed as ransom for the release of the captives.

Abbas, the uncle who was also among the Captives of Badr, appeared before the Holy Prophet (PBUH) and submitted:

"The amount of ransom fixed for my release is not available with me; how then I can produce so heavy an amount."

Thereupon, the Messenger of Allah turned towards Abbas and said:

"What happened to your wealth deposited with Umm FazI with the will that in case of your being killed your wealth will get divided among your offsprings."

At this revelation of the fact, Abbas got embarrassed and said to the Prophet:

"How did you come to know this for nobody knew about the wealth except Umm FazI and myself." Thereafter, Abbas paid the ransom from the money brought from Umm FazI.

Baihaqui reports from Hazrat Urwah (R.A.A.):

"Once a dromedary of the Holy Prophet (PBUH) was lost and could not be found out inspite of tremendous searching.

Thereupon, a hypocrite tauntingly said:

"Muhammad (PBUH) claims to reveal the unknown things; why the bringer of revelation does not reveal the whereabout of the lost dromedary."

Thereupon, Hazrat Jibrail came and informed about the taunting of the hypocrite and trace of the lost dromedary.

Thereafter, the Messenger of Allah came out and said:

"I don't claim to know the hidden facts, but my Lord has disclosed to me about the taunting of the hypocrite as well as the lost dromedary. My dromedary is there in so and so ravine and her bridle has got entangled with a tree."

Hearing this, the Companions of the Prophet of Allah rushed towards the ravine and found the lost dromedary in a state described by him.

Ibn Asakar reports from Wathila bin Athqa:

Once I appeared before the Holy Prophet (PBUH) and found him sitting in the assembly of his Companions. I sat in the middle of the circle. The Companions of the Apostle asked me not to do so. Thereupon, the Messenger of Allah said to his Companions:

"Let him sit here, for I know his intention."

"Tell me O Prophet of Allah as to why have I come to you?" Wathila asked.

"You have come to know about the difference between "Certainty" and "Uncertainty," the Apostle explained. "Yes, O Messenger of Allah, I have come to know exactly what you said.

Thereupon, the Apostle of Allah further said:

'Certainty' is one which sticks to heart and which satisfies the heart of a Believer. "Uncertainty" is that which does not satisfy the heart. Hence, you should do what looks "certain" and avoid what looks "uncertain."

Baihaqui reports from Abu Bardah bin Neyaz (R.A.A.):

I brought three cut off heads before the Holy Prophet (PBUH) and said:

"I have killed the two but fail to know who has killed the third one. I have only seen that a tall and fair–complexioned person has killed him and I have only lifted his head."

Thereupon, the Holy Prophet (PBUH) said:

"So and so angel has killed him."

Baihaqui reports from Sa'b bin Abi Habeesh who had come to fight the Believers in the Battle of Badr. He narrates:

"By Allah I also ran away when the Quraish took to their heels. No one captured me. But all of a sudden, a tall and fair–complexioned person appeared sitting on horse between heaven and earth. He tied me up and left there. In the meantime, Abdur Rahman bin Auf (R.A.A.) came. He saw me tied up and asked the soldiers as to who had tied him up. But nobody claimed to have tied him up. He brought me to the Prophet of Allah (PBUH).

"Who has tied you up?" asked the Apostle.

"I do not recognise the person who has tied me up," I replied; and did not narrate what had happened because its mention meant confessing the truth of Islam and the existence of the angels. But hearing all this, the Messenger of Allah (PBUH) said:

"You have been tied up by an angel."

Imam Ahmed, Ibn Sa'd and Ibn Jarir (R.A.A.) report from Abdullah Ibn Abbas and Baihaqui from Hazrat Ali (R.A.A.):

In the Battle of Badr, Abul Al–Yaser had arrested Abbas although the former was a very weak person and the latter was a very strong man.

The Holy Prophet (PBUH) once asked Abul Al–Yaser as to how he was able to capture Abbas. At this, Abul Al–Yaser replied:

"A certain person I had never come across before helped me in tying him up."

"It was a very respectable angel who helped you in tying him," the Apostle explained.

Muslim reports from Hazrat Abu Hurairah (R.A.A.):

Once Abu Jahl said:

"By Lat and Uzza, if I found Muhammad rubbing his nose on the ground, I shall trample his neck by my feet.

One day, the Holy Prophet (PBUH) was saying prayer. Abu Jahl saw and got up in order to fulfil his design. But he retreated awefully as if anything was resisting him.

When the people asked what happened to him, he narrated:

"I saw between Muhammad and I a blazing trench and a very terrible scene and also some feathers."

Thereupon, the Messenger of Allah said:

"If Abu Jahl would come near me, the angels could tear him into pieces."

Sahihin report from Hazrat Abu Saeed Khudri (R.A.A.):

"One night Hazrat Usaid bin Huzair (R.A.A.) was reciting Surah al–Baqara. His horse standing nearly started jumping and tossing. As Usaid stopped the recital, the horse also became peaceful. And as he started reciting the Quran again, the horse started jumping once again. Usaid kept quiet again and the horse did it again. The excercise was repeated for the third time.

After saying his prayer, Usaid bin Huzair took aside his son, Yahya who was sleeping near the horse for fear of being trampled by the horse.

He then raised his eyes towards the sky and saw something spread like a canopy and display of lights in it. The next morning, he narrated the whole episode to the Messenger of Allah. Thereupon, the Prophet of Allah said twice:

"Go on reciting the Quran."

Thereupon, Ibn Huzair submitted:

"O Messenger of Allah! I was afraid that Yahya might be trampled upon. And when I went near Yahya, I saw a canopy which went on up and up and gradually it vanished.

The Apostle of Allah said to Usaid:

"Do you know what was that? "No, O Messenger of Allah," Usaid replied.

"They were angels. They came near you because of your recital of the Quran. When you stopped the recital, they disappeared. Had you been reciting till the morning, the people would have seen them in the morning."

Baihaqui reports:

"Once during the childhood, Hanzia bin Hazeem came to the Holy Prophet with his father and the Apostle had spread his hand over his head and supplicated for his well–being. As a result of this, whenever a man had his mouth or a she–goat had its udder swollen, got cured after being touched by the head of Hanzia.

Tabarani reports:

"When Ayed bin Amr received injury in the Battle of Hunain, the Holy Prophet (PBUH) cleansed his blood and invoked blessings of Allah for him. As a result of this, his forehead always kept shining.

Baihaqui reports from Amr bin Tholeba Jahni (R.A.A.):

"I met the Holy Prophet (PBUH) at Se Yala and embraced Islam on the spot. The Prophet of Allah spread his hands on my face and head."

As a result of this, Tholeba died at the age of 100 and the hairs of his head and beard touched by the Apostle of Allah never grew white till his death.

Ibn Abdul Barr reports in Al–Istiab:

Once the Holy Prophet (PBUH) was taking bath that his daughter Zainab came across. He sprinkled a little water on her face. As a result of this, her face looked fresh and shining till her old age.

Tabarani reports from Abu Amama:

Once the Holy Prophet (PBUH) was taking his meal. In the meantime, a young girl turned up and asked for some food. The Apostle of Allah gave some food from his dish. But she requested that she wanted to have food from his mouth. The Prophet of Allah took out some food from his mouth and gave it to her. The girl ate it up.

It is said that the girl was notoriously shameless in the whole Madina, but after eating from the food of the Apostle, she came to be known as the most shameful woman of Madina.

Baihaqui reports:

With the blessings of the Holy Prophet (PBUH), Abdur Rahman bin Auf (R.A.A.) grew very rich. He hoped to find gold even if he removed a stone from its place. He had gold in his house so much in quantity that after his death during the Caliphate of Hazrat Uthman Ghani (R.A.A.), it was cut into pieces by an axe and the cutters would get tired.

He had four wives. He divorced one of his wives during his last illness. And she was given one –fourth of the eighth part of the whole property and it amounted to eighty thousand dinars to which she agreed.

Moreover, Hazrat Abdur Rahman bin Auf (R.A.A.) had made a will to give away fifty thousand dinars in the way of Allah. He also donated a garden of four lakh rupees to the holy wives of the Holy Prophet (PBUH) and gave away lakhs of dinars as alms, charity etc.

Baihaqui reports in Dalail–e–Nabawaya:

"Once the Holy Prophet (PBUH) supplicated for Abu Qatadah (R.A.A.) in the following words:

"May your face have success and well–being; and O Allah! bless the hairs and the body of Abu Qatadah."

"As a result of this supplication, Abu Qatadah (R.A.A.) died at the age of 70, without a single hair being white; and his face looked like that of a boy of 15.

Tirmidhi and Baihaqui report:

The Holy Prophet (PBUH) supplicated for Sa'd bin Abi Waq'qas (R.A.A.) in the following words:

"O' Allah, accept the supplications of Sa'd."

As a result of this supplication, every supplication of Hazrat Sa'd bin Abi Waq'qas (R.A.A.) was accepted by Allah, the Almighty.

Sahihin report from Hazrat Abdullah Ibn Abbas (R.A.A.):

"O Allah! Confer upon Ibn Abbas knowledge and understanding of Islam and that of commentary of the Holy Quran."

As a result of this supplication, Abdullah Ibn Abbas (R.A.A.) used to be called "a man of deep learning" and the "Interpreter of Quran."

Bukhari, Dareqatni and Imam Ahmed report:

The Holy Prophet (PBUH) invoked blessings for Urwah. He narrates:

"As a result of this supplication, I would, by Allah, return from the market of Kufa getting not less than a profit of forty thousand."

As per Bukhari, Urwa profitted from even by purchasing soil.

Baihaqui and Ibn Majah report:

Once the Holy Prophet (PBUH) invoked:

"O Allah! Save Ali from the rigours of cold and heat."

As a result of this, Hazrat Ali (R.A.A.) used to wear warm clothes during summer and thin clothes during winter.

Baihaqui reports from Imran bin Haseen:

One day I was at the service of the Holy Prophet (PBUH) that his younger daughter Hazrat Fatima (R.A.A.) came in. Her face had turned pale because of hunger.

The Messenger of Allah put his hand at the chest of Fatima and supplicated:

"O filler of the hungry and lifter of the fallen, raise Fatima, the daughter of Muhammad and remove her misery."

I saw that her face began to shine and paleness disappeared. From that day on she never felt hungry.

Khatib reports:

"A person belonging to Yamama brought his one day child to the Holy Prophet (PBUH) on the day of Hajjatul–wida'a. The Prophet of Allah asked that child of one day.

"Who am I?" "You are the Prophet of Allah (peace be upon you)."

"You are telling the truth," the Messenger of Allah said and added, "May Allah bless you."

From that day on, the child never uttered a word unless he attained an age when a child starts speaking.

Muslim reports from Asma'a bint Abu Bakr (R.A.A.):

She took out a robe and said:

"This robe was worn by the Holy Prophet (PBUH) and wherever water after washing this robe was made to drink a patient he would get cured."

Tabarani reports from Hazrat Abu Hurairah (R.A.A.):

"Once Hazrat Husain (R.A.A.) was crying for water. The Holy Prophet (PBUH) put his tongue in his mouth and the thirst was quenched and he stopped crying."

Baihaqui reports in Dalail–e Nabuwah and Ibn Barr in al–Istiab from Umm Aasim, the wife of Utbah bin Farqad (R.A.A.):

"We three were the wives of Utbah (R.A.A.) and we used best of the perfumes. But the fragrance coming out of the body of Utbah excelled all of us. One day I asked Utbah about the secret of his odour. He narrated:

"Once I fell sick. The Holy Prophet (PBUH) came to me and having got me undressed, took his saliva; rubbed it on his palms and spread it on my belly and back. And from that day on, my body produces such a fragrance that all others are subdued by it."

Tabarani and Baihaqui report:

Sherjeel Jafi (R.A.A.) had developed hard lumps in his palm so that he could not catch hold of a sword nor could he hold the rein of the horse. When the Holy Prophet (PBUH) came to know, he pressed his hand and the lumps were cured.

Baihaqui reports:

Once Hakam bin Abi–Aas was sitting in the assembly of the Holy Prophet (PBUH); and when the Apostle would utter anything he would cause convulsive motion in his face and make signs towards the hypocrites with the intention of ridiculing the Apostle.

Seeing this, the Messenger of Allah said:

"May you be so!"

As a result of this curse, he would cause convulsive motion in his face the whole life.

Baihaqui reports from Asma'a bint Abu Bakr (R.A.A.):

"When the wife of Abu Lahab came to know about the revelation of Surah Lahab, she took a stone and came to hurl it at the Holy Prophet (PBUH) who was sitting in the mosque with Abu Bakr (R.A.A.).

But when she came near only Abu Bakr (R.A.A.) was visible. She turned blind for the Apostle. She saw here and there and went back saying:

"I have heard Muhammad using bad words for me; had I found him, I would have hurled this stone at him."

Baihaqui reports from Osama bin Zaid (R.A.A.):

Once the Holy Prophet (PBUH) said:

"One who attaches anything wrong to me will find his place in the Hell."

Once the Messenger of Allah sent someone somewhere. He attached something wrong to the Apostle and circulated it to the people.

When the Prophet of Allah came to know about this, he cursed him. As a result of this, his stomach got burst after death and the earth threw him out."

Ahmed and Bizar report from Anas bin Malik

Once the Holy Prophet (PBUH) accompanied by Hazrat Abu Bakr, Hazrat Umar and an Ansari entered a garden. There were some she–goats. They lay in prostration before the Prophet of Allah.

Thereupon, Hazrat Abu Bakr (R.A.A.) submitted:

"It is more obligatory on us to bow down before you."

"None is liable to be worshipped but Allah," the Apostle said.

Muslim and Abu Dawud report from Abdullah bin Jafar (R.A.A.):

Once the Holy Prophet (PBUH) entered a garden. There was a wicked camel and would bite the entrants.

The Messenger of Allah (PBUH) called him. He came near and lay down in prostration before him; and then sat nearby. Then the Apostle said addressing the camels:

"All except the wicked jinn and men know that I am the Prophet of Allah.

Tabarani and Baihaqui report from Umm Salma (R.A.A.):

Once the Holy Prophet (PBUH) was passing through a forest that a doe called him. A villager was sleeping nearby. The Prophet of Allah asked:

"What do you want to say?" "This villager has captured me and two kids of mine are lying hungry in a ravine. If you set me free I shall come back after suckling them," the doe said.

"Will you really come back?" the Apostle asked.

"Yes," she replied confidently.

The Prophet of Allah (PBUH) released her. She came back after suckling her kids. The Apostle tied her up.

When the villager got up he asked the Apostle as to what did he want?

"Set her free," the Prophet of Allah (PBUH) advised him. She left saying:

"I bear witness that there is none worthy of worship and you are the Prophet of Allah."

Abu Yala and Tabarani report from Hasan:

When Halima Sa'dia carried Muhammad (PBUH) for suckling it proved to be a blessing for her.

It was a period of scarcity because of famine. Even pastures were dried up. There was want of grass. In such a case goats used to come back home hungry and weary. But even in such a situation, the goats of Halima would return eating to the fill, fresh and happy.

Hazrat Sa'd bin Abi Waqqas (R.A.A.) reports:

> "During the Battle of Uhad I saw two men in spotless white dress whom I had never seen before. I saw them fighting right and left of the Messenger of Allah. I was later told that they were Jibrail and Mikail."
>
> (Bukhari, Muslim).

Hazrat Ai'sha (R.A.A.) reports:

"After coming back from the Battle of the Trench, the Holy Prophet (PBUH) put off his armour and took bath. When the Apostle was rubbing his head, Jibrail came to him and said:

"You have put off your armour, but I swear by Allah, that the angels have not done so, hence go out to them." On enquiry, Jibrail revealed, "To Bani Quraiza."

Hence, the Messenger of Allah went to them.

(Bukhari; Muslim).

The Predictions

Hazrat Abu Hurairah (R.A.A.) reports:

"After the conquest of Khaiber, a poisoned sheep was presented to the Holy Prophet (PBUH) by the Jews. Thereupon, the Messenger of Allah asked to collect the Jews present there. When the Jews assembled, the Apostle said to them:

"I am going to ask you something, so will you tell me the truth about it?"

"Yes, Abul Qasim," they replied with one voice.

"Who was their father?" the Apostle asked.

"He was so and so," they replied.

"No theirs was so and so and that they were telling a lie," said the Prophet of Allah.

"Thou have spoken the truth," they admitted.

"Will you tell me the truth about a matter I ask you about?," the Prophet of Allah asked.

"Yes, Abul Qasim; and if we tell a lie, you will come to know the truth as you did in case of our father," they replied.

"Who will go to hell," the Apostle asked.

"We shall be in the hell for a time being, then you will go to hell." they replied.

"Go off in shame into the hell. I swear by Allah that we will never succeed you in it," said the Apostle.

"Will you tell me the truth about a matter if I ask you about it?," the Apostle said.

"Yes, Abul Qasim," they replied.

"Have you put poison in this sheep?," the Apostle said.

"Yes, we did so," they replied.

"What had induced you to do so?," the Prophet asked.

"We wanted to get rid of you in case you are a liar;

and as you are telling the truth it will not harm you," they replied. (Bukhari).

Abu Wa'il reports from Hudhaifa:

"Who amongst you remembers the statement of the Messenger of Allah regarding the afflictions?" once Hazrat Umar ibn Khattab (R.A.A.) asked.

"I remember what did the Apostle said about it," said Hudhaifa.

"Tell, you are really a darling man," Hazrat Umar said.

"The Messenger of Allah had said that a man's afflictions regarding his family, his property and his neighbours are expiated by his prayers, charities and enjoining what is good and forbidding what is bad," Hudhaifa replied.

"I don't mean these afflictions but the afflictions that will be heaving up and down like waves of the sea," Hazrat Umar said.

"O chief of the Believers! you need not fear those afflictions as there is a closed door between you and them," Hudhaifa replied.

"Will that door be opened or broken?" Hazrat Umar asked.

"It will be broken," Hudhaifa replied.

"Then it is very likely that the door will not be closed again," Hazrat Umar replied.

Later on the people asked Hudhaifa, "Did Hazrat Umar know what that door actually meant?"

"Yes, Umar knew it as everyone knows that tonight precedes tomorrow and I had narrated to Umar something authentic and not a lie," Hudhaifa said.

"We dared not ask Hudhaifa," said Abu Wa'il. However, he added that once they asked Masruq about it who had asked Hudhaifa about the matter.

When asked, what does the door stand for?"

"Umar," was the reply from Masruq. (Bukhari).

Ibn Mas'ud (R.A.A.) reports the Holy Prophet (PBUH) to have said:

"Very soon others will be preferred to you; and you will come across things you will not like."

"O Messenger of Allah, what do you enjoin upon us to do in such a case?," the Companions of the Apostle asked.

> "Give the rights that are on you and ask your rights from Allah," the Prophet of Allah (PBUH) replied. (Bukhari)

Usama (R.A.A.) reports:

"Once the Holy Prophet (PBUH) stood on one of the high buildings (of Madina) and said:

> "Do you see what I see?" and added, "I see afflictions pouring down your houses like rain drops." (Bukhari)

Uqba bin 'Amr (R.A.A.) reports:

"Once the Holy Prophet (PBUH) offered the funeral prayer for the martyrs of Uhud, and thereafter proceeding to the pulpit he said:

> "I shall be your predecessor and a witness on you; and I am really looking at my sacred Fount now. No doubt, I have been given the key of the treasures of the world. By

> Allah, I am not afraid that you will worship others alongwith Allah, but I am afraid that you will envy and fight each other for worldly fortunes." (Bukhari)

Zainab bint Jahsh (R.A.A.) reports:

Once the Holy Prophet (PBUH) came to me in a state of fear and said:

"None has the right to be worshipped but Allah! Woe to the Arabs because of evil that has come near. Today a hole has been in the wall of Gog and Magog as large as this," pointing with two of his fingers making a circle."

"O Messenger, of Allah! Shall we be destroyed though amongst us there are pious people?" "Yes, if evil increases," the Apostle said.

Hazrat Umm Salama reports:

> "Once the Holy Prophet (PBUH) woke up and said: Glorified be Allah! What great treasures have been sent down, and what great afflictions have been sent down!" (Bukhari)

Hazrat Amr bin Akhtab al–Ansari reports:

"One day, the Messenger of Allah led us in the Fajr' (dawn) prayer, and mounting the pulpit addressed us till the 'Zuhar' (noon) prayer.

Thereafter, he descended from the pulpit, led the prayer and again mounted the pulpit and addressed us till the 'Asr' (afternoon) prayer. He then descended and led the prayer.

After that he ascended the pulpit and addressed us till the sunset. In his addresses the Messenger of Allah informed us of what is to happen upto the day of Resurrection.

Hazrat Ali (R.A.A.) reports:

"I relate the tradition of the Messenger of Allah to you; for I would rather fall from the sky than attribute anything to him (the Apostle) falsely. Once I heard the Holy Prophet (PBUH) saying:

> "In the last days of this world, there will appear some foolish people who will use the best speech (the Quran) for their own ends. Their faith will not go beyond their throats (i.e.), they will have practically no belief; so wherever you find them, kill them; for he who kills them shall gain a reward on the Day of Resurrection."
>
> (Bukhari.)

Hazrat Abu Hurairah (R.A.A.) reports the Messenger of Allah to have said:

"The Day of Resurrection will not be established till there is a war between two groups inflicting great number of casualties, although claiming the same faith.

> And the Hour will not be established till there appear about thirty liars claiming to be the messengers of Allah."
>
> (Bukhari).

Hazrat Abu Hurairah (R.A.A.) reports the Messenger of Allah (PBUH) to have said:

"The Day of Resurrection will not be established till you fight a nation wearing hairy shoes, and till you fight the Turks, who will have small eyes, red faces and flat noses; and their faces will be like flat shields.

And you will find that the best people are those who hate responsibility of ruling most of all till they are chosen to be the rulers."

Last Breath

Hazrat Abdullah ibn Abbas (R.A.A.) reports:

"In his fatal illness, the Holy Prophet (PBUH) came out, wrapped with a sheet and wrapping his head with an oily bandage. He sat on the pulpit, and praising and glorifying Allah, the Almighty, he said:

> "From now on, people will increase but the Ansar will decrease in number, so much so that they will remain just like salt in the meals. So, if anyone of you achieves power by which you can benefit some and harm others; it is better to favour their virtues and excuse their faults." (Bukhari).

Hazrat Abu Hurairah (R.A.A.) reports:

Once the Holy Prophet (PBUH) predicted the following:

> "When Khosroes perishes, there will be no (more) Khosroes after him; and when Caesar perishes, there will be no (more) Caesar after him. By Him in whose Hands Muhammad's life is, you will spend the treasures of both of them in the Cause of Allah, the Almighty." (Bukhari).

Hazrat Hudhaifa (R.A.A.) reports the Holy Prophet (PBUH) to have said:

> "Among my Companions (or people according to another version), there will be twelve hypocrites who will neither enter paradise nor have its odour. Eight of them will be repelled by an internal ulcer which will appear on their shoulders and extend into their breasts." (Muslim).

Hazrat Khabbab bin al–Aratt (R.A.A.) reports:

"One day the Holy Prophet (PBUH) was lying on a stripped cloak in the shade of the Ka'aba. We complained him against the persecution from polytheists and requested him to make supplication to Allah."

Thereupon, the Apostle's face turned red and he sat straight to say:

"Before your time, a man was put in a pit dug for him, then his head was cut in two with a saw, but those sufferings and miseries failed to turn him away from his Faith. Another person was combed with iron combs below his flesh, but he did not break with his Faith.

> "I swear by Allah that this matter (Islam) will reach its perfection, so that a rider will go from San'a to Hadrmaut fearing nothing but Allah, the Almighty; or a wolf which may attack sheep; but you are in quite hurry." (Bukhari).

'Adi bin Hatim (R.A.A.) reports:

"Once I was with the Holy Prophet (PBUH) that a man came to him and complained of his poverty. In the meantime, another person came and complained to him of highway robbery.

Thereupon, the Messenger of Allah turned toward me and said:

"Adi! Have you seen al–Hira? Thereafter, he added:

"If you live long enough you will certainly see a woman travelling from al–Hira to go round the Ka'aba fearing none but Allah, the Almighty.

"If you live long enough, you will see that the treasures of Kisra (Chosroes) will be conquered."

"If you live long enough you will certainly see a man coming out with a handful of gold or silver looking for someone to accept it but he will find none to be accepting it from him."

"One of you will meet Almighty Allah on the appointed day when Allah will ask him: Did I not send you a Messenger to convey My Message to you?"

"Certainly Yes," he will admit.

"Did I not give you property and show favour to you?" Allah, the Almighty, will ask.

"Certainly yes," he will accept without any hesitation.

Thereafter, the said:The person will look towards his right and he will find 'Hell,' then he will look towards his left and will see 'Hell."

"Saying this, the Messenger of Allah warned:Guard against ' Hell' even though it be with half a date, and if one can not get so much he should do it with a good word."

'Adi bin Hatim adds:

"I have seen a woman travelling from al–Hira to go round the Ka'aba fearing none but Allah, the Almighty.

I was among those who conquered the treasures of Kisra, son of Hurmuz; and if you will live long enough you will see what Abul Qasim (the Apostle) had foretold the third thing to happen." (Bukhari).

Hazrat Hudhaifa (R.A.A.) bin Al–Yaman reports:

"The people would ask the Holy Prophet (PBUH) about good, but I used to ask him about evil fearing that it might overtake me. Once I submitted to the Apostle of Allah.

"O Prophet of Allah! We were in ignorance and in evil and Allah has bestowed upon us the present good; will there be any evil after this good?" "Yes." he replied.

"Will there be good after that evil?" I asked. "Yes, but this good will be tainted with a little evil," he said.

"Yes, there will be some people who will invite others to the doors of Hell; and whoever accepts their invitation, will be thrown into it," he said.

"Describe those people to us," I asked.

"They will belong to us and speak our language," he said

"What do you ask me to do if such a thing should take place in my life," I asked.

"Adhere to the group of Muslims and their chief," he said.

"If there is neither a group (of Muslims) nor a chief (what shall I do)?" I asked.

> "Keep away from all those different sects, even if you have to bite (i.e. eat) the root of a tree, till you meet Allah while you are still in that state." (Bukhari).

Hazrat Abu Sa'eed Khudri (R.A.A.) reports:

"We were with the Prophet of Allah when he was distributing the booty. A man from Bani Tamim came to the Apostle and said:

"Act equitably, O Messenger of Allah!"

"Who will act equitably if I do not?" the Apostle said.

Thereupon, Hazrat Umar (R.A.A.) sought permission to cut off his head.

"Leave him," said the Messenger of Allah and added;

"He is better than those who recite the Quran but it does not pass their collar bones. They deviate from the religion as an arrow goes through the animal aimed at. They will be recognised by the presence of a black man of whose upper arms quiver like a woman's breast, or like a piece of meat; and they will revolt against the best section of mankind."

After this Abu Sa'eed (R.A.A.) says:

"I testify that I heard this from the Messenger of Allah, and I testify that Ali bin Abu Talib (R.A.A.) fought with them and I was with him. He gave orders about that man who was sought for and when he was brought in, and I looked at him, he was exactly as the Prophet of Allah had described him.

In another version it is narrated:

"A man with deep–set eyes, a projecting brow, a thick beard, high cheek bones and a shaven head came forward and said:

"Fear Allah, O Muhammad!"

"Who will obey Allah if I disobey him?" the Apostle replied and added, "Allah entrusted me with power over the inhabitants of the earth but you do not."

At this a man sought permission to kill him but the Apostle (PBUH) prevented him from doing so.

When the man turned away, the Messenger of Allah (PBUH) said:

> "From this man's stock there will be people who recite the Quran, yet it will not pass their throats. They will swerve from Islam as an arrow goes through the animal shot at. They will kill the followers of Islam and leave the worshipers of idols alone; but if I live to their time I shall certainly kill them as Aad were killed."
>
> (Bukhari; Muslim).

Sa'eed bin Jaber (R.A.A.) reports from Hazrat Abdullah ibn Abbas (R.A.A.):

"Umar bin Khattab (R.A.A.) had very sympathetic attitude with Abdullah ibn Abbas (R.A.A.) and treated him very favourably.

Once Abdul Rahman bin Auf (R.A.A.) said to him:

"We also have sons that are equal to him."

"It is because of his knowledge," Hazrat Umar (R.A.A.) replied.

Thereafter, Umar (R.A.A.) asked Ibn Abbas to interpret the verse:

"When come the help of Allah and Victory."

"It portends the death of the Messenger of Allah," Ibn Abbas (R.A.A.) said.

Thereupon, Hazrat Umar (R.A.A.) said:

"I do not know from this verse but what you know."

(Bukhari)

Hazrat Abdullah bin Mas 'ud (R.A.A.) reports:

"Once Sa'd bin Mu'adh (R.A.A.) came to Makkah with the intention of performing 'Umra. He stayed at the house of Umaiyya bin Khalaf, for Umaiyya himself would stay at S'ad's house whenever he passed by Madina on his way to "Shamm" (Syria).

When Sa'd (R.A.A.) wanted to go round the Ka'ba, Umaiyya said to him:

"Will you wait till mid–day when people leave for their homes so that you perform "Tawaf" round the Ka'ba peacefully."

But while Hazrat S'ad bin Mu'adh (R.A.A.) was going round the Ka'ba, Abu Jahl turned up and asked:

"Who is there performing Tawaf?" "I am S'ad," replied Hazrat S'ad Ibn Mu'adh (R.A.A.).

"Are you going round the Ka'aba, although you have given refuge to Muhammad (PBUH) and his companions?" Abu Jahl said.

"Yes" Sa'd replied.

Now they started quarreling. At this, Umaiyya bin Khalaf came forward and said advising Sa'd:

"Don't shout Abu Jahl, for he is the chief of the valley (of Makkah)."

Thereupon, Sa'd told Abu Jahl:

"By Allah, if you prevent me from performing the' Tawaf of the Ka'ba, I will spoil your trade with Shaam."

But Umaiyya bin Khalaf kept on saying to Sa'd:

"Don't raise your voice," and took hold of him.

At this, Sa'd grew furious and rebuked Umaiyya, saying:

"Be away from me, for I have heard the Prophet of Allah (PBUH) saying that he will kill you."

"Will he kill me?" Umayyia asked.

"Yes!" Sa'd said with confidence.

"By Allah, when Muhammad says a thing, he never tells a lie," Umayyia also said with certainty. Thereafter, he went to his wife and told her:

"Do you know what my brother from Yathrib (Madina) has said to me?"

"What has he said?" she asked.

"He claims that he has heard Muhammad saying that he will kill me," he said to his wife.

"By Allah! Muhammad (PBUH) never tells a lie," she replied.

When the Meccan army proceeded towards Madina that resulted in the Battle of Badr, Umayyas's wife reminded him the prediction of the Apostle of Allah saying:

"Don't you remember what your brother from Yathrib had told you?"

Thereupon, Umaiyya decided not to join the battle. But Abu Jahl persuaded him by saying:

"You are from the nobles of the valley (of Mecca), so you must accompany us for a day or two."

Thus, very reluctantly Umaiyya bin Khalaf joined the battle and the prophecy of the Messenger of Allah came exactly true.

Anas bin Malik (R.A.A.) reports:

"Once the Holy Prophet (PBUH) found Thabit bin Qais missing from his assembly. When he enquired about him a man said:

"O Messenger of Allah! I shall bring you his news."

So, he went to Thabit and found him sitting in his house brooding his head in sadness.

"What's the matter?" the man asked Thabit.

"An evil situation!" replied Thabit and added.

"A man would raise his voice over the voice of the Prophet of Allah (PBUH) and so all his good deeds have been annulled and he is from the people of Hell."

The man went back to the Messenger of Allah and told him what Thabit had said.

Hearing the utterances of Thabit, the Apostle of Allah said:

> "Go and say to Thabit, You are not from the people of Fire; you are rather from the men of Paradise." (Bukhari).

Hazrat Abu Hurairah (R.A.A.) reports:

"Once the Holy Prophet (PBUH) predicted:"This branch from Quraish will ruin the people."

"What do you enjoin us to do in such a case?" the Companions of the Messenger of Allah asked.

"I would ask you to keep away from such people," the Apostle of Allah said to his companions.

Sayeed Al–Umawi reports:

Once I was with Hazrat Abu Hurairah (R.A.A.) and Marwan and heard Abu Hurairah saying:

"I heard the most trustworthy (the Prophet) as saying:

The destruction of my followers will be brought about by the youngster's from Quraish.

"Youngster's?" Marwan asked with wonder.

"If you wish, I would name them:They are the children of so and so and the children of so and so," Abu Hurairah replied confidently."

Hazrat Abu Sayeed Al–Khudri (R.A.A.) reports:

"Once the Holy Prophet (PBUH) said:"A time will come the people (Muslims) will wage holy war, and it will be asked:

"Is there any amongst you who has enjoyed the company of Allah's Apostle?" They will say "yes" and then victory will be bestowed upon them.

"They will wage holy war again, but it will be asked:

"Is there any among you who has enjoyed the company of the Companions of Allah's Apostle?"

"Yes" they will say and then victory will be bestowed on them."

Hazrat Abdullah bin Umar (R.A.A.) reports:

"The Jews will fight you, and you will be given victory over them."

That time even a stone will say:

> "O Muslim:there is a Jew behind me; so kill him!" (Bukhari).

Hazrat Al–Mughira bin Shu'ba (R.A.A.) narrates:

"Once the Holy Prophet (PBUH) said:"Some of my followers will remain on the right path and hence victorious till the Day of Resurrection."

Mu'awiya (R.A.A.) reports:

"I heard the Holy Prophet (PBUH) say:"A group of people amongst my followers will remain obedient to Allah's orders and they will not be harmed by anyone. And they will remain victorious till the Last Day provided they remain obedient to Allah, the Almighty." (Bukhari).

True Words

Abu Humaid al–Sayeedi reports:

"While accompanying the Holy Prophet (PBUH) on the expedition to Tabuk, we arrived at "Wadi al–Qura." While passing a garden belonging to a woman, the Messenger of Allah asked us to estimate its value. We did as ordered. Then the Prophet of Allah estimated it at ten camel loads. The Apostle then told the woman to calculate the value of her garden till we return, should **Allah** will.

Thereafter, we left the place.

When we reached, the Messenger of Allah told us:"You will have a violent storm tonight, so I tell you that nobody should get up till it is blowing and persons having camels must hobble them firmly."

As predicted by the Apostle of Allah, a violent wind started blowing, and as a man, ignoring the order of the Prophet, got up, and he was carried away by the strong wind and thrown between the two mountains of Tayy.

We then came back and passed the garden at Wadi al–Qura.

When the Messenger of Allah asked the woman how much fruit her garden had amounted to, she replied:

"Ten camel loads!"

Unaisa, the daughter to Zaid bin Arqam reports on the authority of her father:

> The Prophet (PBUH) went to visit Zaid when he was ill.

Consoling him, the Prophet of Islam said to him:

"Your illness will bring about no harm to you," and "how will you do if your life is prolonged but you become blind?" "I shall seek my reward from Allah and show endurance," Zaid replied.

Thereupon, the Messenger of Allah said to him:

> "In that case you will enter paradise without being taken to account," the Prophet of Allah predicted. (Bukhari).

Jabir (R.A.A.) reports:

Once the Holy Prophet (PBUH) asked me, "Have you got carpets?"

"Wherefrom can we get carpets?" Jabir replied.

"But you shall soon have carpet?"

When my wife managed to have carpets, I used to say to her:

"Remove your carpets from my sight," but she would say in reply:

"Didn't the Prophet of Allah tell you that you would soon have carpets?"

Thereupon, I gave up asking her to do so.

8

Holy Prophet's Commands–2

The Holy Prophet (PBUH) informed his companion about the death of Negus (Najashi) in Abyssinia. He also led the prayers for the dead king in absentia in Madina.

At the time of the Battle of Mota in 8 A.H., the Holy Prophet (PBUH) appointed Hazrat Zaid bin Haritha (R.A.A.) commander of the Muslim Army. Before the march of the army, he had prophesied that after the martyrdom of the commander, Ja'far (R.A.A.) shall be the commander and after him Abdullah bin Rawahah will take over and after his departure, the army will select its commander.

When the battle was going on, the Messenger of Allah (PBUH) was monitoring his Companions what was happening in the battlefield. He had tears in his eyes when he was narrating the tragedies. But nothing happened against what he had foretold. Khalid bin Walid (PBUH) was selected as new commander and victory was gained at the end.

In a battle, a person was seen fighting very bravely. The people praised his bravery before the Prophet (PBUH). But he said that the person was a 'jahannami' (belonging to Hell). Later on, the people saw that during the fighting he received wound which hurt him so much that he committed suicide. The prediction of the Apostle came true.

One person was killed in the battle fighting on the part of the Muslims. The people declared him a "jannati" (belonging to Heaven). But the Holy Prophet (PBUH) predicted against what they had said. He said that it was not possible for him to enter paradise because during Miraj he had seen him in the Hell for having stolen a dress from material obtained in booty.

Once Umar bin Wahaab conspired with Safwaan to kill the Prophet (PBUH). He dipped his sword in poison and left for Madina. When he was passing through the streets, he came across Hazrat Umar (R.A.A.), who caught him and produced before the Messenger of Allah (PBUH).

The Apostle disclosed that he had come, in collusion with Safwaan, to kill him (the Prophet). The man got very much surprised as only Safwaan had knowledge about the plan. Thereupon, he confirmed the Prophethood of Muhammad (PBUH) and embraced Islam on the spot.

Piety and Sin

Once Hazrat Wabasaah (R.A.A.) appeared before the Holy Prophet (PBUH) with the intention to request the Apostle to explain what is good and what is evil. As he approached the Apostle, he disclosed the desire of the visitor to his wonder. Later on, the Prophet of Islam explained that 'good' is what gives 'pleasure at heart'; and 'evil' leaves the doer 'sad' or 'doubtful at heart.'

When the Holy Prophet (PBUH) arrived at Madina, a learned Jew, Abdullah bin Salaam met him and asked him three questions and the Apostle replied as under:

(1) The first sign of the approach of 'Qayamat' (Doomsday) is that there shall rage a fire which will drive people to the west from the east;

(2) the first food for the "Jannaties" (men belonging to Heaven) shall be the liver of fish.

(3) a child resembles the father when father's seed is the stronger, and it favours the mother, when mother's seed is the stronger.

Abdullah heard the answers and acknowledged the Prophethood of Muhammad (PBUH).

On another occasion, a learned Jew put three questions to the Holy Prophet (PBUH) for answers because only a Prophet could do it. As the Apostle answered those questions correctly and to the satisfaction of the Jew, he too acknowledged him as a true Prophet.

Once a few Jews asked the Prophet (PBUH) four questions with the promise that if answers to these questions were made correctly, they would embrace Islam. The Apostle answered three questions correctly as they themselves admitted. While answering the fourth one, the Messenger of Allah said that his friend and protector among the angels was Jibrail (Gabriel) and that Jibrail was also the friend and protector of all the Prophets. Thereupon, they said that they could not go along with the Prophet as Jibrail was their enemy.

Some of the Jews met the Holy Prophet (PBUH) and asked about the ten Commandments given to Musa (Moses). When the Apostle answered the question correctly, the Jews were so overwhelmed with joy that they kissed his hands and feet, and acknowledged him as a Prophet. Thereupon, the Apostle asked why did they not accept Islam, they said that they were afraid of being killed on accepting Islam.

On another occasion, the Holy Prophet (PBUH) was asked about "Rooh" (Soul). He kept silent. His Companions were satisfied that the Apostle would answer the question on receiving the 'Wahi' (Revelation). After sometime the Apostle, answering the question said, "Say that the soul is a thing from my Lord and that you have been given but small portion of knowledge." (Bani Israel)

During the Battle of Trenches, while digging the trench, a hard rock was causing great difficulty for it could not be broken by the pick. When the Holy Prophet (PBUH) was informed, he dropped down into the trench and gave such a blow with the pick that one–third of the rock was hewed asunder. Thereupon, the Apostle said, "Glory be to Allah, the keys of Syria have been given to me."

> With the second blow of the pick, the Apostle hewed another one–third of the rock and said, "Glory be to Allah, the keys of Persia have been given to me. By God, I see the white castle of Medina. (Ctesiphon)."
>
> In the third attempt, the remaining portion of the rock was broken to pieces, the Apostle then said, "Glory be to Allah, I have been given the keys of Yemen. By God, I can now see the gate of San'a."(Ibn Kathir vol.III, p.194).

While digging the trench, whenever any party felt a difficulty owing to the existence of any hard rock which could not be broken or removed by them, the Holy Prophet (PBUH) called for some water and put a little of his saliva into it; then he prayed as Allah willed him to pray; and directed to sprinkle the water on the rock which pulverized like a heap of sand.

During the Battle of Trenches, a violent hurricane from the desert uprooted the tents of the enemies of Islam and overthrew their cooking pots. The severe weather, sent by Allah, disheartened the enemy. Calling his men, Abu Sufyan said to them, "O Quraish, it is no longer a fit place to camp here. Our horses have died, Bani Qurayza have not kept faith with us and we have heard dreadful tidings of them. You can see the havoc caused by the gale; we have neither a cooking pot at its place, nor can lit a fire, nor have tent standing, nor yet a shelter to bank on. Get you gone, for I have decided to go.

This was a miracle worked by the mercy of Allah.

During the Battle of Trenches, when the Meccan army left in embarrassment, the Holy Prophet (PBUH) said to Companions:

> "The Quraish shall not come at you after this year, but you would attack them after that."
>
> (Ibn Kathir vol. III, p. 2210.

The terms of agreement of Hudaibia and the obligation to return without performing "Umra' plunged the Muslims into the most profound depression. It seemed incredible to them how the Messenger of Allah had agreed to those seemingly ignominious terms. So dismayed were they that Hazrat 'Umar (R.A.A.) went as far as to speak his mind.

The Apostle then broke camp to return to Madina. He was still in the way when Allah confirmed that the truce of Hudaibia was not a setback but a signal victory.

Hazrat Umar (R.A.A.) asked the Prophet (PBUH), 'Is it a victory, O Apostle of Allah?" The Apostle replied "Yes."

The events that followed proved that the truce of Hudaibia was a decisive step in gaining victory after victory for Islam.

After the Treaty of Hudaibia, the Holy Prophet (PBUH) bought peace and order and started his missionary activities. The

Apostle then sent several letters to the sovereigns outside Arabia and the tribal chiefs within the country inviting them to accept Islam.

When the letter of the Prophet (PBUH) was handed over to Chosroes II of Iran, he was indignant enough to tear the letter into pieces, saying, "My slave dares to write me thus!"

> When his reply was conveyed to the Prophet (PBUH) he remarked, "Even so shall Allah shatter his kingdom to pieces." (Tabari vol.111, pp.90–91).

Chosroes II wrote to Badhan, who was his governor in Yemen, to get the Prophet of Islam sent to him in Ctesiphon. Badhan deputed Babwayh to tell the Apostle what Chosroes II had written to him and that he had come to take him to the King.

But when Babwayh came to Madina, the Apostle told him, "Allah has given Shervh power over his father and he has killed Chosroes II. The prophecy of the Apostle came true exactly in the way foretold by him.

After his return from Hudaibia, the Holy Prophet (PBUH) stayed in Madina for sometimes and then marched off to Khaybar. He passed the night there and ordered to march ahead before the call for prayer was given. The Muslim met the workers of Khaybar coming out with spades and baskets. As soon as they saw the Apostle and the army. they turned on their heels, shouting, "Muhammad and his force."

> The Apostle said, "Allah is Great. Khaybar is destroyed." (Ibn Hisham vol.111, pp.229–30).

The slave of a Jew of Khaybar had been hired to watch over the flocks of his master. When he saw the Jews taking up arms for giving a fight to the Muslims, he asked, "What for do you go?"

The Jews replied that they were going to fight the man who had laid a claim to prophethood. The slave's curiosity brought him to the Prophet (PBUH) whom he asked about the faith preached by him. The Apostle replied, 'I call you to Islam, that is, you bear witness that there is no deity save Allah and that I am the Apostle of Allah, and you serve not aught except Allah."

"If I bear witness as you say," enquired the slave, "and have faith in Allah, what shall I get in return?"

The Apostle replied, "If you die with Faith, you will enter Paradise."

The slave accepted Islam and then asked the Apostle, "What should I do with the flock? I hold it in trust."

The Apostle told him to abandon the goats in the field near the fort and Allah would cause them to reach their owner. The man did so and the goats did find their way back to their master.

Unknown Facts

During the Battle of Khaybar, a Bedouin came to the Apostle and after accepting Islam expressed his desire to accompany him in the expedition. The Apostle asked some of his Companions to take care of him and see his needs. When the Muslims captured one of the forts and won a large booty, the men had taken out a herd of cattle for grazing. The spoil was distributed among the combatants and the share of the Bedouin was also apportioned. When he was given his share, he took it to the Apostle and asked, "What is it?" The Apostle explained that it was his share of the booty of war. Thereupon, he said, "I didn't come to you for it." Then pointing to his throat he continued, "I followed you in the hope that I would be hit by an arrow here and would go to paradise." The Apostle replied, "If you desire it so, Allah will do likewise."

Then, in a subsequent battle at Khaybar, the dead body of the Bedouin was found among those killed in encounter. The Apostle asked, "Is it the same man?" When the Companions replied in the affirmative, the Apostle remarked, "He was true to Allah and Allah made his wish come true."

Hazrat Amr bin Salim al–Khuza (R.A.A.) went to the Apostle in Madina and recited verses describing how the Quraish had violated their pledged word. He asked the Apostle to extend his help by virtue of the treaty of alliance between him and the Khuza'a.

We took the stand that the Quraish had annulled the treaty with the Prophet (PBUH) by attacking his allies when they were at their well and had not spared their lives even when they were performing prayers. After listening to his complaint, the Prophet (PBUH) replied:

"You will be helped, O 'Amr bin Salim."

The Prophet (PBUH) then sent a man to Makkah in order to get a confirmation of the affair and also to allow the Quraish to redress the wrong committed by them.

The Apostle directed to place three alternatives before the Quraish:

(a) they should either pay the blood money for the victims of Khuza'a;

(b) or terminate their alliance with the aggressors belonging to Bani Nifasa of Banu Bakr; but

(c) failing these they shall get in return what they had alone. The terms were communicated to the Quraish but in the fit of their pride they replied: "Yes, we would prefer measure for measure."

The Muslims were thus absolved of their undertaking with the Quraish and it became incumbent on them to get satisfaction of the wrong done to their allies.

When the Prophet (PBUH) was informed of the reply given by Quraish, he said;

"I see if Abu Sufyan has come to you to strengthen the treaty and to ask for more time."

> The events took shape as predicted by the Apostle. The Quraish realised the gravity of the situation and felt sorry for the indiscreet reply given by the thoughtless among them. They charged Abu Sufyan to get the treaty ratified and extended again.
>
> (Zad al–Ma'ad vol.1, p. 120).

When the Holy Prophet (PBUH) decided to proceed for the conquest of Mecca, he asked the Muslims to start making preparations for an expedition but also bade them to keep it a secret. Later on, the Apostle informed the men that he intended to go to Mecca and ordered them to get ready for it. He also prayed.

> "O Allah! confound the spies and the informers of the Quraish so that we may take them by surprise in their land." (Zaad–al–Ma'ad Vol.I, p.421)

Hatib bin Abi Balta'a was one of those Muhajireen who had migrated from Makkah and had taken part in the Battle of Badr. It is related that when the Holy Prophet (PBUH) informed his companions about his intention to attack Mecca and they quietly started making preparations for it, Hatib bin Abi Balta'a wrote a letter to the Quraish about the intended attack and gave it to a woman for delivering it to the Quraish. Hatib also promised to give some money to the woman who set off for Mecca after putting the letter in her head and plaiting her locks over it. The voice of

Heaven informed the Apostle about the action of Hatib. He immediately sent Hazrat Ali (R.A.A.) and Hazrat Zubayr (R.A.A.) in her pursuit, saying:

"Go until you come to the meadow of Khaakh, where you will find a woman travelling on a camel who has a letter which you must take from her."

The two went off racing on their horses until they came to the meadow, and there they found the woman going on her camel. They made her dismount and searched her baggage but found nothing. At last, Hazrat Ali (R.A.A.) said to her:

"By Allah, the Messenger of Allah is not mistaken nor are we. You must bring out the letter or we will search your person."

When she saw that they were in earnest, she asked them to turn aside. Then she drew out the letter from her tresses and handed it over to them. The letter, brought back to Apostle, had been written by Hatib bin Abi Batla'a informing the Quraish about the departure of the Muslim army. When summoned by the Apostle, Hatib bin Batla'a said:

"O Messenger of Allah, don't be hasty with me. I swear to Allah that I have faith in Allah and His Apostle; neither I have abandoned nor changed my faith. I had been attached as an ally to the Quraish and was not one of them; I have my family there but no kinsmen to protect them. Other emigrants with you have their relations among the Quraish who will take care of their families. I thought that as I did not have that advantage I should give them some help so that they might protect my relations."

Hazrat 'Umar bin Khattab (R.A.A.) sought permission of the Holy Prophet (P.B.U.H) to cut off Hatib's head whom he charged as being a hypocrite, disloyal to Allah and His Messenger. But the Apostle replied:

"He was present at Badr. Do you know, 'Umar', perhaps Allah has looked favourably on those who were present at Badr"

"Do as you wish for I have forgiven you."

Umar (R.A.A.) dissolved into tears, saying:

"Allah and His Messenger know better."

The Apostle set out from Madina, during Ramadhan, at the head of ten thousand companions. The army made camp at Marr al–Zahraan. The Quraish were, however, still uncertain, for Allah had kept them completely ignorant of the advance of the Muslim army.

After the Conquest of Mecca, the Holy Prophet (PBUH) first cleared the Ka'ba of three hundred and sixty idols after the return of normalcy.

Thereafter, the Holy Prophet (PBUH) went round the sanctuary. Then he sent for Uthman bin Talha, who had the charge of the Ka'aba's keys. He took the keys from 'Uthman and got the doors opened.

Once, before his migration to Medina, the Apostle had requested 'Uthman' to give him the keys of the Ka'aba, but Uthman had not only refused his request but had also been impertinent to him. With exemplary forbearance, the Apostle had then said to him;

"Uthman, the day will come when you will see this key in my hands. I would then give it to whom I would like."

"If the day comes, the Quraish would be humiliated and crushed that day."

"No," the Prophet (PBUH) had said calmly,

"It would be the day when they would be honoured and secured."

> It is related that the prediction had so haunted the mind of 'Uthman that he had come to believe that it would happen exactly as foretold by the Apostle.
>
> (Zaad–al–Ma'aad vol.1, p.425, Bukhari).

Fadala bin 'Umayr wanted to kill the Holy Prophet (PBUH). He made up his mind to attack the Apostle when he would be busy in circumambulating the Ka'ba. When he drew near, the Apostle (PBUH) called out:

"Fadala" to invite his attention.

He replied, "Yes, O Apostle of Allah."

The Apostle then asked him:

"What are you thinking about?"

"Nothing" replied Fadala, "I was recollecting Allah."

The Apostle smiled and said:

"Seek forgiveness from Allah," and at the same time he put his hand on Fadala's chest. His heart was at once set at ease and, as Fadala related later on:

"The Holy Prophet (PBUH) had not yet removed his hand from my chest that I found him dearer to my heart than every creature of Allah."

Fadala further says:

> "Then I went back to my house and passed the woman with whom I used to converse. She asked me to sit down and talk with her, but I replied, "No, Allah and Islam do not permit it now." (Ibn Hisham vol.11, p.417).

The people of Mecca who had joined the Holy Prophet (PBUH) in this battle were fresh from paganism. Now, in the days of pagan past, some tribes of Arabia used to venerate a great green tree known as Dhat–u–Anwaat under which they stayed for a day, suspended their weapon to its branches and offered sacrifices beneath it. When these men were going with the army they happened to pass by a big shady tree which reminded them of the past fetishism. They immediately requested the Apostle:

"Make us a tree as they used to have Dhat–u–Anwaat, O Messenger of Allah."

The Prophet (PBUH) replied:

> "Allah is great! By Him who holds my life in His hands, you say what the people of Musa (Moses) said to him:Make for us a God even as they have gods. He (Musa) said:Lo! you are a folk who know not." (Q.7:138).

The Apostle then added:

> "Verily, you would follow every custom of the people before you." (Ibn Hisham, vol. II, p.442).

It was the 10th of Shawwal, 8 A.H. when the Muslim army reached Hunain, descending the 'wadi' (valley) in morning twilight. The enemy had already taken its position in the glens and hollows and craters of the valley. A valley of arrows was all that the Muslims saw of the enemy, then suddenly the enemy followed up the attack with full force. Hawaazin were celebrated archers.

The sudden onslaught forced the Muslim flanks to fall back and they fled in terror none heeding the other. The battle had taken a dangerous turn; a complete rout of the Muslims was in sight without any possibility of an orderly retreat or rallying of their forces again. Like the Uhad, when the rumour of the Apostle's death had disheartened the Muslims, the troops were once more driven to despair in Hunain by a similar misgiving.

Some of the rude fellows from Mecca who had joined the Muslim army but were still not strong in faith started talking in a way that let out their antipathy to Islam. One said:

"Their flight will not stop before they get at the sea."

Another man remarked:

"The spell of their sorcery has ended today."

The Muslim had to suffer this defeat after the brilliant victory of Mecca as if by way of punishment for their reliance on numbers instead of the succour of Allah. Their faith needed to be strengthened by a misadventure for they had to learn the lesson that both victory and defeat came from Allah; neither the one should make man exultant nor the other despondent. The Muslims were all over with their trepidation when the peace of Allah appeared to be descending on them and the Apostle. The Prophet (PBUH) had all the while stood firm on his place, riding his white mule, without any fear. Only a few of the Ansar and Muhajirin or his relatives were then with him. Abbas bin Abdul Muttalib was holding the bridle of his mule while the Apostle of Allah was calling aloud:

"Verify, I am the Prophet without falsehood; I am son of Abdul Muttalib."

(According to Bukhari Abu Sufyan bin Harith was holding the bridle).

In the meantime, a detachment of the enemy advanced towards him. The Apostle took a handful of dust and threw it into their eyes.

When the Holy Prophet (PBUH) saw his men in confusion, he said:

"O Abbas call out, O Ansar, O comrades of the ocacia tree." All those who heard the cry, respondend:

"Here are we."

Abbas had a loud voice. Whoever heard him calling got off from his camel and came to the Holy Prophet (PBUH).

When sufficient number of men had gathered, they bore down upon the enemy. A combat between the two parties started afresh. The Apostle then took to a height alongwith some of his companions. He saw the two sides grappled with one another. He said:

"Now the battle has grown hot." He threw a few pebbles on the enemy. Abbas relates:

"I saw the enemy becoming slack thereafter and losing the day to the Muslims."

Both the armies fought bravely. However, before all those Muslims who had fled away had come back, the enemy was discomfited and a party of handcuffed prisoners was brought before the Holy Prophet (PBUH). Allah helped the Apostle with the hosts of heaven to win the day and brought Hawaazin to their knees.

The Holy Quran narrates it as under:

"Allah has given you victory on many fields and on the day of Hunain, when you exulted in your multitude but it availed you naught, and the earth, vast as is, was straightened for you; then you turned back in flight;

> Then Allah sent His peace of assurance down upon His Messenger and upon the believers, and punished those who disbelieved. Such is the reward of Disbelievers."
>
> (Q. 9.25–26).

After distributing the spoils and captives of the Battle of Taif at Jirrana, the Apostle put on the "Ihram" for performing 'Umra' for this was the place from where the people going for pilgrimage to Mecca from Taif changed into "Ihram". Having completed the lesser pilgrimage the Apostle returned to Medina.

The Apostle came back to Madina in Dhi Q'ada, 8 A.H. While the forces were returning from Taif, the Apostle of Allah asked the men to recite–

"We are those who revert and repent and worship and glorify our Lord."

Some of the people then asked the Holy Prophet (PBUH) to call down evil on Thaqif.

The Apostle raised his hands to entreat:

"O Allah! Guide Thaqif on the right path and bring them here."

Urwa bin Mas'ud al Thaqafi met the Apostle while he was on his way back to Madina. He became a Muslim and returned to his people for inviting them to Islam. He was very popular and enjoyed the esteem of his clansmen but when he broke the news that he had accepted Islam, the people turned against him. They shot arrows at him from all directions; one hit him and he died.

The Thaqif held out for a few months after killing Urwa but after taking counsel among them they reached the conclusion that it would be beyond their power to fight all those tribes which had already taken the oath of allegiance at the hands of the Apostle. Ultimately, they decided to send a deputation to the Apostle.

When the deputation of Thaqif came to Madina, a tent was pitched for them in the Prophets's Mosque. They requested the Apostle not to destroy their chief deity, the idol of al–Laat, for three years. The Apostle refused; then they continued to reduce the period by one year, but the Apostle remained firm in refusing their request until they finally asked for a period of one month after they had returned to their homes. The Apostle again rejected their request and ordered Abu Sufyan and Mughira bin Sh'uba al–Thaqafi to destroy al–Laat. Thereafter, the Thaqif asked the Prophet (PBUH) that they might be excused from offering prayers. To this the Apostle replied:

"Nothing remains of a religion which has no prayer."

> Abu Sufyan and Mughira bin Sh'uba accompanied the deputation of Thaqif when they returned to Taif. Mughira smote al–Laat with a pickaxe and broke it into pieces. Thereupon, the people of Taif accepted Islam; not one of them remained attached to paganism.
>
> (Zaad–al–Ma'ad vol.1, pp. 458–59).

Spread of Islam among the tribes further aggravated the resentment of the Quraish. They came together and decided to draw up a decree ostracising Bani Hashim and Bani Abdul Muttalib.

1. It was decided that nobody should marry the women of these two clans nor give their women to them in marriage;
2. Neither anybody should buy from them nor sell to them.

Having solemnly agreed to these points, the agreement was put into writing and parchment was hung in the K'aba in order to give it a religious sanction thereby making it mandatory for all.

Bani Hashim and Bani Abdul Muttalib joined Abu Talib after the boycott was enforced and withdrew to a narrow glen or 'wadi' known as Sh'eb Abi Talib. It was the seventh year of the Prophet's mission.

Weeks and months passed, and the people of Hashim lived in misery and hunger. The ban was so rigorously imposed that the Prophet's clan was reduced to eating leaves of acacia and the cries of hungry children echoed all over the valley. The caravans passed peacefully through the streets of Makkah but the Quraish told the merchants not to buy or sell anything to the forsaken clans with the result that they pegged the prices so high that it was well nigh impossible for the beleaguered people to purchase even the bare necessities.

The decree of proscription lasted for three years — for three years Bani Hashim and Bani Abdul Muttalib lived in exile and endured the hardships of blockade.

But all the people of the Quraish were not utterly deprived. Those among them who were well–natured and kind–hearted occasionally supplied food secretly to the exiles. However, the Apostle never ceased preaching the message he had brought to his own people, and, even to others, whenever he got the opportunity. Bani Hashim on their part, endured every trouble with exemplary patience and fortitude.

The pitiable condition of the exiles gave rise to feelings of indignation against the ban among the gracious and genial sons of the desert. Hisham bin 'Amr bin Rabi'a took the initiative to end the boycott. He was amiable and kind–hearted as well as highly esteemed by the Quraish. He contacted some other considerate and well–disposed persons and put them to shame for allowing the tyranny to linger on.

At last, Hisham supported by four other persons agreed to stand together till the decree of boycott was cancelled. On the morrow, when the Quraish had assembled in the sanctuary, Zuhayr whose mother 'Atika was daughter of Abdul Muttalib, cried out to the people:

"O ye people of Makkah, shall we eat and drink while Bani Hashim should die of hunger, unable even to buy or sell? By Allah I will not take rest until this cruel and unjust decree is torn to pieces."

Abu Talib was also sitting in the corner of Ka'aba. He disclosed that Muhammad (PBUH) had already told him that Allah has given white ants power over the document. He also declared that had not come true he would give up support to Muhammad (PBUH). This disclosure made the matter very interesting and sensational. All those assembled there waited to know the truth.

When, inspite of intervention from Abu Jahal, Mut'im bin Adiy went up to tear the document into pieces, he found that with the exception of the words "In Thy name, O Allah" the rest of the document had already been eaten up by white ants.

The blighted document was, however, taken out and thrown away and thus ended the boycott and what was written on it. (Ibn Hisham vol.1, pp.350–51).

The Dilemma

The number of the Prophet's followers increased day by day threatening to turn the tide against Quraish; they felt the situation highly embarrassing but were unable to do anything to stem the tide of Islam.

Utba bin Rabi'a the old and wise patrician of the Quraish realised that he must find a way to patch up the differences with the Apostle. He consulted the Quraish to make some concessions to the Apostle so that he might give up his mission. The Quraish thought it to be workable proposition and allowed him to negotiate with the Prophet on their behalf.

'Utba went to the Apostle and sat by his side. Then he said:

"O my nephew, you know the worthy position you enjoy among us. But you have created a rift in your people by ridiculing them, insulting their gods as well as their religion, declaring their forefathers as heathens and denying their customs. Now, listen to me, I will make some suggestions, happily you may find one of these acceptable."

The Holy Prophet (PBUH) replied,

"O Abul Walid, go on, I am listening."

'Utba continued:

"My nephew, if you want to have wealth by what you preach, we will collect enough of it that you will be the richest of us; if you desire honour, we will make you our chief and leave every decision to your choice; if you aspire for kingship, we will recognize you as our monarch; and if you are possessed of a ghost or a jinn of which you have no remedy, we will find a skilful physician for you and spend our wealth lavishly until your health is completely restored."

The Apostle (PBUH) listened patiently. When 'Utba had finished, he asked,

"Is it all that you have to say?"

"Yes", replied 'Utba.

"Now listen to me", said the Prophet (PBUH):

"In the name of Allah, the Compassionate, the Merciful...

and he continued to recite the Sura Fussilat,

ending the recitation at prostration."

When 'Utba heard the revelation, he listened with rapt attention, putting his hands behind him and leaning on them. The recitation ended, the Prophet (PBUH) prostrated and then said to Utba:

"Abul Walid, you have heard what you have heard, now it is for you to decide."

As the Quraish saw Utba returning, they said:

"Honest to God, he comes with an altered expression of his face."

And when he came near they asked him what had happened.

"I have heard a discourse the like of which I had never heard before. I'll swear to God, O Quraish, that it is neither poetry, nor spells, nor witchcraft. Take my advice and let this man alone."

The Quraish reviled 'Utba, and said:

"You have been bewitched by his tongue."

> "This is my opinion," replied Utba, "Now you may do whatever you think fit."
>
> (Ibn Hisham, vol.I, pp. 293–94).

The Quraish offered a reward of one hundred camels to anyone who brought back the Apostle, dead or alive, while he was on his way to Madina. On the other hand, the Apostle spent three nights in the cave and then guided by Amir bin Fuhayrah went along the road by the sea coast.

Suraqa bin Malik bin Ju'shum heard of the price set by the Quraish on the head of the Apostle (PBUH) and hurried after him. The reward of a hundred camels was too much for him; he got up on his mare and went after the fugitives tracking their footsteps. He let his mare go in a canter until he nearly overtook the fugitives. But his mare stumbled abruptly, and he was thrown off. He rose, got hold of his quiver, and remounted the mare, and let her go ahead. His mare again stumbled and he was again thrown off, but he continued the chase until he could see the three men going ahead. Suddenly, his mare stumbled for the third time, its fore–legs sinking up to the knees in the ground, and he was thrown off again. He also saw dust rising from the ground like a sandstorm.

Suraqa was now convinced that the Apostle was protected against him and he would not in any case triumph over him. He called but saying that he was Suraqa bin Ju'shum and that no harm would come to them from him. The Apostle asked Abu Bakr:

"Ask him what he wants from us?"

Suraqa answered:

"Write for me a warrant of security."

Thereupon, the Holy Prophet (PBUH) ordered Amir bin Fuhayrah to write the warrant which he wrote on a piece of tanned leather or bone. Suraqa preserved the writing for long as a memorial.

While migrating to Madina, Hazrat Abu Bakr and the Holy Prophet (PBUH) passed by the tent of Umm M'abad, a woman of Khuza'a, who had a milch ewe but its udder had dried up owing to draught.

Allah's Messenger wiped its udder with his hand and mentioning the name of Almighty Allah, he prayed that Umm M'abad might have a blessing in her ewe. It then gave a flow of milk. He first gave Umm M'abad and others a drink until all of them were fully satisfied; he drank himself last of all.

He milked it a second time, and when the vessel was full he left it with her.

When Abu M'abad came back and his wife told him about the prodigious happening and the angelic stranger, he replied:

"By Allah, he appears to be the same man of the Quraish whom they are prowling after."

After the death of Abdul Muttalib, Abu Talib took the Apostle (PBUH) under his care for he and Abdullah, the Apostle's father, were brothers by the same mother. Abdul Muttalib had also been insisting upon Abu Talib to take care of the Apostle. Accordingly,

Abu Talib took the Apostle under his protection and treated him with more care and affection than his own sons, Ali, Ja'far and Aqil (R.A.A.).

Once, when the Apostle was nine years old, Abu Talib planned to go in a merchant caravan to Syria. The Apostle approched his uncle, and nestling close to him, insisted on accompanying him in the journey. Abu Talib felt moved and agreed to take him to Syria.

When the caravan reached Busra in Syria, it broke the journey for a short stay, where lived a monk, Buhaira by name, in his cell. He came out, against his practice, to welcome the merchants and made a great feast for them. The caravan found favour with Buhaira, so they relate, because of something he had seen while in his cell. When Buhaira saw the Apostle of Allah, he satisfied himself of the signs of apostleship he had known, and advised Abu Talib:

"Return to your home with this youth, and guard him from the Jews; for great dignity awaits your nephew."

Abu Talib took the Apostle (PBUH) off quickly to Makkah as advised by Buhaira.

In accordance with the Arabian custom, in order to learn the pure Arabic dilect (and to enjoy the pleasant atmosphere of the countryside at the same time) the baby (Muhammad PBUH) was given in the custody of the nurse Halimah, who visited Makkah during those days in search of a rich baby to bring up but was not successful; hence was obliged to accept orphan Muhammad (PBUH) as it was heavenly destined for her.

In all, baby Muhammad (PBUH) spent six years with her among the Banu Sa'd, during that time he developed the purest dialect of Arabic about which he spoke later:

"Verily, I am the most eloquent Arab amongst you;

My descendant is from the Quraish and I speak the tongue of Banu Sa'd."

Once when Muhammad (PBUH) was playing with children, two angels in snow–white dress came down from the heaven and opened his holy chest. They took out some black pieces of flesh from it. Then they washed the heart and inner side of the chest from the "snow water" they brought with them in a gold dish from the Heaven.

It is also narrated that they also fixed the "Seal" of the Prophets at the same time in between the two shoulders on the back and then went back.

Seeing all this, his foster–brother and other boys with whom he was playing were frightened and ran to Lady Halimah, but when she reached there the angels had left.

However, Muhammad (PBUH) told her all the story and said that they filled a kind of divine light but he was not hurt at all.

In those days, reading and writing was not in vogue in Arabia and the business-minded Quraish regarded it a task for menials, therefore, he was not educated. Afterwards this unlettered orphan became the repository of the highest wisdom. Though himself untaught by a worldly teacher, he became the teacher of mankind which was one of his Great Miracles.

The Holy Quran speaks about it:

"Those who follow the Apostle, the unlettered Prophet, whom they find mentioned in Torah (Old Testament). He commands them what is just and good, and forbids them what is evil; he allows them as lawful what is good (and pure) and prohibits them from what is bad (and impure). He releases them from their heavy burdens and from the yokes that are upon them. So it is those who believe in him, honour him, help him, and follow the Light which is sent down with him — it is they who will prosper."

> "Say, O men! I am sent unto you all, as the Apostle of Allah, to whom belongs the dominion of the heavens and the earth, there is no god but He. It is He that gives both life and death. So believe in Him and His Apostle, the unlettered Prophet, who believes in Allah and His words; follow him that you may be guided."
>
> (Q.7:157–58).

After the death of Abu Talib, the oppositon of Makkah grew greater day by day and the enemies of Islam began to redouble their persecution. The Holy Prophet (PBUH) was then forced to turn his attention towards the next biggest city of Arabia:Taif.

He travelled to Taif and invited its inhabitants towards Islam. But all the chieftains of the clan refused even to listen to the Holy Prophet (PBUH) and treated him most contemptuously and rudely. When he was leaving the town they told a gang of vegabounds to pelt him with stones. He was so much pelted that his whole body was besmeared with blood and his shoes were clogged to his feet.

The Holy Prophet (PBUH) left the town in this woeful plight while praying to Allah:

"O Allah! To Thee I complain of the feebleness of my strength, of my lack of resourcefulness and my insignificance in the eyes of people. O 'Most Merciful of all, capable of showing mercy! Thou art the Lord of the weak and Thou art my own Lord. To whom art Thou entrust me, to an unsympathetic foe who would sullenly frown at me, or to an alien to whom Thou hast given control over my affair. Not in the least do I care for anything except that I may have Thy protection for myself. In the light of Thy face do I seek shelter — the light of which illumines the Heaven and dispels all sorts of darkness, and which controls all affairs in this world as well as in the Hereafter. May it never be that I should incur Thy wrath, or that Thou should be displeasure with me. I must remove the cause of Thy displeasure till Thou art pleased. There is no strength nor power but through Thee."

Bleeding and exhausted, the Holy Prophet (PBUH) marched onward to Makkah. His shoes were besmeared with blood. On his return to Makkah during the night, he offered Salaat at Nakhla, a place in suburbs of Makkah.

While he was offering Salaat, a group of Jinns passed by him. They were seven in number. The Jinns listened to the Holy Quran which was being recited by the Holy Prophet (PBUH). After he completed his Salaat, they requested him to allow them to enter the folds of Islam. The Holy Quran points out towards this as under:

> "Say (O Muhammad!):It is revealed to me that a company of the Jinns gave ear, and they said:Lo! it is a marvellous Quran which guides to righteousness, so we believed in it and we shall not join (in worship) any (gods) with our Lord." (Q.72:1–2).

God's Support

In the Battle of Badr, the Quraish reached the battlefield earlier and occupied the points of advantage. The Muslims could not get any well or spring. Moreover, the sandy soil was causing the feet of camels to sink. Then it was suggested by Hubaab bin Mundhir (R.A.A.) to take possession of a nearly big spring. The suggestion was accepted by the Holy Prophet (PBUH) and he asked the Muslims to take over the spring. By the grace of Allah, it rained heavily and small reservoirs were improvised for storing water.

The Holy Quran speaks about this as follows:

> "And He sent down water from sky that thereby He might purify you." (Q. 8:2).

The Holy Prophet (PBUH) prayed all the night at Badr, weeping and repeating the following words:

> "O Allah, should You suffer this small band of Believers to perish this day, no one will be left on earth to worship Thee." (Ibn Hisham Book 1 Vols. 1+ 2).

> Allah answered the prayer and gave glad tidings of victory through the following revelation: (Bukhari).

> "Soon shall the enemy be routed and will then turn and flee...." (Q. 54:45).

Great Success

The victory at the Badr was a clear help of Almighty Allah. Indeed, it was a glorious spiritual victory of the Truth ('Haq') over the Falsehood ('Batil')—with marvellous Divine Help. The Holy Quran speaks about this as under:

> "Indeed there was a sign for you in the two Hosts which met together in encounter; one party fights in the Way of Allah, and the other unbelieving and Allah strengthens with His aid whom He pleases; most surely there is a lesson in this for those who have eyes to see."(Q. 3:12).

The Holy Quran again says:

> "Allah had helped you at Badr, when you were contemptible little force; then fear Allah in order to show your gratitude." When you did say to the believers:Does it

> not suffice you that your Lord should help you with three thousand angels sent down." (Q. 3:123–24).

According to the historians, the angels referred to in the above verse (3:124) came down with three arch angels viz. Jibrail, Micka'il and Isra'fil, each of them was accompanied by 1,000 angels.

Help from the Skies

Coming down of the angelic warriors is attested by a peasant (who had not accepted Islam by then) who was attending sheep on an adjacent hill. He says:

"I was with a companion, my cousin, upon the fold of mountain watching the battle and waiting to join with the conquerors and share the spoil. Suddenly, we beheld a great cloud sailing towards us, and within it were the neighing of steeds and braying of trumpets. As it approached, squadrons of angels sallied forth, and we heard the terrific voice of archangel as he urged his more Haizum, "Speed! Speed! Oh Haizum!" Due to that awful sound, the heart of my companion burst with terror, and he died on the spot, and I had well nigh shared his fate."

This miraculous aid is repeatedly mentioned in the Holy Quran as also quoted above.

When the Battle of Badr began, the Holy Prophet (PBUH) prayed, and threw a handful of dust (or sand) at enemy, symbolical of their rushing blindly to their fate. Every act in the battle is ascribed to Allah, as it was in His cause, and it was not undertaken except by His Command. The Holy Quran points out towards it as under:

> "It was not you who slew them, it was Allah:When you threw (a handful of dust), it was not your act, but

> Allah's:In order that He might test the Believers by a gracious trial from Himself:for Allah is He who hears and knows (all things)." (Q. 8:17)

> Ukkashah bin Mihsan, a companion, was fighting in the battle. During the fight his sword broke down. The Holy Prophet (PBUH) gave him a piece of rod which turned into a sword, as soon as he took it from Prophet's hand. He fought with that sword. He named that sword as "Al–Awn" which remained with him in all the following battles. (Ibn Hisham Book 1, vol.1+ 2 p.637)

Once Addi bin Haatim (R.A.A.) was sitting with the Holy Prophet (PBUH) that two persons came along. One complained of starvation and the other of highway robberies;

"The Holy Prophet (PBUH) turned towards Addi and said:

"If he (Addi) lived till then, he would see that a veiled (purdahnasheen) woman would travel on camel back from Hira and reach the K'aba unmolested fearing none but Allah that the treasures of Iran will be conquered and that a person may walk around with fistfuls of gold and silver for distribution among the poor but none would be interested!"

Addi (R.A.A.) narrated that he wondered greatly at the predictions, but he lived to see the first two predictions fulfilled and he was one of those who plundered the treasures of Iran.

And the third prediction too, according to reliable tradition came true during the time of Bani Umayyah.

Before the Battle of Badr began, the Holy Prophet (PBUH) toured the battleground and pointed out to his companions the places where each of the Quraish chiefs was to fall.

After the battle, the Companions found to their wonder that each and every prediction came true.

It is considerable that before the battle there was no hope for such a poorly armed army of three hundred Muslims to win the battle.

During his last illness, when the Holy Prophet (PBUH) found his beloved daughter Hazrat Fatimah (R.A.A.), he called her near and whispered something that made her weap; but when he again whispered something she began to smile.

When Hazrat Aisha (R.A.A.) asked Hazrat Fatimah (R.A.A.) as to what the Apostle whispered in her ears, she declined to disclose the matter. But after the demise of the Holy Prophet (PBUH) when Hazrat Aisha (R.A.A.) insisted again, Hazrat Fatimah (R.A.A.) revealed that when the Apostle predicted his death she started weeping; but when she was told by the Messenger of Allah that she (Fatimah) will be the first from his family to join him, she smiled.

Both these predictions of the Holy Prophet (PBUH) were found to be correct.

During the last Hajj, the Holy Prophet (PBUH) told the gathering that he may, perhaps, not be seen there next year.

The year of his death, the Holy Prophet (PBUH) told Sa'ad bin Mua'dh (R.A.A.), who was proceeding on to Yemen, that he might not see him on his return.

Again, a few days before his demise, he said that Almighty Allah had given a choice between the world and the life of the Hereafter; and that he had chosen the later.

Victories All Over

The Holy Prophet (PBUH) had predicted conquests of Syria, Yemen and Iran while digging the trench at the Battle of Trenches. These predictions came true later.

> Syria was conquered by Hazrat Khalid bin Walid (R.A.A.) during the Caliphate of Hazrat Umar ibn Khattab (R.A.A.).
>
> Yemen was conquered in 8 A.H. during the Caliphate of Hazrat Umar bin Khattab (R.A.A.).
>
> Iran was conquered by Hazrat Sa'ad bin Abi Waqqas (R.A.A.) during the Caliphate of Hazrat Umar ibn Khattab (R.A.A.).

The Holy Prophet (PBUH) had predicted a high place of honour for Hazrat Sa'ad bin Abi Waqqas (R.A.A.) and said that many will gain by his acts and many others lose.

This was an indication of his conquest of Iran when the Muslims gained and the Magis lost.

The Holy Prophet (PBUH) had predicted that Egypt would soon be conquered by the Muslims. He had further said that Egyptians should be treated kindly as they were related to Arabs (Hazrat Ibrahim's wife and mother of Hazrat Ismail was from Egypt).

The Holy Prophet (PBUH) had predicted the fall of Bait–ul–Maqdis to Muslims. He had also predicted that it would fall after his death.

> This prediction came true during the Caliphate of Hazrat Umar ibn Khattab (R.A.A.).

One day, the Holy Prophet (PBUH) was in deep sleep. All of a sudden, he woke up smiling and said:

"I saw some of my Ummah sitting on a royal throne and sailing the Mediterranean for Jehad."

This dream came true during the time of Amir Mu'wiyya (R.A.A.) when the Muslims sat on the royal throne for the first time in Damascus; and Prince Yazeed sailed to Constantinople.

The Holy Prophet (PBUH) had predicted that 'apostasy' will raise head after his final departure and a number of false prophets will rise in various parts of Arabia and be joined by some Muslims.

The prediction proved correct during the time of Caliph Hazrat Abu Bakr Siddique (R.A.A.).

Umme Waraqa (R.A.A.) had requested permission to join 'Jihad' at the time of Badr. But the Holy Prophet (PBUH) had asked her to stay at home to die as a 'Shaheed' (martyr).

The prediction came true at the time of Caliph Hazrat Umar Ibn Khattab (R.A.A.), when a slave man and a slave girl strangled her to death. And this tragedy occurred at her home and thus she got the status of 'Shaheed' as predicted by the Apostle.

Once the Holy Prophet (PBUH) pointed his finger towards the east and predicted that evil shall come to the Muslims from this direction (Iraq falling in the east).

The prediction came true in more than one way.

The murderer of Caliph Hazrat Umar ibn Khattab (R.A.A.) was an 'Ajami'.

The evil during the third Caliph Hazrat Uthman bin Affan (R.A.A.) rose from Iraq and spread up to Egypt.

Both the Battle of Jamal and Battle of Siffin fought between fourth Caliph Hazrat Ali (R.A.A.) and Amir Mu'awiyyah (R.A.A.) took place in Iraq.

Khwarij–e–Islam rose from Iraq.

The Jabriah and Qadriah sects which shattered the unity and purity of Muslim beliefs were born there.

Karbala falls in Iraq. The evil of Mukhtar took place there.

Hajjaj bin Yusuf perpetrated his cruelties on the same soil. The depredations of the Mongols and the Turks took place there.

Once the Holy Prophet (PBUH) had predicted before his wives that one of them shall have barking dogs at her at Howaab.

When Hazrat Aisha (R.A.A.) joined the Battle of Jamal in Basra (Iraq) and reached the period of Howaab, the dogs started barking at her. Thus, the prediction of the Apostle proved to be correct.

Times to Come

Once the Holy Prophet (PBUH) took his maternal grandson Hazrat Hasan (R.A.A.) with him on to the pulpit of the Prophet's Mosque and told the congregation:

"One day, Hasan will bring about compromise between two groups.

Six months after the "Shahadat" (martyrdom) of the fourth Caliph of Islam Hazrat Ali (R.A.A.). Hasan effected a compromise between the camp followers of Hazrat Ali (R.A.A.) and Amir Muawiyyah (R.A.A.).

Once the Holy Prophet (PBUH) had predicted that the upstart Quraish will bring about untold miseries to Islam.

This prediction also came true because martyrdom of the third Caliph of Islam, Hazrat Uthman Ghani (R.A.A.), was the result of their ambition; so also the Battle of Jamal between Hazrat Ali (R.A.A.) and Amir Muawiyyah (R.A.A.) was fought because of their high ambitions once again. History bears witness to this fact. And thus the prediction made by the Apostle proved truthful.

Once the Holy Prophet (PBUH) told his Companion Hazrat Abu Hurairah (R.A.A.) that spiritual and moral decline of the Muslims would start by 60 A.H.

Hazrat Abu Hurairah (R.A.A.) says:

"I used to wish publicly that I might not live to see 60 A.H."

He died in 59 A.H. Moreover, the prediction of the Apostle came true with the coming of Yazeed on the throne.

The Holy Prophet (PBUH) had once said that there would be born a 'lier' and a "killer" in the Thaqeef tribe.

When Hajjaj Thaqafee hanged Hazrat Abdullah bin Zubair (R.A.A.), he sent for his (Abdullah bin Zubair's) mother, Hazrat Asmaa (R.A.A.). But she refused the summons.

At last Hajjaj himself called on Hazrat Asmaa (R.A.A.). She said to him:

"Mukhttar Thaqafee was known as a "liar" and that, according to the prophecy of the Prophet (PBUH), she thought that Hajjaj was the "killer."

On hearing this, Hajjaj went away without saying a word.

Once the Holy Prophet (PBUH) had declared publicly that there were four periods—his own time, one after that, then after that and followed by another—when people would give evidence at their own initiative without being called:who would be guilty of misappropriations; who would not be trustworthy; who would not keep their promises.

The four periods mentioned by the Holy Prophet (PBUH) were:The period of the Apostle himself; that of his Companions (Sahaba); that of the Tabi'yeen; and the one of the Taba–tabiyeen.

These four periods were productive of the moral, and religious excellence of the Muslims. They produced pious persons, Imams and great spiritual leaders one after another. In these periods, Islam was at its peak.

Thereafter, Islam went on declining day by day. Innovations were introduced, oppression started, evil acts prevailed, learned persons became victims of false desires. Philosophies of Greece, India and Persia exerted influences among the Muslims bringing about weaknesses in the beliefs, creeds and deeds of the Muslims as a whole, with the result Islam saw disorder and general disorganisation.

Once the Holy Prophet (PBUH) had predicted that a time would come when even women would take part in business and trade with men that business would be a widely-practised profession.

The Holy Prophet (PBUH) had once predicted that a time would come when the nations of the world would unite against the Muslims, although they would be large in number. He added that they would fall victim because of their involvement with the world, fear of death. Fears of the Muslims will leave the hearts of the unbelievers. We now see the prediction of the Apostle come true.

Prophet's Successors

Once Ibn Haban said to Safina, the freed man of the Holy Prophet (PBUH) that when the Apostle started construction of the Mosque in Madina, he laid the foundation stone himself and then asked Abu Bakr (R.A.A.) to put his stone. Thereafter, Umar and Usman (R.A.A.) were asked to do the same in succession.

The above–mentioned tradition was reported by Hakam and Baihaqui. And the Caliphs of the Faithfuls Abu Bakr, Umar and Uthman took charge in the same order.

Hakam Reports Hayat Anas (R.A.A.) (noted servant of the Apostle) to have said:

"Once he was sent by Bani al–Mustaliq to the Holy Prophet (PBUH) to inquire of him on their behalf that to whom should they take their presents to after him; so he came to the Apostle and asked him the question.

"To Abu Bakr," the Holy Prophet (PBUH) replied. When he informed them to what the Apostle had said, they again sent him to ask the Apostle as to what should they do in case anything ill befalls Abu Bakr (R.A.A.)?

"To Umar," the Apostle replied.

They again sent him to the Holy Prophet (PBUH) to ask that if something serious by dangerous befell Umar (R.A.A.), then whom should they go with their presents to?

"To Osman?" the Holy Prophet (PBUH) replied.

When they sent him again to the Holy Prophet (PBUH) to ask what should they do in case a peril befalls to Osman?

"If peril befalls Osman, then there will be ruin and destruction, and so forth," the Apostle said in reply.

Once Hazrat Abu Hurairah (R.A.A.) saw the following in dream:

"I was on a well and there was a bucket on it also. I drew as much water out of the well as it pleased Almighty Allah. Thereafter, Abu Bakr took the bucket and with ease drew one or two bucketful of water. The bucket then became a large one and it was taken by Omar ibn Khattab (R.A.A.). I never saw such a strong person drawing out water. Now the people were fully satisfied with water while there were multitudes of them around the well.

Abu Dawud and Hakam report from Jabbar bin Abdullah that once the Holy Prophet (PBUH) said:

"A righteous person saw in a dream that Abu Bakr was suspended with the Apostle and Omar with Abu Bakr and Osman with Umar (R.A.A.)."

Jabir goes on to say that when he and others left the Holy Prophet (PBUH), they said among themselves:

"The righteous person who dreamt was the Prophet himself and the suspension of one with the other signified that they should be inheritors of the trust for which Allah had sent the Apostle, and so forth."

Hakam cites Safina as saying:

"It was a habit of the Prophet (PBUH) every day after the morning prayers to ask his companions if any one of them had a dream. Once a certain person told him that he had dreamt as if a balance descended from above and that the Apostle was put in one pan of it and Abu Bakr in the other, that the Apostle's pan was heavier; then Umar was put against Abu Bakr in the other pan, Abu Bakr's pan proved heavier; and then was put Osman against Umar and Umar's pan counter poised. The balance was then drawn up again. On hearing this the complexion of the Apostle's countenance was changed and he said:"The Caliphate would last for thirty years only and the monarchy would prevail."

Abu Dawud cites from Samura bin Jundab (R.A.A.) that a man said to the Holy Prophet (PBUH):

"O Prophet of Allah, I saw in a dream that something like a bucket was hung from the heaven, and then came Abu Bakr (R.A.A.) and held the bucket by its strings and drank a little water; then Umar came and caught the bucket by its ropes and drank to his fill and then came Osman and did the same and was amply satisfied. Thereafter, Ali did the same, but the strings of the bucket were to loose and a little water fell upon Ali (R.A.A.)."

Hazrat Anas bin Malik reports:

"Once the Holy Prophet (P.B.U.H..) ascended the hill Uhad accompanied by Abu Bakr, Umar and Osman (R.A.A.). The hill began to shake and shook them also. The Apostle stamped it and asked it to be at rest and said to it that there were on it one Prophet, one 'Siddeeq' (truthful) and two 'Shaheeds' (martyrs). By the Prophet he meant himself; by the Siddiq, Abu Bakr; and by the two martyrs, Umar and Osman (R.A.A.)."
(Bukhari).

Hazrat Abu Musa Ash'ari (R.A.A.) reports:

"Once I was with the Holy Prophet (PBUH) in one of the gardens of Madina. In the meantime, a certain person came and wished the gate opened:The Apostle directed me to open the gate and gave the comer the good news of the Paradise. I opened the gate and saw Abu Bakr, whom I gave the glad tidings as ordered by the Apostle. He thanked and praised Allah.

Abu Huraira (R.A.A.) reports:

"Once the Holy Prophet (PBUH) was on Mount Haray and there were with him Abu Bakr, Osman, Ali, Talha and Zubair. The rock shook and the Apostle commanded it to be at rest for there were on it none else but the Prophet, the Siddeeq, and the martyrs." (Muslim). The prediction came true later on.

Imam Ahmed, Tirmizi, Ibn Majah and Hakam report from Hazrat Aisha (R.A.A.) that once the Holy Prophet (PBUH) told Osman (R.A.A.).

"O Osman! certainly Allah will put on you a chemise, which you, though the antagonisms might wish you to do so, should not put off till you meet me."

In this tradition, the chemise typifies the Caliphate and Osman is warned that Allah would give Caliphate to him and that if the unbelievers should desire a portion of the Caliphate he should not mind them and should not severe from the Caliphate till death; and so it came to pass that Osman became the Caliph and the unbelievers demanded a portion of the Caliphate, but he did not, according to the direction of the Holy Prophet (PBUH), accept their proposals, but told them he was content with the agreement which the Apostle made him to make.

Tirmizi cites from Abdullah ibn Omar (R.A.A.):

"Once the Holy Prophet (PBUH) made mention of a quarrel and pointing to Osman (R.A.A.) said that he would be innocently killed in it."

And so it came to pass that Osman (R.A.A.) was faultlessly slain in an uproar of the Egyptians and the Iraqis.

Baihaqi reports:

One day, the Holy Prophet (PBUH) saw Ali and Zubair laughing together and he asked Ali if he loved Zubair. Ali replied how could he not love Zubair who was his aunt's son and his co-religionist. The Apostle then asked Zubair if he loved Ali, he replied how could he do otherwise he being his uncle's son and his co-religionist. Thereupon, the Holy Prophet (PBUH) told Zubair that it would soon happen that he would wage war with Ali and that he would be the aggressor."

The prediction came true at the Battle of Jamal when Ali and Zubair came face to face. Hazrat Ali (R.A.A.) made him swear and asked him if he had not heard the Apostle say that he would wage war against him and that he would prove cruel. Zubair said:

"Certainly I had heard but I had forgotten."

Saying this Zubair retreated from the battlefield.

Imam Ahmed reports from Ali (R.A.A.):

"Once the Holy Prophet (PBUH) told him that your case would be like Jesus, whom the Jews took as their enemy so far that they blamed his mother and the Christians took as a friend so far they exalted him to a position which did not belong to him.

So in your case, there would be exaggerations too; some people would become enemical to you and would depreciate you so much as to talk ill of you and accuse you falsely, and some people would befriend you and extol you so far that you would not merit it, they would call you God."

And so it was, that there crept in discrepancies about Hazrat Ali. The Nawasib and Khwarij talk ill of him and accuse him of ill–treatment with Hazrat Aisha and accessary to the murder of Hazrat Osman, and the Rafizi congregations call him God.

Imam Ahmed reports:

"Once the Holy Prophet (PBUH) asked Umar ibn Khattab (R.A.A.) if he knew who of the ancient religious sects was the most wretched and who is the most wretched of our sect. Umar (R.A.A.) said that the most wretched of the former sects was the ruddy man of Samaod tribe, i.e. Qudar bin Salif who cut the tendons of the leg of Naqatullah, and the most wretched of our sect is the man who would give sword–cut on your head so that your beard would be drenched with blood and the sword should make a martyr." In this tradition the Holy Prophet (PBUH) foretells that the executioner of Ali (R.A.A.) shall inflict a sword wound on his head and that the blood shall redden his beard and that he shall thereby be martyred, and so it came to pass that Abdul Rahman bin Maljam Kharji smote his forehead with a sword in the morning and blood flowed down his beard and he was therefrom made a martyr.

Through the conversation of the Prophet (PBUH), Ali (R.A.A.) was made so fully acquainted with the circumstances of his martyrdom that in the night preceding the morning when Ibn Maljam would attack him, Ali (R.A.A.) came out several times and gazed upon the sky and said:By Allah, he never told a lie, nor a lie was ever told to him, that it was the same night of which a promise was given him, and at dawn the geese began to crackle before him, the people drove them away. But he told them to let them alone for they lamented. The "muazzin" then came and told him of prayer. He came out to lead the prayer. Ibn Maljam was sleeping in the mosque. Hazrat Ali (R.A.A.) got him awakened and himself engaged in prayer. Ibn Maljam got up and as Hazrat Ali (R.A.A.) lay in prostration, he struck forcefully at his head so that a very deep injury was inflicted and blood flowed down his beard turning it red. Thus, the prediction of the Holy Prophet (PBUH) about Ali came true.

Imam Ahmed and Baihaqi report from Huzaifa:

"Once the Holy Prophet (PBUH) said that there should be a prophetic age among you as long as Allah would wish, and then He would remove it. Thereafter, Caliphatic age would start for a time as Allah would wish; and this should also be removed by Allah when He would like, then it should be supplanted by an iron monarchy which should last and be removed as Allah would be pleased; and after monarchy the caliphate should prevail after the prophetic fashion, and then the Prophet (PBUH) became silent."

Habib the transcriber of this tradition reports that when Umar bin Abdul Azeez became the Caliph of Islam, he sent him a copy of this tradition writing that on the expiration of the cruel and biting monarchy he would be the chosen Caliph, on hearing this, he praised Almighty Allah.

Thus, the prophecy of the Holy Prophet (PBUH) came true. After the demise of the Prophet (PBUH) the prophetic age came to an end; then began the era of four Caliphs one after another. It was followed by an oppressive and iron monarchy. Thereafter, prophetic type of Caliphate was restored once again when Umar bin Abdul Azeez became the Caliph.

Thoban reports the following:

"Once the Holy Prophet (PBUH) said that Almighty Allah gathered the whole land and showed its eastern and western ends to him. Thereafter, he added:as far as he saw the sovereignty of his followers would cover these areas."

And accordingly, it came to pass that in a very short period, that is during the Caliphate age the extent of the kingdom of the followers of the Prophet had so widened and enlarged that no other king on the face of the earth had so much territory. And till the days of Osman (R.A.A.) the breadth of the Muslim empire stretched from Constantinople to Aden, and the length from Indus to Balkh. (Muslim).

In Sahihin there is a tradition as reported by Sa'ad bin Abi Waqqas (R.A.A.):

"I was sick in Makkah on the occasion of Hajjat–ul–Wida, and the Holy Prophet (PBUH) went to see him. I thought that I would die of that malady. I, therefore, prayed the Apostle that my heir would be my only daughter and I would, therefore, bequeath two–thirds of my having towards charity or alms. But the Apostle declined the proposal. I then said about 'half' but received the same answer; whereupon I said 'one–third' and the Apostle asserted.

Thereafter, the Holy Prophet (PBUH) predicted that he hoped. I would live so long that many others should derive great benefit through me and many more suffered injuries."

In this prophecy, the Holy Prophet (PBUH) foretold that Sa'ad bin Abi Waqqas should be cured of his illness and he could live so long that many a man should have good and bad at his hands. And so it happened that after the recovery from illness, he lived more than fifty years and the Muslims were benefited plentiful by him and the infidel Magies were subjected to great losses.

In the Caliphate of Hazrat Umar ibn Khattab (R.A.A.) Persia was vanquished by him and that great battle of Qadsia was won by him. In this battle 32,000 Muslims and a lac and a half of Magies were engaged, Rustam bin Farakhzad was made the Magain Commander by Yazdgird, the king of Persia. Rustam was slain and Median, the ancient capital of the Iranian kings came to Muslim possession, and immense treasures of the Iranian Emperors were transferred to the Muslim.

The infidel Magies were inflicted great losses by Sa'ad bin Abi Waq'qas (R.A.A.) because thousands of them were slain and hundreds made slaves and their country and treasures were snatched from them. Thus, the prophecy of the Holy Prophet (PBUH) proved to be correct.

Bukhari reports from Auf bin Malik (R.A.A.):

"I came to the Holy Prophet (PBUH) during the Battle of Tabuk, when he was in a tent of leather. He told me to count six incidents before the Last Day:

1. my death;
2. the conquest of the holy city Jerusalem;
3. an epidemic among them like that of goats;
4. abundance of riches so that a man would not gladly accept 100 dinars if he is given;
5. a meeting to be joined by all Arab families without exception;
6. there would be a treaty between Nasaras (Christians) and them which they would break leading to war."

1st, the conquest of Jerusalem after the demise of the Holy Prophet (PBUH): It came to pass at the hands of Hazrat Ubaida bin Jarrah, the Commander of Syrian Army during the Caliphate of Umar (R.A.A.) besieged the Holy city, there was in the fort a bishop, who said to Ubaida (R.A.A.) on seeing his face that the fort was to be conquered by him; that the name and speciality of the conqueror was with one whose name was Umar. Ubaida informed Umar of this. Hence Umar ibn Khattab (R.A.A.) went to Jerusalem in person and the bishop in looking at his face said that he was the man appointed to subdue the stronghold and immediately he caused the castle to be evacuated. So from this conquest of Jerusalem two proofs of Muhammad (PBUH) being Prophet are seen:

(a) occurring of things accordingly as they were foretold; and

(b) that a detailed account of the Prophet and his companions had been given in former scriptures.

2nd, the prevalence of an epidemic after the conquest of Jerusalem: It also happened in 16 A.H. near Jerusalem where the forces of Abu Ubaida were encamped. Such a virulent pestilence broke out that 70,000 men died in three days and Abu Ubaida (R.A.A.) died in the same epidemic.

3rd, the plenteousness of wealth:This also came to be the state during the days of the leading Caliphs especially in the Caliphate of Osman (R.A.A.).

4th, a great rebellion warfare which should possess all the Arab clans. This refers to the uprising against Osman (R.A.A.) which caused horrible strifes and slaughter among the Muslims, and hardly anybody escaped this catastrophe.

5th, the conclusion of a treaty between the Muslim and the Christians, and then its violation by the latter and their invasion upon the former which forms the 6th prediction of the Apostle.

Bukhari quotes Umm–i–Haram (R.A.A.) as reporting:

"One day the Holy Prophet (PBUH) slept at my residence and awaked laughing. I asked him the reason of his laughter. He (the Apostle) said that he saw in the dream that his Companions sailed in ships for 'jihad.' I said, 'O Prophet of Allah, may I be among those crusaders?" The Apostle replied, "You are already among them." Thereafter, the Apostle slept again and re–awaked laughing. I asked again the reason of his laughter. He replied, "The first army that would wage war with the Roman Emperor would have its sin forgiven." Here the Holy Prophet (PBUH) foretold of three things: First, of the crusade by his followers in the Mediterranean; second, the inclusion of Umm–i–Haram among the crusaders against Constantinople, the capital of Roman Empire.

Bukhari quotes from Hazrat Abu Bakr (R.A.A.)

"Once the Prophet (PBUH) pointing to Hasan (R.A.A.) said that his son was Sayed and that it is hoped that through him Allah will bring about a reconciliation between two great multitudes of Muslims." This prophecy came true when after the martyrdom of Hazrat Ali (R.A.A.) the Muslims swore allegiance to Hazrat Hasan (R.A.A.) and he was made the Caliph. Later, a battle took place between the soldiers of Hasan (R.A.A.) and Amir Muawiyya. Hazrat Hasan (R.A.A.) presuming bloodshed of the Muslims on a large scale on both sides, entered into a peace treaty and thus became an instrument of peace and tranquillity to Muslims.

Baihaqui reports from Umm–ul–Fazl:

"Once I came before the Apostle and said that I had a very bad dream. The Holy Prophet (PBUH) asked me about the dream. I narrated that a part of my blessed body severed and fell into my lap. Thereupon, the Apostle revealed that the dream had a good news. It meant that Fatima should give birth to a son who would be in her lap. Accordingly, Imam Husain was born and was put in my lap. Thus, the prophecy of the Holy Prophet (PBUH) came true."

Baihaqui reports from Umm–e–Fazl:

"Once I had Imam Husain in my lap that the Holy Prophet (PBUH) came and staring him burst into tears. I requested him to give the reason of his shedding tears. Thereupon, the Apostle revealed that Jibrail (Gabriel) had informed him that his followers would kill his son, Husain."

Later Imam Husain was slain in Kerbala making the prophecy true."

Abu Noam reports:

"Once I was with Ali and Imam Husain in the Saqar Sateen. When we came to the town of Tainvi, Ali warned Husain to stop on the banks of the Euphrates. When I asked the reason, Ali revealed that he had been forewarned by Jibrail that Husain should be killed on the banks of the Euphrates, and he (the Apostle) had been shown a handful of dust of that place by the arch angel."

Ibn–i–Asakar reports from Mohammad bin Umar bin Hasan:

"Once I was with Imam Husain in the Kerbala. The Imam said on seeing Shimar, 'Allah and his Messenger told the truth." On enquiry he revealed, "The Holy Prophet (PBUH) told that he saw a white–spotted dog putting his snout in the blood of his skin; and Shimar had white leprosy and was spotted white.

Hazrat A'isha (R.A.A.) reports:

"Once the Holy Prophet (PBUH) told his chaste wives that among us she should meet him (the Apostle) first whose hands were the longest. We (the wives) conjectured what the length of the hand meant. We measured the length of our hands with a stick.

But when Zainab died we came to the conclusion that by large hand the Holy Prophet (PBUH) meant munificence, alms–giving, charity, etc. Since Zainab excelled all in these qualities, the prophecy of the Apostle came true." (Sahihin).

Abu Nairn reports from Ibn–i–Abbas:

"Once my mother, Umm–ul–Fazl, passed in front of the Holy Prophet (PBUH). He called her and revealed that from that conception of hers she should bear a son and when the boy should be born, she should bring him to him. Thus, when I was born she took me to the Apostle who called "Azan" in the right ear and "aqamat" in the left one. Thereafter, he tasted me his spittle of the mouth and named me, "Abdullah." Then he asked my mother to take me away — the father of the Caliphs.

When my mother narrated the matter to my father Abbas, he went to the Apostle and mentioned what he heard from his father. The Holy Prophet (PBUH) told him that the boy was in reality the Father of the caliphs."

The prophecy of the Holy Prophet (PBUH) proved to be correct because the Abbaside Caliphate had been in ascendancy for five hundred years.

Urwah and Sa'eed bin Mus'ab (R.A.A.) report:

"The Holy Prophet (PBUH) had told Abi bin Khalaf that he would be killed by him (the Prophet)."

"The prophecy came true in that he was wounded by the Apostle and died of the wound. (Baihaqui). It is narrated that Abi bin Khalaf was too deadly inimical to the Prophet to have a horse whom he gave gram and grass saying that mounting on it he might slay him.

When the Messenger of Allah heard, he replied, "if Allah so pleased, he (the Apostle) would kill him."

Now during the Battle of Uhad, Abi bin Khalaf challenged by saying, "Where is Muhammad, today he will not be spared from his hand." While he was advancing, the Companions of the Apostle wanted to prevent him. But the Holy Prophet (PBUH) said, "Let him come." When he came close, the Apostle hit him with a lance taken from a Companion. The lance hit an exposed part of his chin and inflicted a scratching wound which did not even bleed; but he fell down his horse and ran towards the Qurashi'ite. When they told him that there was no danger to him, he replied that the wound was from none but Muhammad's hands, and he would not remain alive even if he spat upon him. And, accordingly, he died on his way to Makkah.

Abi Qatada reports:

"During the Battle of Trench Amaar bin Yaser was digging a trench that the Holy Prophet (PBUH) moved his hand over his head and said:

"Regretful, a band of rebels shall kill thee, O son of Sumaiya."

> The above prophecy came true in the Battle of Siffin when Amaar bin Yaser was slain by the force of Muawiya. (Muslim).

During the days of Ignorance, Ka'aba used to be opened on Mondays and Thursdays. The key of Ka'aba remained in the possession of Uthman bin Talha.

One day, the Holy Prophet (PBUH) wanted to enter it for prayer. But Uthman refused to open the door of Ka'aba and uttered harsh words. The Apostle listened all patiently, and said to Uthman bin Talha:

"One day you shall see that key in my possession and I may give it to anyone I will like."

Thereupon Uthman replied,

"Shall the Quraishi'ite become extinct and disparaged that day?"

"That day the Quraishi'ite shall be more exalted," said the Holy Prophet (PBUH) in reply.

> On the day of the conquest of Makkah, the Messenger of Allah sent for Uthman bin Talha, and he came before the Apostle with the key of Ka'aba." (Tabqat–Ibn Sa'd).

In the above tradition there are two prophecies of the Holy Prophet (PBUH) proving to be correct.

Firstly, that one day the key of Ka'aba shall be in his hand. Secondly, the Prophet of Islam while giving back the key of Ka'aba to Uthman had predicted that it should remain with his family in future too. Now the second prophecy also came true as the key was still in possession of the family of Uthman bin Talha.

Sahl bin Hanzala reports:

"A cavalier came to the Prophet (PBUH) during the Battle of Hunain that he ascended a certain hill and saw that the whole Hawazin clan came to Hunain with their camels and cattle. Thereupon, the Messenger of Allah smiled and said:

"The next day if Allah be pleased, all that would be the booty of the Muslims." (Abu Dawood).

The prophecy came true the day following. The Battle of Hunain was won with a large booty that fell into the hands of the Believers.

When the Holy Prophet (PBUH) sent Hazrat Khalid bin Waleed (R.A.A.) against Ukaider, Governor of Damat–ul–Jandat, he had already told Khalid that Ukaider would surrender to him.

Hazrat Khalid bin Waleed, Commander of the Islamic Army arrived at the fort of Ukaider bin Abdul Mulk in a moon–lit night. Ukaider was very fond of Neelghai hunting. When he was reeling over his balcony in that moon–lit night, some Neelghais came to the wall of his stronghold and began to rub themselves with the wall of the fortress.

> On hearing the whiz so produced he looked down and found four animals near the fort. He rushed towards the animals with his brother Hassaun to hunt them as soon as possible. Khalid was waiting for the opportunity. As he came out of the fort, Khalid fell upon him suddenly and made him a captive; while his brother was killed. Ukaider was produced before the Messenger of Allah, was left after being levelled Islamic tax upon him."
>
> (Baihaqui and Ibn Ishaq).

Hazrat Anas (R.A.A.) reports:

"Once the people of Madina were afflicted by famine during the lifetime of the Holy Prophet (PBUH). Now when the Apostle was delivering his Friday sermon, a nomadic Arab got up and said:

"O Prophet of Allah! the animals are perishing and the children are hungry; so make supplication to Allah for us."

Thereupon, the Messenger of Allah raised his hands at once. While there was not a speck of cloud in the sky, but I swear by Allah in whose hand my soul is, that he had not lowered his hand before the clouds were appearing like mountains and before he descended from his pulpit, I saw the rain coming down on his beard.

We had rain that day, the next, the following day, and till the next Friday. Then (during the Friday Sermon) that nomadic Arab or someone else got up and said, "O Messenger of Allah! the buildings are being broken down and the animals are being drowned, so make supplication to Allah for us."

The Apostle then raised his hands and said:

"O Allah! (Send rain) round about us, but not on us."

> The Messenger of Allah did not point to any region in the clouds without their breaking up; and Madina became like gap. The "wadi" (valley) had a channel flowing in it for a month, and no one came from any region without speaking of plenty." (Bukhari; Muslim)

Hazrat Anas (R.A.A.) reports:

"Once a learned Jew 'Abdullah bin Salam came to know that the Messenger of Islam had arrived. He was then in his orchard gathering dates. He left his work, appeared before the Prophet of Islam and said:

"I shall ask you about three things which only a prophet knows. What is the first sign of the Last Hour? What is the first things the inhabitants of Paradise will eat? What makes a baby look like its father or its mother?"

The Messenger of Allah (PBUH) replied:

"Jibrail has just informed me about them (i.e. your questions). The first sign of the Last Hour will be a fire which will drive mankind from the east to the west. The first thing the inhabitants of Paradise will eat will be the liver of a fish. When liquid of the man comes before the woman's, he attracts the child to his likeness; but when the liquid of the woman comes first it attracts it to her likeness."

Thereupon, Abdullah bin Salam said."

"I testify that only Allah has the right to be worshipped and that you are Messenger of Allah. O Apostle! the Jews are slanderous people, and if they know of my acceptance of Islam before you ask them will slander me."

When the Jews came, the Holy Prophet (PBUH) asked:

"What kind of man is Abdullah among you?"

"Our best one and the son of our best one, our chief and the son of our chief," they replied.

"Tell me what you will do if he accepts Islam." the Apostle asked, "May Allah preserve him."

Thereupon, Abdullah came out and said:

"I testify that none has right to be worshipped but Allah, and that Muhammad is the Messenger of Allah."

They said:

"He is the worst of us and the son of the worst of us."

"This is what I feared, O Messenger of Allah,"

Abdullah bin Salam said.

Hazrat Abu Hurairah (R.A.A.) reports:

"A wolf came and took away a sheep. The shepherd ran after it and snatched it from it. Thereafter,1 the wolf climbed on a mound and having sat on its haunches with its tail between its legs said, "I took the sheep as a provision of Allah but you snatched that from me." The shepherd wondered at the sight and said, "By Allah, I have never seen like it before, a wolf talking."

"But more wonderful is the man among the palm–trees between the two "harras" who can tell what has already happened and what is going to be happened after your time," the wolf replied.

> The shepherd was a Jew. Having heard from the wolf, he came to the Holy Prophet (PBUH) and embraced Islam. (Sharh–al–Sunnah).

Unais bin 'Aim reports:

"Ahban bin Aus narrates, "I was amongst my sheep. All of a sudden a wolf appeared and caught a sheep. Thereupon, I shouted at it at the top of my voice. At this, the wolf sat on its tail and addressed me, saying:

"Who will look after the sheep when you are busy and not able to look after it? How can you forbid me the provision which Allah, the Almighty, has kept for me?"

Ahban further said, "Clapping with both hands I said with wonder that I had never seen something more wonderful and striking during my whole life."

"But there is something more wonderful than this," the wolf said with confidence and added, "It is this that the Prophet of Allah is inviting people to Almighty Allah."

"Hearing this, Ahban went to Allah's Apostle and informing him about his wonderful site, accepted Islam."

'Amr said. (Fatah al–Bari).

Acknowledged Prayers

Abdullah bin 'Amr (R.A.A.) reports:

"The Holy Prophet (PBUH) went out at the Battle of Badr with his three hundred and thirteen Companions. Most of them were in a very wretched condition. The Messenger of Allah felt disturbed at their state of life and their sacrifice for the cause of Almighty Allah, and raised his hands in prayer, saying:

"O Allah they are hungry, so satiate them; they are naked, so clothe them; they are bare–footed, so provide mount for them."

> Allah, the Exalted bestowed victory on them and almost all his Companions went back home with provision, cloth and camels. (Abu Dawud).

Anas (R.A.A.) reports Hazrat Umar (R.A.A.) to have narrated:

"After the Battle of Badr, the slain among the unbelievers were put into a well on top of one another. After sometime, the Holy Prophet (PBUH) went near the well and called, "So and so and son of so and so! have you found true what your deities had promised you to be?" I have found true what my Allah had promised me to be true?" Thereupon, I (Umar) asked the Messenger of Allah, "How can you speak to bodies which contain no spirits?"

9

Historic Speech

Last Sermon

Prophet Muhammad (peace and blessings of Allah be upon him), the Prophet, was now in the sixty-third year of his life which coincided with the close of the tenth year of the Hijrah. His mission was completed. To a people steeped in ignorance, the Holy Prophet gave light and inspired them with belief in Allah, the sole Creator, Master and Sustainer of the universe. To a disunited mass, engaged in perpetual warfare, he gave unity of thought and action and locked them in ties of brotherhood and love. His life is the noblest record of mission nobly and faithfully performed and "he performed it with an enthusiasm and fervour which admitted of no compromise, conceived no halting; with indomitable courage which brooked no resistance and allowed no fear of consequence; with a singleness of purpose which thought of no self."

The completion of his mission implied his departure from his earthly home to his heavenly abode. The Prophet visualised it clearly and, therefore, spent most of his time in making preparations for the journey on which he was about to set.

The month of pilgrimage was at hand, and the Prophet decided to avail himself of this opportunity. The Ka'bah had been completely purified and there was no vestige of an image left which could offend his eyes. He set on what is called the Farewell Pilgrimage, because it was the last pilgrimage performed by him. Messengers were sent to all the parts of Arabia inviting people to join him in this great pilgrimage. It was necessary for them since they should learn by first-hand knowledge the several injunctions and practices of pilgrimage— free from all taints of ignorance—an ideal pattern which was to be kept intact in its pristine glory for all times to come.

Five days before Dhul Hijjah, the Prophet (peace be upon him) put on the pilgrim's garb and set out to Mecca with more than 114, 000 Muslims along with him. All his wives accompanied him. As he rode, he recited "Labbaik! Labbaik! " signifying, "Here I am at Thy service, here I am O Lord! Here I am to declare that there is no partner with Thee. All praise and blessings belong to Thee and all sovereignty is Thine. I am here at Thy service, and Thou has no partner, O Allah! As the Holy Prophet recited the above call, all his companions repeated the same loudly.

What the psychologists call the sudden outburst of crowd psychology was changed into sublime spiritual expression. There is something marvellously sacred with this ritual of Islam which raises a man to the lofty heights of love for God. It symbolises self-sacrifice and devotion to the Great Master. It is an assembly where human equality reigns supreme and where no mark of distinction between a king and peasant is seen, where all meet as brethren to do homage to their Lord.

The Holy Prophet reached Mecca on the 5th Dhul Hijjah. He made seven circuits (tawaf) of the Ka'bah, offered two raka'hs of prayer at the "station of Ibrahim" and climbing up the Mount of Safa declared, "There is no god, but Allah. He has no partner. All sovereignty and praise belong to Him. He gives life and brings death. He is All-Powerful and Supreme over everything. He fulfilled his promise, He helped His servant, and He alone crushed all the forces of disbelief." Meanwhile 'Ali (Allah be pleased with him) also joined the Prophet with pilgrims of Yemen.

On the 8th of Dhul Hijjah, the Prophet left with his companions for Mina and passed the night there, and on 9th, after the morning prayer, he proceeded to Arafat where he delivered the following celebrated address:

> "All praise be to Allah. We glorify Him and seek His help and pardon; and we turn to Him. We take refuge with Allah from the evils of ourselves and from the evil consequences of our deeds. There is none to lead him astray whom Allah guides aright, and there is none to guide him aright whom He leads astray. I bear witness that there is no god but Allah alone; having no partner with Him, and I bear witness that Muhammad is His bondman and His Messenger. I admonish you, O bondmen of Allah! to fear Allah and I urge you to His obedience and I open the speech with that what is good.
>
> Ye people! Listen to my words: I will deliver a message to you, for I know not whether, after this year, I shall ever be amongst you here again. O people! Verily your blood, your property and your honour are sacred and inviolable until you appear before your Lord, as this day and this month is sacred for all. Verily you will meet your Lord and you will be held answerable for your actions. Have I not conveyed the message? O Allah! Be my witnesses.
>
> He who has any trust with him he should restore it to the person who deposited it with him.
>
> Beware, no one committing a crime is responsible for it but he himself. Neither the son is responsible for the crime of his father, nor the father is responsible for the crime of his son.

O people! Listen to my words and understand them. You must know that a Muslim is the brother of the Muslim and they form one brotherhood. Nothing of his brother is lawful for a Muslim except what he himself allows willingly. So you should not oppress one another. O Allah! have I not conveyed the message?

Behold! all practices of paganism and ignorance are now under my feet. The blood-revenges of the days of Ignorance are remitted. The first claim on blood I abolish is that of Ibn Rabi'ah Ibn Harith who was nursed in the tribe of Sa'd and whom the Hudhayl killed.

Usury is forbidden, but you will be entitled to recover your principal. Wrong not and you would not be wronged. Allah has decreed that there should be no usury and I make a beginning by remitting the amount of interest which Abbas b. 'Abd al Muttalib has to receive. Verily it is remitted entirely.

O people! fear Allah concerning women. Verily you have taken them on the security of Allah and have made their persons lawful unto you by words of Allah! Verily you have got certain rights over your women and your women have certain rights over you. It is incumbent upon them to honour their conjugal rights and, not to commit acts of impropriety which, if they do, you have authority to chastise them, yet not severely. If your wives refrain from impropriety and are faithful to you, clothe and feed them suitably.

Behold! Lay injunctions upon women but kindly.

O people! Listen and obey though a mangled Abyssinian slave is your amir if he executes the ordinances of the Book of Allah among you.

O people! Verily Allah has ordained to every man the share of his inheritance. The child belongs to the marriage-bed and the violator of wedlock shall be stoned. He who attributes his ancestry to other than his father or claims his clientship to other than his masters, the curse of Allah, that of the angels, and of the people be upon him. Allah will accept from him neither repentance nor righteousness.

O people! Verily the Satan is disappointed at being ever worshipped in this land of yours, but he can be obeyed in anything short of worship he will be pleased in matters you may be disposed to think of little account, so beware of him in your matters of religion.

Verily, I have left amongst you the Book of Allah and the Sunnah of His Apostle which if you hold fast, you shall never go astray.

"And if you were asked about me, what would you say?" They replied: "We bear witness that you have conveyed the message, and discharged your ministry."

The Holy Prophet addressed the assembly again on Friday, Dhul Hijjah 10 A. H. and besides repeating some of the important points of the previous address, he threw a good deal of light on some new questions.

As usual, he opened his oration with praising Allah and expressing his gratitude to Him.

O people! Verily the intercalation (of a prohibited month) aggravates infidelity. Thereby the unbelievers are led to wrong. For they make it lawful one year and forbid it in another year to be in conformity with the number of months which Allah declared unlawful so they consider violable that which Allah declared to be inviolable and they consider inviolable what Allah declared to be violable.

Verily the time has revolved in its own way from the day when the heavens and the earth were created. The number of months to Allah is twelve of which four are sacred; three are consecutive—Dhul Qa'dah, Dhul Hijjah, Muharram, and Rajab which is between Jumadah and Sha'ban.

O people! Do you know what day it is, what territory it is, what month it is?

To this the people answered: The day is the day of sacrifice; and the territory is the sacred territory, the month is the sacred month. At each reply the Holy Prophet said:

So I apprise you that your lives, your property and your honour must be as sacred to one another as this sacred day, in this sacred month, in this sacred town.

And your slaves! See that you feed them with such food as you eat yourselves and clothe them with the clothes that you yourselves wear. And if they commit a fault which you are not inclined to forgive, then part with them for they are the servants of Allah and are not to be chastised.

Behold! Listen to me. Worship your Lord; offer prayers five times a day; observe fast in the month of Ramadan; make pilgrimage to the House (Ka'bah); pay readily the Zakat (poor-rate) on your property and obey whatever I command you, only then will you get into the heaven.

"Let him that is present convey it unto him who is absent. For happily, many people to whom the message is conveyed may be more mindful of it than the audience."

The Holy Prophet picked up the thread of his oration on the next day also and added:

> O people! Verily your Lord is one and your father is one. All of you belong to one ancestry of Adam and Adam was created out of clay. There is no superiority for an Arab over a non-Arab and for a non-Arab over an Arab; nor for white over the black nor for the black over the white except in piety. 'Verily the noblest among you it he who is the most pious.' (xlix: 13)

> Behold, the nearer ones of you should convey the message to the remoter ones. I have conveyed the message. Then looking up to the heaven, he said:

> "O Lord! I have delivered the message and discharged my ministry."

> "Yes," cried all the people crowding round him, "Yes, verily you have."

> "O Lord! I beseech Thee bear Thou witness unto it."

And with these words, the Prophet concluded his address.

He alighted from his camel and offered the noon and afternoon prayers together. It was at this time that the verse regarding the completion of religion was revealed to him:

> This day I have perfected for you your faith, And completed my favour upon you, And I am well-pleased with al-Islam as your religion. (v: 4)

The Prophet immediately recited this verse to all those who were present on this occasion.

The Muslims were happy on receiving this information, but Abu Bakr was sad as he perceived in it a clear indication of the departure of Holy Prophet (peace and blessings of Allah be upon him) to his eternal abode. Abu Bakr rightly realized that the Prophet had been raised in order to bring the religious truth to perfection. Evidently when the mission of Muhammad (peace and blessings of Allah be upon him) had been fulfilled, it meant that his physical presence on the earth was no longer needed and that the time had come for him to take eternal rest in his heavenly abode far from the cares and worries of worldly life.

The farewell address of the Holy Prophet is not only remarkable for its eloquence, but also for its sublime message for the whole of human race. The world has not been able to lay down better principles of ethics than those enunciated in it. Every word of it breathes a spirit of magnanimity and aims at establishing righteouess and fair dealings among men on a workable basis. It establishes brotherhood among Muslims irrespective of the divergences of their geographical, racial and colour backgrounds and puts finishing touches to a social order, perfectly free from oppression and injustice:

> "Three days were allowed for the Medina contingent to recuperate before returning home. The atmosphere was cordial and different from what it had been at the time of the last visit. Relatives met relatives and friends recognized friends without that watchful glance for the concealed sword. Parties were given and the brothehood of which Muhammad had preached was put into practice. It was perhaps less gay than in the days of Abu Jahl and Abu Lahab, but it was more sincere."

Muhammad (peace be upon him) was happy. His mind was at peace. He had completed the pilgrimage and established a religious practice in ideal form, free from all taints of paganism. He had delivered the message which sums up beautifully the fundamentals of Islam and the responsibilities which fall upon the shoulders of Muslims as the standard-bearers of the Divine faith. "The Prophet", observes Ibn Hisham, "completed the Hajj and showed to the people the rites and ceremonies which are essential and taught them what God had made incumbent upon them with regard to pilgrimage, the "station", the throwing of stones, the circumambulation of the House, and what He had permitted and forbidden in this connection. It was the pilgrimage of message and proclamation and that of the Farewell also, since it was the last Hajj which the Holy Prophet performed in his life."

After the Farewell Pilgirmage, the concourse broke and returned to Medina. The Holy Prophet accompanied his men in their homeward journey and reached the city of Medina at the end of Dhul-Hijjah.

He had no doubt realized that he would soon be called back to his heavenly abode, but he was not to be disheartened or dismayed. He was entrusted with a heavy responsibility by Allah and he was therefore very anxious to spend every moment of his sacred life in the discharge of his ministry. The idea of fast-approaching death did not droop his spirit; it rather provided him incentive to give finishing touches to the work assigned to him, so that nothing should be left undone before he presented himself to his Lord in heaven.

The Holy Prophet in the last year of his life spent most of his time in Medina. He settled the organization of the provinces and tribal communities which had adopted Islam and become the component parts of the Muslim state. Officers were sent to the provinces and to various tribes for the purpose of teaching the people the precepts and practices of Islam, administering justice according to the Qur'an and the Sunnah and collecting zakat.

The Arabs had embraced Islam, he thought, but what about Syria, Egypt and Abyssinia? These countries and in fact the whole world must bear the message of Islam. Arrangements were made to send missions to these countries also.

The Holy Prophet was up till now in good health and had performed all his duties with zeal and fervour; leading prayers, issuing despatches, appointing governors, and arranging administration throughout Arabia. He, however, became indisposed during the middle of Safar, 11 A.H. after his return from Mecca. The poison which had been given to him by a Jewess at Khaybar and which had slowly penetrated into his system, began to show its effects and his health deteriorated with alarming rapidity.

The Holy Prophet had said good-bye to his people at Mecca but his mind was occupied with the thought that he had not prayed for the martyrs of Uhud; and so to their graves he now turned his steps. There, standing besides the graves of his brave and faithful companions, he prayed and with such earnestness that although they were now buried for eight long years, one would have believed as if a departing soul was bidding farewell to living persons. Then he went to the pulpit and said:

> I am to precede you and I have been made a witness upon you. By God, you will meet me at the "Fountain" very soon. I have been given the keys of the worldly treasures. By Allah, I do not fear for you that you will turn polytheists after me. But I do fear that you may strike one another's necks for the acquisition of worldly riches.

On the 18th of Safar, he went to Baqi' al-Gharaqad in the middle of the night and prayed for the dead. He, then, returned to his wife Maimunah's apartment. The fever became violent and the pain considerably increased. But he bore all these sufferings with remarkable calmness and serenity. He led the prayers in the mosque as long as his health supported him but he could not continue that as his health was failing alarmingly. One day water had to be poured over his head before he could come out and he had a bandage round his head to relieve headache. He called his wives and said: "You see that I am very sick. I am not able to visit you in turn. If it be pleasing unto you, I may be permitted to stay in the apartment of 'A'ishah." They all agreed and he walked with the support of 'Ali and Abbas (Allah be pleased with them) to her apartment.

Abu Bakr was commanded by the Holy Prophet to lead the prayer during his illness. 'A'ishah suggested to her husband that her father should be relieved of this for he had a tender heart and might burst into tears while reciting the Holy Qur'an. The Holy Prophet insisted on his continuing to officiate for him so that Abu Bakr had no other choice but to lead the prayers.

Final Guidelines

On Thursday, he again asked his family to pour water upon him. Refreshed by the bath he felt relieved and went forth to the mosque, supported by 'Ali and Abbas, to offer his noonday prayer. At the conclusion of the prayer he seated himself upon the pulpit and addressed the people around him:

> There is a servant whose Lord has given him option between this life and that which is nigh unto the Lord, and the servant has chosen the latter.

Abu Bakr seems to have been the only one in the mosque who recognised what Muhammad (peace be upon him) really meant and tears filled his eyes at the idea that soon the Prophet would be no more among them.

Then the Apostle of Allah (peace be upon him) said:

> There is none more bountiful to us for his unwavering loyalty and devotion and for his sacrifice of wealth then Abu Bakr. If I were to choose a bosom friend it would be he; but Islam has made a closer brotherhood among us all.
>
> The fact is that your companion is the friend of Allah. Let every door that leads into the mosque be closed, except the door of Abu Bakr.
>
> O people! It has reached me that you are afraid of the approaching death of your Prophet. Has any previous Prophet lived for ever among those to whom he was sent? So think not that I would ever live among you?
>
> Behold, I am about to go to my Lord. You too will go sooner or later. I instruct you to do good to the first Emigrants and I recommend the Emigrants to do good among themselves.

Verily Allah, the Exited says:

> "By the time, Verily man is in the loss, except those who themselves believe and do righteous works, and enjoin upon each other the truth and enjoin upon each other endurance."

Verily, the affairs take their course according to the Will of Allah. Delay in dispensation should not in any way urge you to be impatient in demand. Allah—the Mighty and the Great-does not submit to the haste of anybody. He who contends with Allah—Allah overpowers him. He who tries to play fast and loose with Allah he is outwitted by Him. In the near future, if you get power in the world, then do not spread mischief on earth and do not cut off your blood relations. I instruct you to do good to the Helpers. They are those who provided facilities for the Promotion of the faith. So you should behave unto them well. Did they not provide accommodation for you in their homes? Did they not give you preference over themselves, while they were confronted with poverty?

The number of believers would increase, but the Ansar would decrease to the extent that they would be among men as salt in the food. They are my family and with them I found shelter.

By Him in Whose Hand my life is, verily I love you. The Helpers have acquitted themselves creditably of the responsibility that fell upon them and now there remains what you have to do.

So he who from among you occupies a position of responsibility and is powerful enough to do harm or good to the people, he should fully acknowledge and appreciate the favour that has been shown by these benefactors and should overlook their faults.

Verily do not give preference to yourselves over them.

Beware, he who is anxious to come to the 'fountain' along with me tomorrow should hold his tongue and restrain his hands.

O people! Verily sins deprive people of blessings and bring about changes in their lot. When people are good, their rulers do good to them and when the people are wrong-doers their rulers oppress them.

There may be some amongst you whom I owe anything. I am, after all a human being. So if there is any man whose honour I have injured, here I am to answer for it.

If I have done any injury to the skin of anybody, here is my skin; he can take his recompense. If I owe aught to anyone, here is my property; he may take it.

Know that among you the most faithful to me is the one who has such a claim against me and then he either takes it from me or absolves me so that I meet my Lord after I have been absolved.

Nobody should say: "I fear enmity and grudge of the Apostle of Allah." I nurse no grudge towards anyone. These are the things which are alien to my nature and temperament. I abhor them."

The Holy Prophet received the news that there was some grumbling in certain quarters about the appointment of Usamah to the post of the commander of the intended expedition to Syria. He summoned the people in question and addressed them in the following words:

> O people! What is this which has reached my ears, that some amongst you murmur against my appointing Usamah as the commander? Now if you criticise my appointing Usamah as amir, [it is not a new thing for] you have indeed criticised my appointing his father [Zayd] as amir before him. And I swear by the Lord, that he verily was well-fitted for the command, and that his son after him is well-fitted also. Truly, Usamah is one of the men most dearly loved by me, as his father was. They both are indeed loved by me.
>
> One day, while he was in a precarious condition, he said to his Companions around him:
>
> Come here, I will cause you to write something so that you may never fall into error. Upon this some of those present said: "The Prophet of God is suffering from accute pain and you have the Qur'an with you; the Book of Allah is sufficient unto us". Others, however, wanted the writing to be made. When Muhammad (peace be upon him) saw them debating over it, he was perturbed and ordered them to go away and leave him alone.

Muhammad (peace be upon him) had a great love for his only daughter Fatimah (may Allah be pleased with her).

She visited her departing father very frequently and received his blessings and love. On one such occasion he whispered to her something and she began to weep. Then he again whispered to her something and she laughed.

'A'ishah questioned her after the Prophet's death, about this weeping and laughing to which Fatimah replied: "The first time, he disclosed to me that he would not recover from his illness and I wept. The second time he revealed that I would be the first of the family to join him and that made me laugh."

The sickness of the Prophet on the Saturday night assumed a serious turn. Fever rose to such a pitch that the hand could hardly be placed upon the Prophet's body owing to the burning heat. His body was racking with pain; but he was still busy in calling people to the path of righteousness. Turning to the women who sat close by he said: O Fatimah! my daughter and thou Safiyyah, my aunt! Work ye out that which shall please the Lord. For verily I have no power with Him to save you in any way.'

Even in this hour of illness, when he had grown very weak, his mind was alert and perceived all that went on around him. Some of the women, who had been in exile in Abyssinia mentioned about the cathedral of Maria and of the wonderful picture on its walls. Overhearing it, the Holy Prophet (may peace and blessings of Allah be upon him) was displeased and remarked:

> These are the people who, when a saint among them dies, build over his tomb a place of worship and they adorn it with his pictures—in the eyes of Lord, the worst part of all creation.

He then raised his hand in prayer and said:

> O Lord! Let my grave be not adopted as an idol. God has cursed the people who have turned the graves of their Prophets into places of worship.

Meanwhile, it occurred to him that he had given to 'A'ishah some gold coins. He desired that these should be given at once in charity to the needy, as he did not like that he should meet his Lord when he had some material wealth in his possession.

The last night of Muhammad's life, i.e. the 11th of Rabi' al-Awwal, 11 A.H. was heavy upon him. He was overheard praying constantly to his Lord for His blessings. The morning brought him some relief. Fever and pain had somewhat abated, and there was some recovery of strength. He moved the curtain of his apartment and saw the Muslims offering their prayers in the Mosque with Abu Bakr as their leader.

Having paused thus for a moment at the door of his apartment, the Holy Prophet, supported by a companion, walked slowly to the place where Abu Bakr stood. People made way for him, opening their ranks as he advanced. Abu Bakr heard the rustle and guessing the cause, stepped backward to vacate the leader's place; but the Holy Prophet asked him by motion of his hand to keep on leading the prayer. When he had finished, Muhammad (peace be upon him) set on the step of the pulpit and addressed, once more his devoted followers:

> By the Lord! As for myself, I have not made lawful anything except that which God has declared lawful; nor have I prohibited aught but that which God has forbidden.

This is the last occasion on which he appeared in public. Muslims were happy that the Prophet had recovered and there was no danger to his life. Usamah came to the Prophet and asked his permission to proceed with his army to Syria. Abu Bakr greeted the Holy Prophet on his recovery and sought his permission to go out of Medina to see his wife at al-Sunah. 'Ali told the eager crowd that the Holy Prophet had recovered and there was no cause for worry. The people, therefore, dispersed well-pleased and happy at this news.

Muhammad (peace be upon him), however, seemed quite exhausted and returned to the apartment of 'A'ishah. As the day advanced, his strength failed rapidly. 'A'ishah, seeing him to be too weak, raised his head from the pillow and laid it tenderly in her lap. She moistened his forehead with damp cloth. His fever was very high. But the Holy Prophet remained calm and forbearing. He had resigned himself to the Will of God and repeated these words again and again:

> "In the company of those on whom is the Grace of Allah." (iv: 69)

He felt as if he was drifting towards the irresistible end but as ever, he was without fear. He did not, for a moment, lost his courage. He constantly called his Master to help him:

> "O Lord! I beseech Thee assist me in the agony of death."

At this juncture 'Abd al-Rahman, the brother of 'A'ishah, entered with a green twig in his hand. Seeing that his eyes rested on it, and knowing it to be such as he liked, she asked whether he would like to have it. He signified assent. Chewing it a little to make it soft and pliable, she placed it in his hand. This pleased him. He brushed his teeth energetically and there put it down.

His strength now rapidly sank and he was heard saying:

> "Lord! grant me pardon! and join me to the companionship on high "

Then at intervals he uttered these words:

> "The most exalted companionship on high."

He also murmured admonition:

"Prayer and the persons who have been entrusted to your care."

This he repeated several times. Then after a pause of silence, his strength ebbed back. His eyes opened widely and he said clearly:

> "Lord! blessed is the companionship on high."

Then his limbs relaxed. His head fell back in 'A'ishah's lap. She fixed her eyes upon him anxiously, almost hopefully to get a response from him but she found to her great sorrow that the faint suggestion of a smile which relaxed her husband's lips did not belong to this world. Muhammad (peace and blessings of Allah be upon him), after having rendered his obligations towards his earthly companions, had now returned to the companionship of the One on high. It was Monday, the twelfth of Rabi' al-Awwal that he left for his heavenly abode, at the age of sixty-three:

> May the Lord shower His choicest blessings on him, his family and his companions!

So ended a life consecrated from first to last, to the service of God and humanity.

The news of the Prophet's death spread to all corners of the city. Consternation and fear blazed through the ranks of the people who had just seen their master alive. Some wept bitterly; some were struck dump; some disbelieved the news of death and held that it was only a swoon. Even 'Umar in the state of agony, forgot that the Prophet was a mortal and death was, therefore, a natural phenomenon with him.

It was an unusal scene, an extraordinary situation. Muhammad (peace be upon him) had never in any manner or by suggestion direct or indirect given any indication that he was immortal. Rather he had emphasised his humanness and mortality time and again. His followers, however, who had received a heavenly life by his teachings, who had developed the consciousness of Allah in full glory through him, and had constantly witnessed the manifestations of Divine help, mercy and power in his words and actions, could not look upon him as a mere human being. They could not associate their master with anything mortal. It was indeed painful for them to imagine that the man who had brought them out of darkness and superstition into light and wisdom; who had changed their lives from gross materialism to sublime spirituality, was no longer within their reach to guide them. Such a feeling was quite natural.

'Umar stood there in the throng with his sword unsheathed and announced that anybody who dared say that Muhammad (may the peace and blessings of Allah be upon him) was dead, would do so at the cost of his life.

Choice of Successor

Just then appeared Abu Bakr. Passing through the mosque and disregarding the crowds which pressed about him, asking a thousand questions, he walked onward into the apartment of 'A'ishah. He did not say anything but lifted the Yamani mantle which had covered the face of the Holy Prophet. For a moment he looked sadly at the finely drawn features of his great and illustrious friend. Then he knelt beside him and kissed the broad forehead, and said: "Sweet you were in life and sweet too in death. Yes, you are dead." He continued, "Alas! my friend, my chosen one, dearer than father and mother to me! You have tasted the death which God had decreed; a second death will never overtake you."

Gently putting down the head upon the pillow, he stooped again and kissed the face; then replaced the covering and withdrew.

He went out and became aware of the tumult outside the Prophet's chamber. He hurried toward it and heard 'Umar's voice reiterating that Muhammad was not dead. Abu Bakr tried to silence him, but it was no use. He would not listen to him. He, therefore, left him to himself and moved towards the people who had thronged round him. He addressed them in his natural calm and soft measured tone:

Has not the Almighty revealed this verse unto His Prophet saying:

> 'Verily thou shalt die, and they shall die.

Again:

> 'And Muhammad is naught but an Apostle; apostles have surely passed away before him. Will ye then, if he dieth or be slain, turn round on your heels.'
>
> (iii: 144)

Let him who worshipped Muhammad know that Muhammad (peace and blessings of Allah be upon him) is dead; but whosover worshipped Allah, let him know that Allah is alive, and He shall never die.

The short sermon had a very salutary effect upon the assembly and it brought solace to the wounded hearts of the Muslims in this unbearably sad bereavement. They submitted, with a cheerful resignation to the Will of Allah with an understanding that like all other mortals the Holy Prophet had also left this earthly abode. They felt that the Quranic verse which Abu Bakr had recited before them was squarely applicable to the situation, as if it had been revealed just then on that occasion.

Abu Bakr in spite of his intense grief, kept his head cool. He knew that at that moment Islam was faced with grave dangers. The shock of Muhammad's death had been great, but the reaction might even be greater. He, therefore, kept a watch over the affairs lest they should take a serious turn. On hearing the report that Ansar had gathered in the Hall of B. Sa'idah in order to decide the issue of Muhammad's successor, he hurried to the spot. He was urgently needed there. 'Umar and Abu 'Ubaydah accompanied him to that place. Abu Bakr listened to the arguments of the Helpers calmly and then placed the matter before them dispassionately and asked them to decide the issue. He told them:

> All that you speak of your excellence is perfectly true.
>
> There is no people upon earth deserving all this praise more than you do. But the Arabs will not accept a cheif other than a man of the Quraysh. Quraysh will be the administrators and you will be their ministers.

He spoke very persuasively, trying to make the Ansar realise the gravity of the situation and make them decide the matter coolly and in the best interest of Islam. Abu Bakr's words touched the chord that vibrated in every heart and thus had the desired effect. The spirit of opposition soon disappeared and he was unanimously elected as the first caliph of the departed Prophet (peace be upon him).

While all this was going on 'Ali and 'Abbas and some other members of the Prophet's family bathed his body. It was wrapped in three coverings and laid in state in 'A'ishah's apartment. People were allowed to catch the last glimpse of their benefactor's face and say the funeral prayers. Each group did that and moved on.

This went on the whole day long: women followed men and children followed women.

When the time for burial approached, it was discovered that no one had a clear idea where the Holy Prophet should be laid to rest. Some were in favour of burying him in the mosque, while others wanted to bury him along with his Companions. Abu Bakr solved the problem by announcing: "I heard the Apostle say, 'No Prophet dies but he is buried where he dies.' So the bed on which he died was removed and a grave was dug there. The sacred body was lowered in the grave by 'Ali, Usamah and Al-Fadl. A vault of unbaked bricks was built over it and the rest was filled in with gravel and sand."

> May Lord shower upon him the choicest of His blessings and favours!

Prophet as an Exemplar

It is proper that before bringing this work to a close, I should sum up the chief traits of the character of the Holy Prophet, which, at different stages of his life and from various points of view, have been presented in these pages. This I will now briefly attempt.

The person of Muhammad (peace be upon him) was extremely graceful. His form, a little above average height, was stately and commanding. The depth of feeling in his dark black eyes and the winning expression of the face gained the confidence and love of strangers, even at first sight. 'He was', says an admiring follower, 'the handsomest, the brightest faced and most generous of men. It was as though the sunlight beamed in his countenance.'

When the Prophet's wife 'A'ishah (may Allah he pleased with her) asked to describe the mode of his life and conduct she replied: "His morals are the Qur'an. In other words, his daily life was a true picture of the Qur'anic teachings." He was an embodiment of all the virtues enunciated by the Holy Quran. The record of his life which sheds light on his conduct as a child, as a father, as a husband, as a neighbour, as a merchant, as a preacher, as a persecuted emigrant, as a friend, as a warrior, as an army commander, as a conqueror, as a judge, as a ruler, as a law-giver and above all as a devotee of Allah was all an exemplification of the Book of Allah.

In his habits he was very simple, though elegant. His eating and drinking, his dress and his household goods retained, even when he reached the apex of his power, their original simplicity. In all matters he stood far too high above to fall a prey to material temptations so much so that he had no wealth or riches with him when he left this earthly abode. For he had set his slaves free and distributed his money in all conceivably good causes. His personal belongings at the time of his death consisted merely of an armour (and even this had been mortgaged with a Jew), a mattress of dried palm leaves and a water-skin.

He was gifted with uncommon power of imagination, sublimity of thought and delicacy and refinement of feeling. He was most indulgent to his inferiors, and would never allow his young servant to be scolded, regardless of what he did. "Ten years," said Anas, his faithful servant, "I was with the Prophet, and he never said as much as 'fie to me." He was very affectionate towards his family. He loved the little children dearly; stopped them in the street and patted their heads with great affection. In times of leisure he even joined them in their innocent games.

Though his living was simple, yet he did not shun the use of the good things of life. He relished tasty food, enjoyed the beauty of flowers, the fragrance of perfumes, and was even fond of light jokes. He gave love for love. He had a large heart, overflowing with the milk of human kindness, especially kindness towards the weak and the oppressed. He admired the good qualities in others and readily accepted good counsel, no matter from which quarter it came.

Muhammad (peace be upon him) was a warmhearted and faithful friend. He loved Abu Bakr with the close affection of a brother. In the same way he loved 'Ali, his cousin and son-in-law and Zayd, his freed slave, with the fondness of a father. This freed slave of the Prophet, in his turn, was so deeply attached to him that he preferred to stay on at Mecca with his kind and affectionate master, rather than return home with his own father. Muhammad (peace be upon him) had a great regard for him and after the death of Zayd, his son Usamah was treated with the same favour and love which his father had received from the Holy Prophet. 'Uthman and 'Umar were also very dear to his heart. He had a very great regard for the Ansar and frankly and gracefully acknowledged their valuable services to the cause of Islam. His affections were in no instance misplaced; they were ever reciprocated by a warm and self-sacrificing love on the part of his followers.

He was very sweet and kind and with the exception of one instance, in which an open challenge was thrown to him, he never struck any one with his own hand.

The worst expression he ever made use of in his conversation was: 'What has come to him? May his forehead become darkened with mud.' When asked to curse someone he replied: "I have not been sent to curse but to be a mercy to mankind." He visited the sicks, followed any bier that he saw, accepted the invitation of everyone, even of slaves, to dinner, mended his own clothes, repaired his own shoes, milked his goats. While shaking hands, he never was the first to withdraw his hand out of another man's palm and turned not away before the other had turned.

> He was the most faithful protector of those he protected, the sweetest and most agreeable in conversation. Those who saw him were suddenly filled with reve-

rence; those who came near him loved him; they who described him would say, 'I have never seen him like either before or after.' He was of great taciturnity, but when he spoke, it was with emphasis and deliberation and nobody could forget what he said.

He was very courteous to all those who met him. He is never reported to have said 'nay' to anyone. He never contradicted anybody unless what he said was opposed to the teachings of Islam, nor did he get angry with any man because of personal matters. He paid equal regard to the humble and the rich. He claimed no distinction for himself and lived amongst his friends as if he was not their leader, but a sincere companion and a devoted brother. When walking, people would walk in front of him and behind him. When seated among his followers, who loved him dearer than their own lives, he would occupy no special seat in order to make himself conspicuous. Strangers were at times puzzled to recognise him from his companions. All his actions and movements were characterized by simplicity and humility. Anything savouring of artificiality was repugnant to his nature.

The Holy Prophet (peace and blessings of Allah be upon him) did not make decisions in hot haste, he decided matters after having weighed their pros and cons carefully and after having taken his companions in full confidence. Once the matter was resolved, he spared no pains in giving it a practical shape.

His generosity not only towards his own friends but even towards his enemies is unparalleled in history. The long and obstinate struggle carried on ceaselessly by the Meccans against him, and the atrocities which they perpetrated without any qualm of conscience, would have induced any other conqueror to take revenge, leaving behind him indelible traces of fire and blood. "But Muhammad, excepting a few criminals, granted general pardon, and nobly casting into oblivion the memory of the past, with all its mockery, its affronts and persecutions, he treated even the foremost of his opponents with a gracious and even friendly consideration. Not less marked was the forbearance shown to 'Abdullah and the disaffected citizens of Medina, who for so many years persistently thwarted his designs and resisted his authority, nor the clemency with which he received the submissive advances of tribes that before had been the most hostile, even in the hour of victory."

Firm Belief

The most striking point in the life of Muhammad (peace be upon him) is his implicit faith in Allah and his constant endeavour to be always in communion with Him. God was the vital spark of his spiritual flame. Such was the Prophet's close relation with his Creator that no one can read the account of his sacred life without having deepened within him a sense of the Majesty of Allah and of His overruling Providence. It was sublime and unshakable faith in Providence which may be called the keynote of the Prophet's character. Prayer and communion with Allah were the basic sources of his strength. His constant and vivid sense of an all-pervading providence influenced all his thoughts and actions. He never took up any work, major or minor, without mentioning the Name of Allah. In trouble and affliction, as well as in joy and sorrow, he always saw and humbly acknowledged the Majesty and Power of Allah, the Benevolent, the Merciful.

Humble and meek to the highest degree, the Holy Prophet had the courage of the bravest man. He had the conviction that the mighty hand of Allah would protect him from all evil designs of the enemies. Filled with this faith he showed unflinching fortitude and unswerving steadfastness under the most trying circumstances. Despair and despondency were unknown to him. He was always calm, self-possessed contented and happy, both in prosperity and adversity. He had to endure privation and, hardships throughout his life. He remained, nevertheless, strong and steadfast amidst the severest opposition and apparent helplessness. "Surrounded by a little group of faithful men and women, he met insults, menaces, dangers and persecutions with a lofty and patient trust in the power of his Maker." He and his family often had to pass several days without food and frequently had to content themselves with a handful of dates, but nobody ever heard a word of complaint from their lips. He was the Messenger of Allah and as such he had made the preaching of the Divine Message the sole purpose of his life. All other considerations were subservient to it. Even in the most adverse circumstances, his heart was aglow with the belief that he would receive a reward from the Creator for all the hardships that he had endured.

Good Deeds

The daily routine of his life was extremely rigorous. After the morning prayer he received people so as to educate them. He even settled disputes and administered justice; received envoys and dictated despatches and then the assembly was adjourned. The public function now over, he used to go to one of his wives, and do any job which she wanted him to do. He even went to the market for shopping. Then another short prayer was performed after which he visited the sick, and the poor, and called at the houses of his friends and then he went to the mosque for the noonday prayer. After coming back from the mosque he took his meal, if it was available, and then retired to his private apartment for some rest and then again went to the mosque for the afternoon prayer.

After the prayer, the Holy Prophet would go to his wives and would sit with them till children claimed his time. He led the evening prayer and then took his supper and attended either to his household affairs or spent his time in the company of his devoted followers and explained to them the teachings of Islam. He led the night prayer in the mosque and then returned to his home for prayers in solitude and rest. He slept for a few hours only and then rose and prayed and meditated and again retired to the bed only for a brief time, rising again for the morning prayer, when the day's work began once again. His energy was extraordinary. He seldom complained of fatigue.

One is simply astonished when one reviews the greatness of the purpose, the meagreness of the sources and yet the astounding results which the Holy Prophet achieved in the brief span of his ministry. "The most famous men created arms, laws and empires only. They founded, if anything at all, no more than material powers, which often crumbled before their eyes. This man moved not only armies, legislation, empires, peoples, dynasties, but millions of men in one-third of the then inhabited world; and more than that, he moved the altars, the gods, the religions, the ideas, the beliefs and souls."

Judged by all standards of human greatness, we find him on the loftiest height which can possibly be conceived of. The most amazing aspect of his life, however, is that in spite of his astounding achievements and his close intimacy with Allah, he never claimed to be anything but a mortal who had been bidden to announce the Message of his Lord to humanity so that it might live in harmony with the Will of the Creator. He not only forcefully disclaimed any divinity for himself, but also warned his followers to attribute any such thing to him. He was entrusted with the sacred task of propagating the Divinity of Allah, the Sole Creator, Sustainer, Master and Sovereign of the universe and this work he performed most eminently.

> May Allah and His angels shower their choicest blessings on him—the Mercy of both the worlds! Amen!

10

Guidelines from the Pious

Hadrat Abu Bakr

In the various accounts about Hadrat Abu Bakr that have come down to us, we come across some anecdotes which illuminate certain aspects of the life of Hadrat Abu Bakr. We refer to some of these anecdotes in this Chapter.

Reaction to praise. Once, someone highly praised Hadrat Abu Bakr. After the man who praised him had left, Hadrat Abu Bakr prayed to God:

> "O Allah, You know me more than myself, and I know myself more than these people who praise me. Make me better than what they think of me, and forgive those sins of mine of which they have no knowledge, and do not hold me responsible for what they say."

Milking the Goats. Before becoming the Caliph, Hadrat Abu Bakr used to milk the goats of the widows in the Mohalla. When he passed through the street after becoming the Caliph, one of the widows remarked, "Now, he would not milk the goats for us". Addressing the widows, Hadrat Abu Bakr said, "No, the Khilafat would make no change. I would continue to milk your goats."

The Two Lions. On an occasion when Hadrat Abu Bakr was busy with the preparation of plans in connection with the campaigns in Syria and Iraq, a companion presented a case concerning his tribe for the decision of the caliph. That irritated Hadrat Abu Bakr, and he said:

> "I am busy considering plans to crush the two lions who are waiting for an opportunity to destroy the Muslims and you are diverting my attention to petty matters".

Revelations about Musailima. After the death of the false prophet Musailima; a deputation of Banu Hanifa waited on Hadrat Abu Bakr. He enquired of them what were the teachings of the false prophet. As a specimen of his teaching they recited the following verse which was alleged to have been revealed to him:

> "O frog ! holy are you. You do not prevent the drinker, nor do you make the water dirty. Half the world belongs to us, and half to the Quraish, but the Quraish are a cruel people."

On hearing this, Hadrat Abu Bakr remarked: "God be praised. Is this the divine word? It has no sublimity of divinity. To what depths he had dragged you".

Necklace of His Sister. On the occasion of the conquest of Makkah, the necklace of his sister was wrenched from her neck by one of the horsemen. To the people assembled in the mosque, Hadrat Abu Bakr said, "I call for the necklace of my sister in the name of God." He repeated this three times, and when there was no response he said, "O sister, reckon upon your necklace as a present to God, for by Allah there is little of honesty among men now-a-days."

Veterans of the Bakr. On one occasion, Hadrat Abu Bakr was asked, "O Vicegerent of the Apostle of God, will you not employ in service those who fought at Badr?" Hadrat Abu Bakr said, "I know their dignity, but I am loath to defile them with the world? "

Doing Things Himself. Once when Hadrat Abu Bakr was riding a camel, the reins of the camel dropped from his hands. He came down from the camel to pick up the reins. He was asked why he had not asked other persons to pick up the reins for him. He said, "My Prophet has ordered me to do my things myself, and not beg anything from any human being."

No Distinction. Once Hadrat Abu Bakr was sitting with a number of persons. A person came, and he said, "Peace be to you, O Caliph of the Prophet". Hadrat Abu Bakr felt irritated and said, "There is no distinction between the Caliph and other Muslims; why have you wished peace to the Caliph alone and not to the other members of the assembly?

No Train of Followers. In the second year of his caliphate, Hadrat Abu Bakr went to Makkah on pilgrimage. On this occasion many persons gathered around him and began to follow in his train. Hadrat Abu Bakr wanted them to disperse for he did not want to be given any undue importance to himself.

Head of Defeated Enemy. Once a commander sent to Hadrat Abu Bakr the head of the defeated enemy. Hadrat Abu Bakr deprecated the practice as un-Islamic. He issued instructions to all concerned that in future the heads of the defeated enemy should not be cut for despatch to him. He urged that due respect should be shown to the dead, even though they were enemies.

Hunting of Game. Once a hunter hunted a raven with large wings. It was presented to Hadrat Abu Bakr. He turned it over and said," No game is hunted and no tree is felled, save it has neglected the praise of God".

Holding the Tongue. Once in anger, Hadrat Abu Bakr said something which he later regretted. He held his tongue and said, 'This it is which has brought me to that to which I have come".

More Poisonous than Poison. Hadrat Abu Bakr was critical of women's passion for gold and perfume. He said, 'The most deadly of things, more poisonous than poison, are the two that are red, gold and saffron."

Unfulfilled Hopes. When Abdullah a son of Hadrat Abu Bakr was on death bed, he kept looking towards the cushion.

When he was dead, the persons who were attending him said to Hadrat Abu Bakr that at the time of death, his son had been looking towards the cushion. When the cushion was moved, some dinars were found thereunder. Seeing them, Hadrat Abu Bakr wrung his hands and said, "Verily we belong to God, and to Him is our return". Thereafter he recited the verse:

> "You shall not cease to announce the death of a friend until you are as he is;
>
> And verily, the youth cherishes a hope and dies without attaining it."

His Reputation and Decorum. Once Hadrat Abu Bakr was asked whether he ever drank wine during the days of Ignorance. He replied, "God forbid, I never touched wine even in the days of Ignorance". He was asked "why"' and he said, "I sought to preserve my reputation and retain my decorum, and verily he who drinks wine destroys his reputation and his decorum".

Joy not Fleeting. Once the poet Labid had a sitting with Hadrat Abu Bakr when he recited the verse "Is not everything but God unprofitable?" Hadrat Abu Bakr said, "You have spoken truly". Then Labid recited, "And every joy is surely fleeting". Hadrat Abu Bakr said, "This is not correct. There is with God a joy which is not fleeting."

Freedom from Accountability. Hadrat Abu Bakr used to say that accountability was a great challenge for man. Once he entered a garden where he saw a ring dove sitting on a tree. Seeing the bird, Hadrat Abu Bakr heaved a deep sigh, and said:

> "Happy you are O bird, that eats of the trees and seeks shelter beneath them, and are not called to account. Would that I were like you?"

His Father's Seat. Once Hadrat Abu Bakr was addressing the congregation in the mosque from the pulpit. Imam Hasan, the son of Hadrat Ali came to the pulpit and addressing Hadrat Abu Bakr said,' Come down from the seat of my father." Hadrat Abu Bakr said. "You speak the truth, this is your father's seat". He put up the child on his lap and wept. Hadrat Ali intervened to say, "This was not said at my instance". Hadrat Abu Bakr said, "I know that."

His Love for the Holy Prophet. Once, addressing the Holy Prophet, Hadrat Abu Bakr said, "O Apostle of God, if you were to ask me to kill myself, I will do that." The Holy Prophet said, "Yes, I know that. I feel proud of you."

Distribution of the Spoils of War. Whenever the spoils of war came, Hadrat Abu Bakr would distribute them equally among all the people. Some of the companions suggested that he should recognise precedence in faith as a ground for preference in distribution of spoils. Hadrat Abu Bakr said, 'The recognition of precedence in faith is for the Lord. It is for Him to reward the piety of such persons who have excelled in faith. These gifts which I distribute are but an accident of the present life."

Honour Comes from Allah. In the second year of his caliphate, Hadrat Abu Bakr went to Makkah to perform the pilgrimage and stayed there with his father Abu Qahafa. On that occasion, the notables of the city came to wait on him. Referring to these notables, Abu Qahafa said, 'They are the notables of our city. Make much of them, and honour them." Hadrat Abu Bakr said, "I will certainty make much of them, but as for honour there is none save that which comes from Allah."

Precedence for Islam. In the Battle of Badr, Abdul Rahman a son of Hadrat Abu Bakr who was yet a non-Muslim fought against the Muslims. Later Abdul Rahman became a Muslim. He told his father that at the battle there were occasions when he could strike at him, but then out of love for him he turned aside. Hadrat Abu Bakr said, "If I had such an occasion, you being an infidel, I would not have spared you."

He asked his son to divorce his wife. Abdullah another son of Hadrat Abu Bakr was so much lost in the love of his wife Atika that he did not participate in the battles against the non-Muslims. He even neglected his prayers. Thereupon Hadrat Abu Bakr asked him to divorce his wife.

He was Asked to Sheathe His Sword. At the Battle of Uhud, Abdul Rahman a son of Hadrat Abu Bakr again fought against the Muslim,. Before the battle began Abdul Rahman stepped forth from the ranks, and threw a challenge to the Muslims to let some one step forward and have a duel with him. Hadrat Abu Bakr accepted the challenge, and was about to fight a duel with his son, when the Holy Prophet commanded, 'Sheathe your sword and do not make us anxious about your person".

***He Slapped a Jew in the Face*.** Finhas, a Jewish rabbi said: "We are rich but your Allah is poor. We are independent of Him but He needs us. Had He been independent of us. He would not have given us interest, which He has denied to you." Hadrat Abu Bakr felt outraged at this blasphemy. He slapped the Jew in the face and said,' Were it not for the treaty between the Muslims and the Jews, I would have cut off your head O enemy of Allah."

***Fight for the Prophet*.** When the Muslims encamped at Hudaibiya, Urwab. Masud came to see the Holy Prophet on behalf of the Quraish. He insinuated that at the time of crisis, the followers of the Holy Prophet were likely to abandon him. Thereupon Hadrat Abu Bakr flared up and said, "May God curse you; how dare you think that we will abandon the Holy Prophet. Rest assured, we will fight to the last for him."

***Hold Fast to the Stirrup of the Holy Prophet*.** Hadrat Umar regarded the treaty of Hudaibiya as humiliating to the Muslims. He saw Hadrat Abu Bakr, and wanted him to persuade the Holy Prophet to withdraw from the pact. Hadrat Abu Bakr said, 'The Holy Prophet knows things more than we do. What the Holy Prophet has done is in the interests of the Muslims. Do not be critical. Hold fast to the stirrup of the Holy Prophet."

***Judging What He did not Know*.** In the case of the ordeal of falsehood, after God had revealed to the Holy Prophet the innocence of HadratAyesha, she said to Hadrat Abu Bakr, "Father would you not have pardoned me if there had been no revelation." Hadrat Abu Bakr said, "What heaven would cover me, and what earth would carry me if I judged that which I did not know?"

***He Wanted God to Forgive Him*.** Mistah was a relative of Hadrat Abu Bakr whom Hadrat Abu Bakr used to pay an allowance. Mistah took active part in spreading the calumny against Hadrat Ayesha. Thereupon Hadrat Abu Bakr swore that he would no longer help Mistah. Thereupon the verse descended on the Holy Prophet, "Let not those in affluence swear not to aid poor kinsmen. Let them forgive. Do you not wish that God should forgive you?" Hearing this Hadrat Abu Bakr restored the allowance to Mistah saying, "Yes, I wish Allah to forgive me."

His Feet Became Dusty in the Service of God. When Usamah's army left for Syria, Hadrat Abu Bakr walked for some distance along with the army to see it depart. Usamah was riding on horseback, and he requested Hadrat Abu Bakr that he should be permitted to dismount or the Caliph should also ride on a horse. Hadrat Abu Bakr said, "No, neither shall you dismount nor shall I mount a horse, for according to a tradition of the Holy Prophet, he whose foot becomes dusty in the way of God will be preserved from hell fire."

He Excelled All in the Matter of Generosity. For the financing of the expedition to Tabuk, the Holy Prophet invited contributions from all his followers. Hadrat Umar made a liberal contribution. When the Holy Prophet asked him, how much he had left for himself and his family, he said that he had given one half of his wealth for the cause of Allah and had left one half for himself and his family. Then Hadrat Abu Bakr came loaded with his contribution, and the Holy Prophet put him the same question as to how much he had left for himself and his family. Hadrat Abu Bakr said, "I have brought all that I had. I have left Allah and His Prophet for myself and my family". Thus Hadrat Abu Bakr excelled every one in generosity.

He Anticipated Hadrat Umar. It is related that a blind old woman lived in a suburb of Madina and had no one to support her. Hadrat Umar used to go in disguise to the house of the old woman, but was always surprised to find that someone else had anticipated him and had supplied the wants of the old woman. One night Hadrat Umar went to the house of the old woman earlier than usual and hid himself to watch as to who attended to the wants of the old lady. He had not to wait long for soon a man arrived who attended to the needs of the old woman, and this man was Hadrat Abu Bakr.

Foremost in Breaking Glad Tidings. Once in the presence of Hadrat Abu Bakr and Hadrat Umar the Holy Prophet said thar the recitation of the Holy Qur'an by Ibn Masud was the most perfect, and had been approved of by God. Later, Hadrat Umar went to the house of Ibn Masud to tell him of the approval of God. He thought that he would be the first man to give the glad tidings to Ibn Masud. When Hadrat Umar reached the house of Ibn Masud he found that Hadrat Abu Bakr had already been to the house of Ibn Masud and has informed him of the glad tidings.

Sweet Dish. It is related that one of the wives of Hadrat Abu Bakr once wished for a sweet dish. The Caliph said that he had no money for such a luxury. She said, "Then permit me to save something daily, and then have a sweet dish when sufficient amount has been collected." This he permitted and in the course of a few days she saved some amount. Hadrat Abu Bakr deposited the amount in the treasury. He had his daily allowance reduced by the amount of the saving, holding that if something could be saved it meant that the allowance sanctioned in his favour was excessive to that extent.

The Physician. During the course of his last sickness, some companions who visited him said, "O Caliph of the Prophet, should we call a physician to examine you?" He said "The physician has already examined me". What did he say, they asked. He said that the physician had said that he would do with the patient what he would will.

Encomium for the Prophet. During the course of his illness while looking at Hadrat Abu Bakr, Hadrat Ayesha recited:

"That bright face whose freshness gives water to the clouds,

Is affectionate towards the orphans,

And protects the honour of the widows."

Hadrat Abu Bakr opened his eyes and said, "No, the Holy Prophet alone deserves this encomium."

The Coffin. When at the point of death, Hadrat Abu Bakr desired that the two pieces of the cloth that he was wearing should be washed and used for his coffin, while the third piece could be purchased. Hadrat Ayesha said that they were not so poor as to be not able to purchase all the three pieces. He said, "New pieces of cloth can be better utilised for the living, than for the dead. The cloth that covers the dead body is for absorbing blood and pus only."

Thus spoke Hadrat Abu Bakr. Hadrat Abu Bakr was of a contemplative bent of mind. He often expressed his thoughts in words conspicuous for their wisdom. A number of his sayings has come down to us, and these show the depths and dimensions of his thought and philosophy. Some of the sayings of Hadrat Abu Bakr which have assumed the character of proverbs are given hereunder:

Greatness. About greatness, Hadrat Abu Bakr said:

(1) Run away from greatness, and greatness will follow you.

(2) There is greatness in the fear of God, contentment in faith of God, and honour in humility.

Good Actions. About good actions, Hadrat Abu Bakr said:

(1) Good actions are a guard against the blows of adversity.

(2) Be good to others, that will protect you against evil.

(3) If you expect the blessings of God, be good to His people.

(4) Every day, nay every moment, try to do some good deed.

Death. About death, he said:

(1) Have an earnestness for death, and you will have life.

(2) Death is the easiest of all things after it, and the hardest of all things before it.

Knowledge. About knowledge, he said:

(1) The more knowledge you have, the greater will be your fear of Allah.

(2) Without knowledge action is useless, and knowledge without action is futile.

(3) Knowledge is the life of the mind.

(4) When a noble man learns knowledge he becomes humble; when an ignoble person gains knowledge he gets conceited .

(5) When knowledge is limited, it leads to folly; when knowledge exceeds a certain limit, it leads to exploitation.

Advice. In the matter of advice, he said:

(1) When you seek advice, do not withhold any facts from the person whose advice you seek.

(2) When you advise any person you should be guided by the fear of God.

(3) If any body seeks your advice, offer right and since advice.

(4) He who is not impressed by sound advice lacks faith.

Kindness. About kindness he said:

(1) If you expect the blessings of God, be kind to His people.

(2) He who aspires to paradise should learn to deal with the people with kindness.

(3) He who fears to weep should learn to be kind to those who weep.

Self-control. About self-control he said, "If you want to control other people, first control your self."

Patience and Confidence. With regard to patience and confidence, he said:

"Patience is half faith, and confidence is full faith."

Society of Evil Persons. About the society of evil persons he held, "Solitude is better than the society of evil persons."

Honesty. About honesty he said, "The greatest truth is honesty, and the greatest falsehood is dishonesty."

Treatment of Muslims. About the treatment of Muslims he said, "Do not look down upon any Muslim, for even the most inferior believer is great in the eyes of God."

Help and cooperation. About help and cooperation, he said:

(1) "God blesses him who helps his brother."

(2) "Do not non-cooperate with one another, and have no grudge or jealousy."

(3) "Muslims should live like brothers."

(4) "God helps those who fear Him."

(5) "Allah will help him who moves in the way of Allah."

Jihad. About "Jihad", he said:

(1) "The people who abandon Jihad fall a victim to humility and degradation."

(2) "Jihad is obligatory for the Muslims."

(3) 'To fight against the infidels is Jihad, but to fight against your evil self is greater Jihad."

Intentions. With regard to intentions, he said, "Intentions count in your actions."

Sadaqah. In the matter of the offering of "Sadaqah" he said, "When you offer any Sadaqah to a beggar, do it with humility and respect, for what you are offering is an offer to Allah".

Mosques. With regard to mosques he said: "He who builds a mosque in the way of Allah, God will build a house for him in the paradise."

Way of Life. About the way of life he said, "Follow the way of life, which the Holy Prophet has shown you, for verily that is the right path."

Prayers. With regard to prayers, he said, "He who prays for five times a day is in the protection of God, and he who is protected by God cannot be harmed by anyone."

Neighbours. About neighbours, he said, "You should not quarrel with your neighbour, for he will remain where he is, but your high handedness will become the talk of the people."

Appearance of Things. About the outward appearance of things he said:

(1) "Maybe a thing that you do not like is really in your interest."

(2) "It is possible that a thing that you may desire may be against your interest."

Love of God. About the love of God, and the love of the world, he said, "He who comes to take the love of God can have no taste for the love of the world."

Becoming a Muslim. About becoming a Muslim, he said, "He who becomes a Muslim does so in his own interest."

Falsehood. About falsehood, he said, "He who indulges in falsehood will find the paths of paradise shut to him."

Boasting. About boasting, he said, "He who boasts lowers himself."

Pride. About pride he said, "Pride in the case of a rich man is bad, but pride in the case of a poor man is worse."

Elation. In the matter of elation, he said, "Do not get elated at any victory, for all such victory is subject to the will of God."

Avoidance of Complaints. With regard to the avoidance of complaints he said, "He who avoids complaints invites happiness."

Attraction of the Things of the World. About the attraction of the things of the world, he said, "If an ignorant person is attracted by the things of the world this is bad, but if a learned person is thus attracted, it is worse." He also said, "O man you are busy working for the world, and the world is busy trying to turn you out."

Justice. About justice, he said: "In the matter of justice, all should be equal in your eyes."

Deception and Faithlessness. About deception and faithlessness he said, "Do not deceive or be faithless even with your enemy."

Measure. About the use of measure he said, "Use same measure for selling which you use for purchase."

Sin. About sin, he said: (1) It is good to repent from sin; it is better to avoid sin. (2) It is bad for a young man to sin, but it is worse for an old man to sin.

Evil. About evil he said, "Cursed is the man who dies himself, but the evil done by him survives."

Dyeing of Hair. In the case of the dyeing of hair he said, "Youth is not restored by the dyeing of your hair."

Early Rising. About early rising, he said, "It is a matter of shame that in the morning the birds should be awake earlier than you."

Piety. About Piety he said, "Piety is the most solid goodness, and the vilest of what is evil is vice."

Truth and Falsehood. About truth and falsehood he said, 'Truth is a trust, falsehood a treason."

Vain Desires. About vain desires, he said, "Do not follow vain desires for verily he prospers who is preserved from lust, greed and anger."

The Best. HadratAbu Bakr prayed, "O Lord, render You the best of my life its close, the best of my deeds as the last, and the best of my days the day of Your meeting."

> "O God verily I ask of You that which may be the best for me in the end. O God vouchsafe that the last good that You bestow upon me, is Your approbation."

Deadly Things. Hadrat Abu Bakr said, "The most deadly of things are those that are red, gold and saffron."

Reward of the Believer. Hadrat Abu Bakr said, 'The true believer is rewarded in every thing, even in affliction."

Life of the World. About the life of the world, Hadrat Abu Bakr said, "Our abode in this world is transitory. Our life therein is but a loan. Our breaths are numbered, and our indolence is manifest."

Condolence. While condoling the death of a companion, Hadrat Abu Bakr said to the bereaved family:

> "There is no harm in patience, and no profit in lamentation. Death is easiest to bear than that which precedes it, and more severe than that which comes after it.

> Remember the death of the Apostle of God, and your sorrow will be lessened."

Prayer for a Dead Man. When praying for a dead man Hadrat Abu Bakr said:

> "O God! his people and his goods and his kindred have forsaken this servant of Yours. His sin was grievous, but You are Merciful and Compassionate."

Hadrat Abu Bakr's eloquence. Hadrat Abu Bakr was known for his eloquence and oratory. He used to address the faithful every week on Fridays. His sermons and addresses were the specimen of masterly eloquence, every word thereof vibrated with superb faith and appealed directly to the heart. All his sermons and addresses have not been preserved. Only a few of his sermons and addresses have come down to us, and these classical addresses which are veritable gems of literature evoke our admiration.

Inaugural Address. On assuming office, he delivered the following address, which is a unique document for the guidance of all rulers:

> "Gentlemen, I have been placed in authority, though by Allah I was averse to the assumption of authority. I would have been pleased if any of you had taken over the office, and I would have assisted him. I have been made to rule over you though I am not the most worthy among you. If you expect me to act as did the Holy Prophet of God, know that I cannot do so, for the Apostle of God was a servant whom the Lord honoured with His inspiration and preserved him thereby from error. I am an ordinary mortal and not better than any of you. Therefore, watch over me. When you see that I am steadfast and obey Allah and His Prophet, then obey

me. When you see that I turn aside from the right path do not obey me. Help me if I am in the right; set me right if I am in the wrong. Know that I have a devil that seizes upon me. Therefore, when you see me enraged avoid me for at that time I cannot be influenced by your counsels or glad salutations. We have the Qur'an for our guidance. We have also with us the instructions of the Holy Prophet. These will be our unerring guides. Know O men that piety is the most solid goodness, and the vilest of what is evil is vice. Truth is a trust; falsehood a treason. The weak among you shall be strong with me till God willing his rights have been vindicated; and the strong among you shall be weak with me till, if the Lord wills, I have taken what is due from him."

Guidelines for the Faithful. In the following sermon, Hadrat Abu Bakr set the guidelines for the conduct of the faithful:

"Beware you of following vain desire, for verily he prospers who is preserved from lust, greed and anger; and beware you of pride for what pride belongs to him who is made of earth, and whom the worms devour after death. Today you are alive; tomorrow you may be dead. Therefore act uprightly from day to day and hour to hour. Be you patient for every work is accomplished through patience. Be you watchful for watchfulness is profitable. Act uprightly for a good act is acceptable to God. Refrain from things against which the Lord has warned you under pain of His wrath. Vie you with one another in hastening to obtain the things which the Lord has promised you in His mercy. Be heedful and in fear for the Lord has declared to you things for which He destroyed those that were before you and things through which He delivered those before you. Verily He has manifested to you in His book His commands and His

> prohibitions, the works He approves and that He abhors. God is He Whose assistance should be implored. There is no power or strength but in the Lord. Obey God, preserve your portion of excellence. Make your charitable donations even when you are poor. O Servants of God, think of your brethren and companions who have departed. Verily, the Lord has no co-partner, and between Him and any of His creatures there is no mediatory influence that can bestow good upon him or avert from him evil save in His worship and obedience to His commands for verily there is no good after which comes hell fire, and no evil after which comes heaven."

The Light of the Book of God. In another sermon, Hadrat Abu Bakr said:

> "I commend to you piety to God. Praise Him as befits Him. Mingle desire with fear, for God praised Zikriya and the people of his house and said, "These strove to excel in good works and called upon Us with love and with fear and humbled themselves before Us." Therefore, know, O servants of God, that the Lord holds your lives as a pledge for what is due to Him, and has taken your compacts regarding it, and has purchased of you a little that is perishable, in exchange for eternal abundance; and this Book of God is among you, whose light cannot be extinguished, nor its wonders end. Therefore, seek you illumination from its light, and accept counsel from His Book and seek light from it in the day of darkness. Verily He has created you for His worship and has appointed for you guardian angels honourable in the sight of God writing down actions, who know that which you do. And know O servants of God that you proceed and draw nigh to an appointed time, the knowledge of which, verily, is hidden from you. Vie you

> with one another in fulfilling the obligations of your appointed times before your appointed periods are completed, lest they cast you upon the evilest of your works, and verily there are some who have made over the obligations of their appointed times on others, and have taken no heed of themselves. Therefore, I forbid you to be like them. Then haste, flee, flee for behind you is a nimble pursuer, swift of deed. Where are the comely, beautiful of countenance, exulting in their youth? Where are the monarchs who built cities and entrenched them round about? Where are they who boasted of victories on fields of battle? Verily their pillars were overthrown when fortune betrayed them, and they went down into the darkness of the grave. Haste, flee, flee."

Importance of dreams. Before the Holy Prophet was commissioned as the Messenger of God, the truth was generally revealed to him through dreams. His dreams were always true, and cast a shadow of the events to come. The Holy Prophet accordingly attached great importance to dreams. Dreams were regarded as a species of revelation, and the interpretation of dreams became a matter of spiritual exercise.

Hadrat Abu Bakr's expertise in the interpretation of dreams. According to a tradition, the Holy Prophet said that he was enjoined by God to relate his dreams to Hadrat Abu Bakr. Whenever the Holy Prophet had a dream, he would relate it to Hadrat Abu Bakr. Whenever Hadrat Abu Bakr had a dream, he would likewise relate it to the Holy Prophet. They would then exchange views, and arrive at an agreed interpretation about the dream. In early Islam, interpretation of dreams was regarded as a spiritual exercise, and it was held that only those who had pure heats and possessed an inward vision could have meaningful dreams and interpret their significance. According to Ibn Sirin, who is regarded as the Imam of the science of the interpretation of dreams, Hadrat Abu Bakr was the best interpreter of dreams after the Holy Prophet.

Battle of Uhud. On the eve of the Battle of Uhud, the Holy Prophet saw in a dream that he was driving some cows, and some cows out of these were slaughtered. He also saw a dent on his sword. Hadrat Abu Bakr interpreted this dream to signify that some of the companions of the Holy Prophet would be martyred in the Battle of Uhud. The dent on the sword signified that one of the relatives of the Holy Prophet would be martyred.

Siege of Taff. When after the fall of Makkah, Taifwas besieged, the Holy Prophet saw in a dream that he had with him a bowl of butter. A cock pecked at it and split it. Hadrat Abu Bakr interpreted the dream to mean that the siege of Taif would have to be raised without actual conquest.

Expedition against Banu Jadhima.When Khalid was sent on an expedition against Banu Jadhima of Kinana, the Holy Prophet saw in a dream that he swallowed a morsel of dates mixed with butter and enjoyed their taste. Some of them, however, stuck in his gullet when he tried to swallow them. Then Ali thrust in his hand and pulled them out. Hadrat Abu Bakr interpreted the dream to mean that something would happen in the campaign against Banu Jadhima at which the Holy Prophet would be happy as well as unhappy, and that he would send Hadrat Ali to put matters right. In the campaign against Banu Jadhima, the tribe was overpowered, and at this the Holy Prophet felt happy. The Holy Prophet, however, felt unhappy when he learnt that Khalid had killed some Muslims as well. The Holy Prophet said, "O God I am innocent before Thee of what Khalid has done". Ali was then sent to the tribe to pay blood money.

Herds of Black and White Sheep. On one occasion, the Holy Prophet saw in a dream that he was driving a herd of black sheep.

Then he found himself driving a herd of white sheep. After some time the two herds were inextricably intermingled and all attempts to separate them were of no avail. Interpreting the dream, Hadrat Abu Bakr said that the black sheep signified the Arabs while the white sheep signified the people of other regions. The dream indicated that Islam would spread to other regions beyond considerations of colour and creed.

Hudaibiya Treaty. On the occasion of the Hudaibiya treaty, the Holy Prophet saw in a dream that he was shaving his head after the pilgrimage. Hadrat Abu Bakr interpreted the dream to signify that the main Hajj would have to be deferred to the following year.

Two and a Half Steps. Once the Holy Prophet saw in a dream that he and Hadrat Abu Bakr were walking together side by side. Then the Holy Prophet outpaced Hadrat Abu Bakr by two and half steps. Hadrat Abu Bakr interpreted the dream to mean that the Holy Prophet would be the first to be summoned to God, and that Hadrat Abu Bakr would follow him after two and a half years.

Drawing Water from a Well. On another occasion, the Holy Prophet saw in a dream that he was drawing water from a well. Then he stepped aside and asked Hadrat Abu Bakr to draw water. Hadrat Abu Bakr was able to draw water for two to three rounds only, and then he showed signs of exhaustion. Hadrat Umar then took up the job, and he was able to complete ten rounds. Hadrat Abu Bakr interpreted the dream to signify that after the passing away of the Holy Prophet, the caliphate would vest in Hadrat Abu Bakr whose period of office would be two to three years only. He will be succeeded by Hadrat Umar whose period of office will be ten years.

Wading through Night Soil. Once Hadrat Abu Bakr saw in a dream that he was wading through the night soil of the people. He related the dream to the Holy Prophet who interpreted it to mean that after the death of the Holy Prophet, Hadrat Abu Bakr would be called upon to undertake apostasy campaigns.

Three Moons. Once, Hadrat Ayesha saw in a dream three moons descend on her house. She related the dream to Hadrat Abu Bakr, and he interpreted it that her house would be the burial place of three luminaries of the world. Subsequently the Holy Prophet, Hadrat Abu Bakr, and Hadrat Umar were buried in her house.

Urinating Blood. Once a person waited on Hadrat Abu Bakr and asked for the interpretation of his dream. In the dream he had seen himself urinating blood. Hadrat Abu Bakr addressing him said, "God curse you. It appears that you go to your wife even when she is with monthly course. Desist from that."

Opening of the Sky. Mahrz b. Nuzlah, a companion saw in a dream that the sky had opened for him and that he had reached the seventh heaven. Hadrat Abu Bakr interpreted the dream to signify that he would meet the death of a martyr, and that his abode would be in paradise.

Hadrat Umar

Hadrat Umar was known for his great knowledge and wisdom. He often expressed his thoughts in words conspicuous for their wisdom. A number of his sayings have come down to us, and these show the depths and dimensions of his thoughts and expressions. We give hereunder the various sayings attributed to Hadrat Umar, which we have been able to gather from various sources:

- "He who keeps his own counsel keeps his affairs in his own hands."

- "Fear him, whom you hate".
- The wisest man is he who can account for his actions." "Do not put off today's work for tomorrow."
- "Money cannot help lifting its head."
- "What regresses, never progresses."
- "He who does not know evil will fall into it."
- "When a man puts me a question, I judge of his Intelligence."
- "Don't forget your own self while preaching to others."
- "The less of the world, the freer you live."
- "Avoidance of sin is lighter than the pain of remorse."
- "On every dishonest man, there are two watchmen, his possessions, and his way of living."
- "If patience and gratitude had been two she camels, it would have mattered little on which I rode."
- "May God have mercy on him who sends me my faults as a present."
- "Preserve the sayings of those people who are indifferent to the world. They say only that what God wishes them to say."
- "Fear God, for He alone lives; all other things are liable to perish."
- The wisest among you is he whose sustenance is the fear of God."

- "Praise God, for by praise His blessings multiply."
- "Fear God, for that is fortune; indifference to God is misfortune."
- "Be patient; patience is a pillar of faith."
- "Acquire knowledge and teach it to the people."
- "Be dignified, honest, and truthful."
- "Do not be an arrogant scholar, for scholarship cannot subsist with arrogance."
- "When you see that any scholar loves the world, then his scholarship is in doubt."
- "God forbid, men should be jealous of knowledge as they are jealous of women."
- "May God bless the man who says less and does more."
- The criterion of action is that to-day's work should not be deferred till the following day."
- "Trust is that there should be no difference between what you do and say and what you think."
- "Learn the Arabic language; it will sharpen your wisdom."
- "Luxury is an obstacle, and so is the fatness of the body."
- "A man may be as straight as an arrow, but even then he will have some critics."
- "O Allah do not give me in excess lest I may be disobedient to You, and do not give me less, lest I may forget You."

- "Allah loves moderation and hates extravagance and excess."
- "He who went to the kings to seek favours went away from God."
- "Sit with those who love God, for that enlightens the mind."
- "Before Allah that is the best dinner which people eat together."
- "As long as you are pure of heart, you speak the truth."
- "The pilgrims are the delegations of God."
- "If your ruler is just, praise God; if he is unjust, pray to God to rid you of him."
- "Allah is happy with such rulers whose slaves are under their control."
- "Forgive the people so that God may forgive you."
- "For the people prefer that which you prefer for yourself. Which you do not wish for yourself, do not impose on others."
- "In the eyes of God he is the best ruler who has secured prosperity and comfort for the people."
- "That ruler is most accursed whose misconduct leads to the distress of the people."
- "Every ruler should keep his door open to the people."

- "Understand the teachings of the Holy Qur'an for that is the source of knowledge."
- "Relate as few traditions as possible, lest by being involved in traditions the people overlook the Qur'an."
- "All the injunctions of Islam are based on reason."
- "The way to express gratitude to God is to give Zakat out of the property that He has bestowed on you."
- "In my view your greatest obligation is to offer prayers.
- He who fulfils this obligation with great regularity will be secure in his religion."
- "He who sleeps without offering the night prayer, may he never enjoy a sound sleep."
- "Women should offer Zakat on their ornaments."
- "Blessed are those who are martyred in the way of Allah."
- "In the preparation of Islam, commit no excess."
- "Without consultation, the caliphate is unlawful."
- "The ruler whose Intention is good will have the help of God in the administration of his affairs: he whose intention is bad will come to dlsgrace."
- "Do not accept gifts; that is bribery."
- "The Judge should always uphold the principle of equality before law."

- "May God curse the people who hesitate to dine with the slaves."

- "Do not be misled by a person's prayers and fasting: look to his sincerity and wisdom."

- "Do not be misled by hearing of any one's reputation."

- "He trusts in God who sows seed in the ground then depends on God."

- "Earning of livelihood by following some profession is better than living on charity."

- "He who has any public responsibility should perform his duties without caring for criticism."

- "He is to be preferred who has the urge to sin, but does not sin."

- "Do not depend upon the morality of a person until you have seen him behave while in anger."

- "I am surprised at three things. Man runs from death while death is inevitable. One sees minor faults of others, but overlooks his own major faults. When there is any defect to one's cattle he tries to cure it, but does not cure his own defects."

- 'To flatter is to slaughter."

- "He, who pretends to be what he is not, is a hypocrite."

- "If a person has ten habits out of which nine are good and one bad, that bad one will destroy the good ones."

- "Do not overeat: that invites disease."

- "He who wins through fraud is no winner."

- "He who wants paradise should hold fast to the community."

- "The efficacy of a prayer depends not on the words but on the sincerity of intention."

- "In the narration of facts refrain from poetising."

- "When you do not know of a thing say so plainly."

- "O I am not worried about the poverty of the Muslims. I am afraid lest by getting rich they might become proud and thereby Invite destruction."

- "In the performance of your duties neither be over zealous, nor indifferent."

Before the conquest of Mecca, Abu Sufiyan was the leader of the Quraish in Mecca. He was very hostile to Islam. He led the Quraish at the battle of Uhud. He was the leader of the Quraish at the battle of the Ditch. The Muslims suffered considerably at the hands of Abu Sufiyan. Umm Habiba a daughter of Abu Sufiyan, however, accepted Islam and was married to the Holy Prophet.

As Abu Sufiyan was the bitter enemy of Islam, Hadrat Umar was very bitter against him. At the time of the conquest of Mecca when Abu Sufiyan came to the Muslim camp for negotiation, Hadrat Umar sought the permission of the Holy Prophet to kill Abu Sufiyan. The Holy Prophet asked Hadrat Umar to wait and watch further developments.

Thereafter Abu Sufiyan and all the Quraish of Mecca became Muslims. As Abu Sufiyan was an aristocrat, even after becoming a Muslim he could not get rid of his past arrogance.

In Madina a complaint was lodged before Hadrat Umar against Abu Sufiyan. It was complained that Abu Sufiyan had constructed a house, and blocked the drainage so that the drainage water was diverted to the houses of neighbours thereby creating a nuisance and damaging such houses.

Hadrat Umar decided that when he visited Mecca on the occasion of the Hajj he would see the site, and pass the necessary orders on the spot. When Hadrat Umar came to Mecca he visited the site. It transpired that Abu Sufiyan had placed some stones in the drain in such a way that the flow of the sullage in the proper direction was obstructed and was instead diverted to the houses of the neighbours. Hadrat Umar felt convinced that the conduct of Abu Sufiyan was not fair.

Hadrat Umar summoned Abu Sufiyan and asked him to remove the stones so that the sullage should now be unobstructed. Abu Sufiyan contended that he had acted within his rights and as such was not going to comply with the orders of the Caliph. Hadrat Umar flourished his whip and said, "Abu Sufiyan I command you to remove these stones forthwith, otherwise I will whip you, your status not with standing."

Without further contention, Abu Sufiyan removed the stones in the manner desired by Hadrat Umar.

Thereupon turning his face to the Ka'aba Hadrat Umar said:

> "Praise be to God, Who, because of the power of Islam, made an ordinary man like Umar dominate over a chief like Abu Sufiyan."

Abu Sufiyan said:

> "All praise is due to God Who blessed me with the light of Islam which has shown me the true path, and made me bow before the truth".

Hadrat Umar said:

> "Abu Sufiyan! Congratulations, for Islam has shown you the true path."

Jabala bin Aiham was a Ghassanid prince. He became a convert to Islam and came to Madina. At Madina, Jabala stayed as the personal guest of Hadrat Umar. A few days later Hadrat Umar and Jabala travelled to Mecca for the purposes of pilgrimage. In Mecca too, Jabala was the State guest.

As Jabala was circum-ambulating the Holy Kaaba, his pilgrim scarf was accidentally trodden by a poor Arab of the Banu Fazara. That aroused the wrath of Jabala. Without waiting to listen to any explanation, Jabala buffeted the Arab in the face bruising him severely in the nose.

The Arab lodged a complaint with Hadrat Umar. Hadrat Umar sent for Jabala and asked him whether the charge levied against him by the Arab was true. Jabala answered haughtily "This rascal trod on my reverence for the Kaaba and, but for the prohibition to shed blood within the sacred premises, I would have slain the man on the spot, instead of merely thrashing him."

Hadrat Umar put the Arab to explanation and he said on oath that due to extraordinary rush, he trod on the scarf of Jabala accidentally.

Turning to Jabala, Hadrat Umar said. "Do you agree that what happened was accidental, or did this man deliberately offend you."

Jabala said, "I am not concerned with that. It might have been accidental but the fact remained that he trod on my scarf, thereby uncovering me. It must be borne in mind that I am a prince while he is a commoner."

Hadrat Umar said, "In Islam there is no distinction between a prince and a commoner. You could not take the law in your own hands merely on the ground that you are a prince, and he is a commoner."

Jabala felt annoyed and said, "I had thought that Islam would add to my dignity and prestige, and here Islam is becoming an instrument for my humiliation".

Hadrat Umar said, "Law must have its own course, and I am obliged to do justice. There are two alternatives. Either patch up with the man and satisfy him, or be prepared to face my verdict."

When Jabala saw that Hadrat Umar was serious in invoking the penal provisions of law he said, "Give me one day to ponder over the matter".

Hazrat Umar deferred his judgement for one day. That very night Jabala left for Syria secretly along with his retinue. From there he proceeded to Constantinople. In Constantinople he become a Christian. He said, "I denounce Islam because it does not discriminate between a prince and a commoner."

When Hadrat Umar came to know on the following day that Jabala had slipped away, he allowed the poor Arab adequate compensation from the Bait-ul-Mal.

It is related that when one night, Hadrat Umar was on his usual round in the streets of Madina, he heard a girl in a house singing:

> "Can I get some wine to drink ;
>
> Can I ever find access to Nasr bin Hajjaj
>
> A young man known for his beauty, youth and manners,

He who is of noble birth,

He whose company was a matter of joy".

Another girl friend sitting by her enquired who was Nasr.

The girl said, "Nasr is the most beautiful young man in Madina. I long that he should spend a night with me, when he and I should be alone."

The following day, Hadrat Umar summoned Nasr. When he saw him he wondered at his beauty. Undoubtedly he was the most beautiful young man in Madina. He had beautiful curly hair. Hadrat Umar called a barber and had the hair of Nasr cut.

Thereupon Nasr composed the following verses:

"Umar could not see my curls,

My hair which when combed waved like a chain ;

He made that head bald where once there were profuse hair ;

He who was bald headed felt jealous of him who had hair,

As he could not be proud of his hair, he deprived me of my hair. "

Hadrat Umar called Nasr again. Even though deprived of his hair he looked still more attractive. Hadrat Umar ordered that he should wear a turban.

Hadrat Umar called him again, and with turban he looked more manly and attractive. Thereupon Hadrat Umar said:

> "You cannot live with me in this city where women long for you."

He ordered that Nasr should go to Basra.

When Nasr went away to Basra, the girl Zulfa who had sung about him felt worried about her fate. She wrote verses to the effect that she had sung of wine and Nasr only in an imaginary mood; otherwise she was a girl of excellent character, and did not actually crave for wine or Nasr.

Hadrat Umar made enquiry about the girl, and it transpired that she commanded good character. Hadrat Umar assured her that he proposed no action against her, but warned her that as a good girl she should not think of things forbidden by law."

At Basra, Nasr became the guest of Mujasha bin Masud. When Mujasha's wife Shameela saw Nasr, she felt attracted. Nasr reciprocated her love. When Mujasha came to know of this clandestine love affair he turned out Nasr from his house and divorced his wife.

From Basra, Nasr wrote a letter to Hadrat Umar supplicating that the orders of his exile should be rescinded, and he should be allowed to come to Madina. Nasr's mother waited on Hadrat Umar and said, "Your sons are with you, but you have exiled my son. That is not fair." Hadrat Umar said, "Your son is a source of danger to the morals of the maidens of Madina. As long as I live, I would not allow him to come, and tempt innocent maidens with his looks."

When Hadrat Umar died, Nasr returned to Madina.

It was the year of the famine. Hadrat Umar took pains to ensure that adequate relief reached all people, and that there were no persons in the city who went to sleep hungry.

One night as usual Hadrat Umar went on his round. He was accompanied by his slave Aslam. As he strolled from street to street all was quiet and the people seemed to be asleep. Hadrat Umar thought to himself, "Thank God, there is no one in this city whom the famine has afflicted."

Then as he turned a corner he saw a cottage where light was burning, and from where the sound of the weeping of the children was heard. Hadrat Umar went to the cottage. He saw that the lady of the house was cooking something on the hearth, and the children were crying.

Hadrat Umar knocked at the gate, and addressing the lady of the house Hadrat Umar enquired why were the children crying. She said that they were crying because they were hungry. "And what are you cooking", asked Umar. The lady said that in the kettle there was only water and stones. That was to while away the children that food was being cooked for them. She hoped that exhausted the children would go to sleep.

Hearing this tale of woe, Hadrat Umar felt guilty. He had thought that because of the arrangements made by him, no one was afflicted in the city and here was a family which was starving. Hadrat Umar said to the lady that he would arrange relief for her family immediately.

Hadrat Umar went to the Baitul Mal. There he put the necessary provisions in a bag and carried the bag to the cottage. His slave insisted that he would carry the bag, but Hadrat Umar said that he would carry his burden himself. Hadrat Umar handed over the bag of provisions to the lady. Hadrat Umar sat by the hearth and helped the lady cook the meals. When the meals were ready the children were awakened and served with the delicious meals. As the children ate to their fill and were satisfied they smiled the smile of happiness. Seeing the destitute children smile Hadrat Umar also felt happy.

Hadrat Umar enquired of the lady whether there was none to support. She said that the father of the children had died, and there was no body to support. Whatever little was in the house had been gradually used up and they were starving since the last three days.

Hadrat Umar asked the lady why she had not brought her distress to the notice of the Caliph. The lady said that in spite of her poverty she had some sense of self-respect and she could not go and beg the Caliph for any favour. She added that it was incumbent on the Caliph to ascertain that there was no one in his charge who was starving.

Hadrat Umar said, "You are right. Please excuse me for the remissness in the past. For the future it will be my responsibility to see that your wants are satisfied."

And when the lady realised that the man who had come to her relief was the Caliph himself, she felt satisfied that the Caliph had discharged his onerous responsibilities creditably.

Once the dead body of a beardless youth was found in an isolated place in Madina. Hadrat Umar wanted the relatives of the dead boy to take care of the body and give it a burial. No one came forward to claim the body. Hadrat Umar had the body buried. Thereafter he initiated an inquiry to trace the murder, but the murder could not be traced. Hadrat Umar prayed to God that he may facilitate his task by providing some clue to trace the murder.

After about nine months, a new born baby was found at the same site where the dead body of the young man had been found. Hadrat Umar entrusted the foundling to a wet nurse at State expense. He instructed the nurse that if any lady came to enquire about the baby, or caressed it, he should be informed. Hadrat Umar felt sure that ere long the mystery of the dead young man would be solved.

After a few months the nurse reported that a lady so and so had come to see the baby, and caressed it as if she was its mother. Hadrat Umar noted the name and address of the lady, and after having girded his sword, went to see the lady.

It transpired that the lady was unmarried and was the daughter of a respectable Ansar chief. Hadrat Umar took the chief into confidence, and said that he wanted to talk to her daughter as he suspected her to be guilty of murder.

Hadrat Umar went inside the house and then branding his sword said, "You are according to my investigation guilty of murder. If you have any defence to offer, let me hear what you have to say."

The girl said, "It is true that I mudered the young man. You may listen to my story, and then you may pass whatever verdict you may pass".

Hadrat Umar said, "Yes. You may narrate your story. But mind you, speak nothing but the truth".

The girl said, "A few years ago I engaged an old woman as a maid servant. She was very kind and affectionate. She treated me as a daughter, and I looked to her as a mother. Some time later she said that she would be going to her village but would like to leave her young daughter with me." She brought her daughter and left her with me. The girl was of my age, and we soon became intimate friends. She would sleep in the same room as myself and we would talk of pleasant things till late hours in the night.

One night we talked of love and allied matters till midnight. Then feeling heavy with sleep I dozed while she kept sitting on my bed. After some time I found to my horror that whom I had taken to be a girl was a boy, and was doing foul action with me. In the heaviness of sleep I did not know what had happened, but when I regained my senses and found that I had been betrayed, I took the dagger and killed the boy. Thereafter I had thrown the dead body at a solitary spot.

Nine months later a baby was born. I did not kill it but had it thrown at the spot where the dead body of its father had been thrown previously."

After hearing the story, Hadrat Umar said, "You have spoken the truth. You were betrayed and in killing the boy you vindicated your honour. You acted within the bounds of law, and I pronounce the verdict of 'non-guilty'. You can even keep the baby with you, if you like."

It is related that once while riding a camel, the whip of Hadrat Umar dropped. Many persons who saw the whip fall rushed to pick up the whip to hand it over to the Caliph. Hadrat Umar asked them to mind their own business, and not to bother about his whip. Hadrat Umar dismounted and picked up his whip himself.

Iqbal has dramatised the episode in his classic poem The Secrets of the Self. Iqbal exhorts:

"Like Umar, come down from the camel,

Beware of incurring obligations, beware."

From this episode, Iqbal deduces a code of conduct, the highlights whereof are:

"Do not incur the obligation of any person,

Do not debase yourself by receiving benefits.

> Self is weakened by asking ; asking disintegrates the Self,
>
> By asking, poverty is made more abject.
>
> By begging, the beggar is made poorer,
>
> Even if you are poor and overwhelmed by affliction,
>
> Do not seek your bread by the bounty of another."

Iqbal further elaborates:

> "God loves a man that earns his living ;
>
> Woe to him that accepts bounty from another's table.
>
> The more your hands are empty, the more you are master of yourself.
>
> Seek no favours and walk with your head erect like the pine.
>
> Sweet is a litlle dew, gathered by one's own hand,
>
> Be a man of honour, and like the bubble
>
> Keep the cup inverted even in the midst of the sea."

By 638 A. D., the whole of Syria was under the occupation of the Muslims. Heraclius, the Byzantine emperor had left Syria and withdrawn his forces. His parting words were:

> "Farewell Syria, never again will I come to this beautiful land. What a fine country I am leaving for the enemy."

Some of the Christian Arabs felt grieved at the discomfiture of the Christians at the hands of the Muslims. In a spirit of fanaticism they vowed vengeance against the Muslims. Having failed to defeat the Muslims on the battlefield they decided to resort to underhand means and murder some high ranking Muslims. A Ghassanid Arab Wasiq by name undertook to murder Hadrat Umar the Caliph of Islam.

Wasiq waited on Heraclius at Constantinople, and volunteered to rid the Byzantine emperor of his enemies. The scheme appealed to Heraclius. He paid Wasiq a huge sum and promised to pay much more when he succeeded in his mission. Thus patronised, Wasiq decided to proceed to Madina.

Arab as he was, Wasiq found no difficulty in coming over to Madina in cognito. He posed himself as a Muslim coming from the interior of the desert to pay a visit to Madina. Wasiq carried a poisoned dagger carefully hidden in the folds of his cloak. Having reached Madina, he was on the look out for a suitable opportunity when he could come face to face with the Caliph of Islam, and kill him with his dagger in an unguarded moment.

He had thought that the ruler of the Muslim State would be surrounded by heavy body-guards at all times and it would be difficult to reach him. He was surprised to learn in Madina that there were no body-guards around the Caliph of Islam. Wasiq felt happy that unguarded as the Caliph was, he could easily get an opportunity to fulfil his mission.

Wasiq waited for a suitable opportunity. One day at noon Wasiq found Hadrat Umar sleeping under a tree, all alone and without any guard. There was nobody near at hand. Wasiq thought that this was a golden opportunity for him and he could despatch the Caliph of Islam without any difficulty.

Cautiously with measured steps and hushed breath Wasiq stepped upto Hadrat Umar and took his sword. He was about to plunge his sword in the body of Hadrat Umar when his eyes fell on the face of Hadrat Umar. The sight of the unadorned majesty of the pious Caliph sent a shudder through the body of Wasiq, and the sword dropped from his trembling hands. With the noise of the dropping of the sword, Hadrat Umar opened his eyes. He was quick to take hold of the fallen sword and then rising up faced his would be assassin.

Wasiq fell at the feet of the Caliph, implored his forgiveness and embraced Islam.

In the wars that were conducted during the rule of Hadrat Umar, the soldiers on the front remained absent for considerable periods. Hadrat Umar introduced the reform that leave should be granted to every soldier after he had served on the front for four months. A story is recorded as to how this reform was brought about.

It is related that one night Hadrat Umar went on his round in Madina as usual. It was the dead of night, and every where was quiet. From one of the houses in the street, Hadrat Umar heard a lady lamenting. She said:

> The night is wearisome and keeps me sleepless ;
>
> For I have none to keep me company.
>
> I fear Allah, Who keeps watch over our souls,
>
> And would not take another companion,
>
> But who could tell Umar,

That he should not be so cruel,

As to keep my husband away from me,

For such a long period."

Hadrat Umar knocked at the door, and when the lady came to the door he said:

"I have heard, what you wanted to be conveyed to Umar. How long has your husband been away?"

The lady said, "About a year."

Hadrat Umar said, "Rest assured your husband would come back to you shortly."

Hadrat Umar consulted Hadrat Hafsa as to the maximum period for which a man might remain separate from his wife. She suggested a period of four months. Hadrat Umar accordingly issued orders to the effect that unless a man of the armed forces could take his wife with him, he should be allowed a spell of leave after every four months of active service on the front.

Abul Siara was a native of Madina. He fell in love with a beautiful lady who was the wife of one Abi Jandab. Abul Siara saw the lady and pressed his suit vehemently. The lady warned him to desist from such a course. She told him that if her husband came to know of his approach he would murder him. In spite of the warning, Abul Siara continued his suit. The lady reported the matter to the younger brother of Abi Jandab. He warned Abul Siara in strong terms, but he took no heed and persisted in his erroneous course.

Exasperated, the lady reported the matter to her husband Abi Jandab. Abi Jandab laid down a trap for catching Abul Siara.

He gave out that he was going out for the grazing of his camels, and he would return after a few days. At night thinking that Abi Jandab was not at home, Abul Siara knocked at the door of his beloved. The lady asked him to go away as she was married and could not reciprocate his love. He sighed and sobbed and made declarations of love in pathetic terms. He said that he was so much lost in her love that he would even welcome death. Apparently moved by the frenzied state other lover, the lady admitted Abul Siara to her house. She advised him to hide himself in the room. In the meantime she would decorate herself and then come to him.

As soon as Abul Siara entered the room, Abi Jandab who was already there started beating Abul Siara with sticks and whips. Abul Siara cried and shrieked. The lady asked the younger brother of Abi Jandab to intervene lest the man might be killed. At his intervention, Abi Jandab withdrew his hand. Badly bruised with his bones broken, Abul Siara was carried out and thrown in the way of camels. When Abul Siara came to consciousness and the people asked as to what had happened he said that he had fallen from a camel and broken his bones.

The matter came to the notice of Hadrat Umar. He sommoned the parties and recorded their statements. The lady stated how Abul Siara tried to seduce her and how she resisted his love. Abi Jandab stated how a trap had been laid to catch Abul Siara red handed. Abul Siara confessed his guilt. Hadrat Umar highly praised the conduct and character of the lady. He absolved Abi Jandab of the charge of violence against Abul Siara. Abul Siara was pronounced guilty and awarded punishment.

It was noon of a Friday. The faithful at Madina had gathered in the Prophet's mosque to offer the Friday prayers.

Hadrat Umar, the Caliph arrived to lead the prayers. He said his preliminary prayer and then proceeded to deliver his address to the congregation. He began by reciting some verses from the

Holy Qur'an. Then addressing the congregation he said "Now listen".

A young man from the congregation stood up to say, "We will not listen to you, until you give us the explanation that you owe to us."

The people were startled at this audacious interference. Hadrat Umar paused for a moment, and then turning to the young man said, "Explanation for what?"

The young man said, "The other day each one of us obtained a piece of cloth from the Baitul Mal. Today I find two pieces of cloth on the person of the Caliph. I want to know what right had the Caliph to get a share twice the share of an ordinary Muslim?"

Before Hadrat Umar could explain, Abdullah the son of Hadrat Umar rose up and said, "Friends, the truth of the matter is that like every other person my father and myself obtained a piece of cloth each from the Baitul Mal. My father is so tall that the piece of cloth that he got from the Baitul Mal did not suffice him. So I gave him my piece of the cloth".

This explanation satisfied every one. The young man who had interrupted the Caliph said, "We are satisfied. You can now proceed with your address. We will listen to you and obey your commands."

Turning to the audience Hadrat Umar said, "What will you do, my friends, in case I deviate from the truth one day?"

Thereupon a man rose up and said, "When you wilfully deviate from the truth, we will withdraw our allegiance to you and I for one would feel it my duty to kill you with my sword."

The Caliph said with an apparent show of anger "Man, do you know to whom you are speaking?"

The man said, "Yes. I am talking to Hadrat Umar, the Commander of the Faithful."

"Then how dare you threat him with your sword?" said the Caliph.

The man said, "You are our Caliph and Commander as long as you follow the truth. When you deliberately deviate from the path of the truth you no longer command our allegiance. Then we have the right to kill you, because you lead us in the wrong way."

At this the face of Hadrat Umar lit up, and a smile of satisfaction played on his lips. Raising his hands towards the heaven he said in a voice choked with emotion "Great Allah, I offer you my thanks that there is no dearth of men among the faithful who have the courage to lift the sword even against the head of Umar when he deviates from the Truth."

Turning to the faithful, Hadrat Umar said: "I enjoin you to follow me as long as I follow Allah and his Prophet. When there is any deviation on my part correct me. If I deliberately deviate from the Truth do not follow me. Pray that you and I may steadfastly keep to the path of the Truth enjoined by Islam."

True to the title 'Al-Farooq', Hadrat Umar was an embodiment of truth. He did not hesitate to speak the truth, in the best interests of the Muslim State. Such truth was sometimes bitter, and the people held him in awe.

Some people understood him, and appreciated his sterling qualities of courage, conviction, and truthfulness. Some people misjudged him and felt that he was unduly hard and harsh with the people.

Hadrat Umar knew that he was more feared than loved. Under a stern exterior, Hadrat Umar had a heart full of the milk of human kindness. Whenever Hadrat Umar came across a person who was in distress or was in any way oppressed, Hadrat Umar was all sympathy for him, and he did all he could to alleviate his distress.

Hadrat Umar did often reflect and ponder over the responsibilities that had come to vest in him and the way he discharged them. He did not feel very happy with the equation between himself and the people. He regretted that the people did not understand him properly.

Hudhaifah a prominent companion has left on record that one day he went to see Hadrat Umar and found that he was feeling much perturbed. Seeing the disturbed state of the mind of Hadrat Umar, Hudhaifah enquired as to what was the matter.

Hadrat Umar said:

> "I was feeling unhappy that the people have awe of me. They generally avoid me, and hesitate to bring my shortcomings to my notice. I was just thinking as to what would happen if I were to fall in erroneous ways, and because of the awe that the people have of me, no one comes forward to restrain me."

Thereupon Hudhalfah said:

> "Your awe is because of the truth at your command. If you deviate from the path of truth, the people will not be afraid to call you to account. Verily if I see that you are in the wrong, I will fix you up, and straighten you."

At this Hadrat Umar felt very happy. He said:

> "Thank God, there are friends who will straighten me when I err. If I have such friends around me, I need have no fear of falling into error."

Once Hadrat Umar was busy with some important affairs of the State, when a person came to him and, complaining about some petty grievance, asked for immediate redress.

Thus disturbed, Hadrat Umar felt very much annoyed. He took the lash and struck the man saying:

> "When I sit for redressing the grievances of the common men you do not come, and when I am engaged in other important work you come with your grievances to disturb me."

The person walked away in a sullen mood. When the man went away, Hadrat Umar felt struck with remorse for having treated the man shabbily.

Hadrat Umar ran after the man, and overtaking him handed him his lash and said:

> "I have been hard on you and lashed you. You take this lash, and strike me so that the account maybe squared."

The man was overwhelmed with the sense of justice of Hadrat Umar. He said:

> "O Commander of the Faithful, how can I raise my hand against you. I seek no revenge. I forgive you. May Allah forgive you."

Hadrat Umar went home and offered a special prayer of repentance. He upbraided himself loudly:

> "O Umar, you were low but Allah elevated you. You were wandering astray but Allah guided you. You were base but Allah ennobled you and gave you sovereignty over the people. Now one of them comes and asks you for requital for the harm done to him, and you beat him.

What answer would you give before Allah?"

Hadrat Umar kept chiding himself long. Holding a straw in his hand he said:

"I wish, I were a straw like this." Turning to himself he said, "I wish my mother had not given birth to me."

Hadrat Othman

As Caliph Hadrat Othman had to deliver frequent addresses. No record of such addresses has been preserved. Only some stray remarks of Hadrat Othman here and there have come down to us. It appears that Hadrat Othman was a man of few words but whenever he spoke his words were surcharged with wisdom. Hereunder are presented some of the sayings of Hadrat Othman by way of example.

Useless Things: Hadrat Othman said that four things were useless and these were,

(1) Knowledge without practice,

(2) Wealth without expenditure in the way of Allah,

(3) Piety for the sake of show prompted by worldliness.

(4) Long life with no stock of good deeds.

The Things He Loved: Hadrat Othman said that he loved three things, namely;

(1) To feed the hungry,

(2) To clothe the naked.

(3) To read and teach the Holy Qur'an.

Fear Allah: In his addresses, Hadrat Othman tried to inculcate in the people the fear of Allah. He said, "Fear Allah, for to Him you are to be gathered".

Quarrels and Disputes: He always advised the Muslims to avoid quarrels and disputes and maintain unity in their ranks. He said, "Do not quarrel and do not create differences among yourselves. Hold fast to the rope of Allah and maintain unity in your ranks."

Spiritual and Terrestrial Worlds: He distinguished between the spiritual and the terrestrial worlds in the following terms:–

> "The thought of the spiritual world sheds light on the soul but the thought of the terrestrial world casts darkness thereon."

Patience. Hadrat Othman highlighted the virtues of patience in the following terms:–

> "Under all circumstances, a person should be patient, otherwise disgrace would be his lot".

Habits to be Acquired: Hadrat Othman exhorted the people to acquire two habits, namely.

(1) The habit to speak the truth and

(2) The habit to do good deeds.

Hadrat Othman conceived history as a means of acquiring wisdom. He said "Acquire wisdom from the story of the dead".

Pride: Hadrat Othman condemned pride in the following terms:–

> "The world is proud. Leave it alone lest it entraps by its guises and teaches you pride which will keep you away from Allah".

Essential Things: Hadrat Othman held the following four things as essential, viz'.

(1) To associate with the worthy is laudable but to follow them is essential.

(2) To read the Holy Qur'an is virtue but to act according to its injunctions is essential.

(3) To visit the sick is meritorious but to cause them to make their behests is essential.

(4) To visit the shrines of holy men is piety but to be prepared for death is essential.

Hadrat Othman said that he was surprised at the conduct of a Person:

(1) Who knows the world to be transient, yet loves it.

(2) Who knows death to be certain, yet does not take it seriously.

(3) Who believes in hell, yet commits sin.

(4) Who believes in the existence of Allah, yet seeks assistance from others.

(5) Who is aware of paradise, yet is engaged in worldly pleasures.

(6) Who knows Satan to be his enemy, yet obeys its dictates.

(7) Who believes in predestination, yet feels aggrieved with what happens and

(8) Who knows that account is to be rendered on the day of resurrection, yet hoards wealth.

Hadrat Othman said:

(1) When the Muslims are disunited they would falter in their faith and would be bereft of their inherent strength.

(2) O people, if I give you all the world, that would not suffice as the price for your faith.

(3) You will not be conscious of the reality of faith till love for Allah is held dearer than the passion to acquire wealth.

(4) The highest degree in faith is that you always regard yourself in the presence of Allah.

***Fears for a Man of Piety*:**

A man of faith and piety is always subject to the following fears:–

(1) The fear of Allah, lest by any disobedience there is any faltering in faith.

(2) The fear of the angels lest they may record anything against you which may be a cause of remorse for you on the day of resurrection.

(3) The fear of the Satan lest he may tempt you to any evil.

(4) The fear of the angel of death, lest your life is taken before you have sought pardon for your sins.

(5) The fear of the world, lest by its temptation it make you oblivious of the next world and

(6) The fear of the family members lest by your attachment to them you become oblivious to your duty to Allah.

Happiness and Grief: Hadrat Othman said, "One should not feel happy at the acquisition of wealth, nor should be feel grieved at its loss".

Delicious Food: Hadrat Othman said, "He who is fond of delicious food, let him bear in mind that ultimately he is to be food for worms."

Justice: Hadrat Othman laid down the criteria of justice in the following terms: "The dictates of justice demand that a proper equation should be maintained between the rights and obligations of the people. Whatever is their right should be conceded to them and steps should be taken to ensure that whatever is their obligation is duly fulfilled."

Backbiting: Hadrat Othman condemned backbiting in the following terms:–

> "A backbiter harms three persons, firstly himself, secondly the person whom he is addressing and thirdly the person whom he is backbiting".

Heedlessness: Hadrat Othman said:

> "O people, do not be heedless of your obligations for Allah is ever heedless. If you are heedless of your

obligations, Allah is aware of what you do. He is ever watchful".

Drinking: About drinking, Hadrat Othman said, "Drinking is at the roots of all evils."

Good Deeds and Death: Exhorting the Muslims to good deeds, Hadrat Othman said, "See that during your lifetime you amass a number of good deeds, for after death it would not be possible for you to do any deed."

Hadrat Othman said, "He who makes the Book of Allah as his guide would remain safe from sin and he would be counted among the best of men."

Cause of Contempt: Hadrat Othman said, "No one is to be held in contempt on account of poverty. Only he is to be held in contempt who is oblivious of his religious duties."

Rights of the People: Hadrat Othman said, "Allah has created the people to establish the truth and do the right Allah accepts only what is true and right. Therefore give to the people what is their right and is due to them and see that they perform whatever are their obligations to Islam."

Tyranny: Hadrat Othman said, "See that there is no tyranny against the people particularly the poor and the orphans. If they are aggrieved, bear in mind that Allah Himself would take up their cause."

Distress: Hadrat Othman said "In the event of distress, a man depends solely on his own plans and relies on the people. When he is disappointed from all sides, then alone he turns to Allah."

Testing People: Hadrat Othman said, "On testing people, I have found some of them more poisonous than poisonous animals".

Anger: Hadrat Othman said, "Silence is the best cure of the malady of anger."

Extravagance: Hadrat Othman said, "Extravagance amounts to thanklessness to Allah for His gifts".

Knowledge: Hadrat Othman said, "That knowledge is of no avail which is not put into practice." There can be no practice without knowledge and any knowledge without putting it to practice is useless. That knowledge is blameworthy which is used solely to acquire wealth.

The Lord: Hadrat Othman said, "It is painful to realise that while an animal recognises its master, human beings do not recognise their Lord."

Distress or Difficulty: Hadrat Othman said, "He who is not put to any distress or difficulty for an year at a stretch let him realise that Allah is displeased with him."

Obedience: Hadrat Othman said, "Obedience to Allah is that one should remain within bounds fixed by Allah, promises made should be fulfilled, one should be satisfied with what he has and should be patient in respect of what he does not have."

Hadrat Ali

Hadrat Ali was an embodiment of knowledge and wisdom. Some of the sayings of Hadrat Ali which breathe wisdom and have attained the dimensions of aphorisms are on record. Some of these are quoted hereunder:

- Fear God and you will have no cause to fear anyone.
- Resignation to the Will of God is the cure of the disease of the heart.
- The word of God is the medicine of the heart.
- Lead such a life that when you die, the people may mourn you and while you are alive they long for your company.
- The days of life pass away like clouds, so do good while you are alive.
- Of all the follies the greatest is to love the world.
- Opportunity is swift of flight but slow to return.
- Pride, cowardice and miserliness are bad for men but good for woman.
- The most happy is he to whom God has given a good wife.
- He who knows himself knows God.
- Do not sell your conscience for anything but Heaven.
- The disease of the heart is worse than the disease of the body.
- To fight against one's desires is the greatest of all fights.
- The strongest amongst you is he who subdues his self.
- Wealth and greed are the roots of all evils.

- Riches without faith are the greatest poverty.
- A man's worth depends upon the nobility of his aspirations.
- Knowledge enlivens the soul.
- The learned lives, although he dies.
- The sum total of excellence is knowledge.
- To respect the learned is to respect God.
- Generosity hides shortcomings.
- The wealth of a miser is as useless as a pebble.
- Desire is one's most inveterate enemy.
- Those who walk on the surface of the earth shall one day be interned in it.
- Every breath of man brings him nearer to death.
- People are asleep as long they are alive, they are awakened when they die.
- Patience is the fruit of faith.
- Virtue never dies.
- A man's glory from his virtue is greater than the glory of his pedigree.
- No shelter is safer than piety.

- A man's behaviour is the index of his mind.
- Courtesy costs nothing but buys everything.
- Clemency graces power.
- Jealousy devours virtue as fire devour fuel.
- He that lends a listening ear to reproach is one of those that deserve reproach.
- Forgiveness is the crown of greatness.
- Carnal appetites are nets spread by the devil.
- Every arrow does not hit the mark, nor is every prayer granted.
- Ostentatiousness spoils prayers.
- Fear none but your sins.
- He who praises you murders you.
- A man who praises himself displays his deficiency of intellect.
- Honour your parents and your sons will honour you.
- A man is hid under his tongue.
- The tongue of a wise man lies behind his heart.
- The tongue pierces deeper than the spear.
- He who purifies his heart from doubt is a believer.

- The opinion of a wise man is an oracle.
- To seek counsel is to go to the fountain of guidance.
- Association with a fool is tyrannical to the soul.
- God hasten the fall of tyrants.
- Tyranny leads to moral cowardice.
- A tyrant's success is his moral defeat.
- It is better do die than to beg.
- When a man begs he loses his faith.
- Hajj is the Jihad of every believer in faith.
- A wise enemy is better than a foolish friend.
- Silence is the best reply to a fool.
- The best speech is one which is short and reasonable.
- Speech is like a medicine, a small dose of which cures but an excess of which kills.
- He that has no courage has no religion.
- His grief is long whose hope is short.
- The right of freedom of speech consists in speaking the truth.
- Repentance washes away sins.

- Folly is an incurable disease.
- To assist the wrong is to oppress the right.
- Sinning is a disease, repentance is its medicine and abstinence from it a sure cure.
- Sorrow makes a man old before his time.
- Pride impedes progress and mars greatness.
- To forgive is the crown of greatness.
- He who understands humanity seeks solitude.
- Right is the best argument.
- Misrepresentation spoils narration.
- As a man's wisdom increases, so his desire to speak decreases.
- He who seeks to do justice with men, let him desire for them what he desires for himself.
- The greatest sin is the sin which the sinner considers to be ordinary.
- Contentment is the asset which is never exhausted.
- Government is a trial for men.
- He who fights against the truth, the truth will defeat him.
- Finding fault in others is one's greatest fault.

- Haste is a species of madness.
- Greed is perpetual enslavement.
- He who does not know his own worth is doomed to destruction.
- The best investment is one with which duties are performed.
- Anger is a fire kindled, he who restrains anger extinguishes the fire, he who gives vent to it is the first to be consumed by such fire.
- Jihad is the highway of prosperity.
- None is more solitary than a miser.
- Knowledge is the ornament of the rich and the riches of the poor.
- Knowledge is the sum total of excellence.
- He who teaches you a letter binds you with a fetter of gratitude.
- As long as we do not hope, we do not fret.
- He who indulges in jokes and loose talk loses a part of his wisdom.
- Truth is bitter, but its result is sweet, falsehood appears to be sweet but it is poisonous in its effect.
- Miserliness is the root of many evils.

- Knowledge and practice are twins and both go together.There is no knowledge without practice and no practice without knowledge.

- He who dissembles plays with his honour.

- When God wants to humiliate a person he deprives him of knowledge.

- When your power increases, decrease your desires accordingly.

- He who listens to a back-bitter loses a friend.

- It is no justice to decide a case on mere conjecture.

- He who does not know his own worth is deemed to ignomy.

- He who practises thrift would never be in want.

- He who does not know should not be ashamed to learn.

- Patience is to faith, what head is to the body. When patience goes faith goes, when head goes, the body goes.

- The grace of God is the best guide.

- A good disposition is the best companion.

- Wisdom is the best friend.

- Good breeding is the best inheritance.

- There is nothing more hateful than pride.

- Be among men like bee among birds.
- Mix with the people with your tongue, but be separate from them in your deeds.
- Be generous but do not be a spendthrift.
- Do not run after the world, let the world run after you.
- A wise man is he who does not despair of the bounty and mercy of God.
- He who is aware of his own faults is oblivious of the fault of others.
- What the eye sees the heart preserves.
- The vision of the eye is limited; the vision of the heart transcends all barriers of time and space.
- Do not be misled by appearances for these are apt to be deceptive.
- Do not have too many irons in the fire; concentrate on one thing at a time.
- What you do not like for your self, do not like it for others.
- Contentment is the treasure which is never exhausted.
- The advice of old men is dearer than the bravery of young men.
- That knowledge is superficial which is merely on the tongue; that knowledge is real which demonstrates itself in your practice.

- Waste of time is one's greatest loss.
- He who knows to keep his secret knows the way to success.
- Foresight is the way to safety.
- No relationship is stronger than the relationship that exists between man and God.
- Enlighten the heart with prayers.
- Strengthen your heart with faith.
- Suppress all lust with piety.
- Do not sell the Hereafter for the world.
- Do not speak in a state of ignorance.
- Refrain from unnecessary talk.
- Do not tread the path from which you can apprehend the danger of running astray.
- In the affairs of God, do not be afraid of the accusations of the evil mongers.
- In all that you do seek the protection of God.
- Do not covet what is undesirable.
- If you seek the truth neither stray from the right path, nor be assailed by doubts.
- Do not become a slave of your desires.

- That wealth is no wealth which brings dishonour.

- Whatever harm accrues of silence can be remedied but whatever harm is done because of speech cannot be remedied.

- It is better to restrain your desires than to stretch your hand before others.

- A little that is earned because of honest labour is better than a larger amount gained through dishonest means.

- Guard well your secret.

- He who seeks more than what is necessary indulges in error.

- To oppress the weak is the worst tyranny.

- Do not bank on false hopes for that is the capital of the dead.

- A wise man takes a lesson even from a minor lapse.

- Overpower desires and suspicions by patience and faith.

- He who does not take the middle course strays.

- A stranger is he who has no friends.

- When hopes are frustrated despair becomes the way of life.

- He who trusts the world, the world betrays him.

In his various sermons conspicuous for the depth of learning Hadrat Ali had dwelt on the various attributes of God in a most masterly way. Extracts from some of his sermons are given hereunder:

> "All praise is due to the Creator of the world whose wisdom is hidden. The various objects of nature openly confirm His existence. It is impossible to the physical eye to behold. His Majesty thus one who has not seen Him has no right to deny. His existence; He surpasses in strength and superiority. He is nearest to us. No one can be nearer to us than He. His distant height has not segregated Him from His creation and His nearness has not established His equality with His creation. He is that sublime and matchless. Being in comprehending when the intellect cannot reach the bottom of his attributes, yet noting prevents a person from comprehending Him. He is that Being Whose existence even an atheist feels in his heart of hearts. Undoubtedly God is free and sublime and bears no comparison with anyone, then how can anyone have the audacity to deny Him."

> "God is higher and superior to all things to such an extent that even the wildest imagination cannot have a definite idea about him. He is the beginning which has no end. He is Infinite. God is one. He has no partner. He is the first cause of everything. There was nothing before Him. He existed when nothing existed. He is Unique. We can have only glimpses of His greatness. His effulgence is so dazzling that we cannot face it. Our intellect is finite and He is Infinite. We cannot describe Him with any degree of exactitude. He is beyond description. He is Almighty. All things in the heavens and on earth are subject to His command."

> "We thank God for what He has taken, for what He has given, for what kindness. He had done, and what tests

He has taken. He is aware of all that is hidden. He knows every secret. Whatever is concealed in one's heart is known to Him. He is omnipotent and omniscient. None is to be worshipped except Him. He has no partner. He has no parallel. He is Unique. He is might, majesty and mercy. He is our Creator. We come from Him and we have to ultimately return to Him. His bounties are unlimited."

A Jew once went to Hadrat Ali and asked him, when did God exist Hadrat Ali said that God is above considerations of time and space Creation was not and He was, He was while there was no being. He existed without cause. He has beginning and no end. He is subject to no limitations. He is Infinite. He is the end of all souls. The Jew next asked, "What is fate" Hadrat Ali said, "It is a gloomy road, tread it not". The Jew repeated the questions and Hadrat Ali said, "It is a deep sea, avoid it". The Jew repeated the question for the third time and Hadrat Ali said, "It is a mystery of God which is hidden from you, do not probe into it." The Jew insisted on a reply and Hadrat Ali asked him, "Has God created you for what? He has willed, or what you have willed?". The Jew said, "Indeed, for what. He has willed". Thereupon Hadrat Ali said, "Then He will do with you as He thinks fit and that is fate "This impressed the Jew and he was converted to Islam at the hands of Hadrat Ali.

Once a Jew came to Hadrat Ali with a view to ridiculing Islam. The Jew was very rich and he disparaged the Islamic way of austerity. He tried to enter into argument with Hadrat Ali and declared that if his questions were answered to his satisfaction he would accept Islam Hadrat Ali said that he would be glad to answer any question that was put to him. The Jew said, "Suppose you are standing on the roof of a high building at a dizzy height, who will protect you'?" Hadrat Ali said, "Of course, God will protect me". The Jew thereupon said, "Do you feel confident that

God would really protect you" Hadrat Ali said, "Certainly, it is our faith that as long as we are ordained to live, God will protect us. "The Jew observed, "If you are sure of the protection of God, would you be prepared to climb to a high building and then jump therefrom in order to test how God protects you." Hadrat Ali said that he was not a fool to jump from a high building for nothing. The Jew said that he was not asking him to undertake the exercise for nothing, for if God actually protects him, he would thereby get a Jew converted to Islam. Hadrat Ali said that such stipulation was erroneous and fallacious. How was that? enquired the Jew. Hadrat Ali said that God is the master and man is His servant. It is open to the master to put the servant to test but it does not behove the servant to put the master to test Hadrat Ali added "If we put God to any test, that means our lack of faith and when faith is lost everything is lost."

The Jew said, "This means that you are afraid that if you take a jump, you will die and God will not protect you" Hadrat Ali said, "I am not afraid of death, but as a servant I cannot defy the Master. Everything in the universe is subject to the will of God. That will is the law and man has been endowed with reason and intelligence to discern such law. If knowing the law I choose to defy it, I will have to suffer for breaking the law. When I deliberately break down the law laid down by the Master, I lose the right of His protection Moreover. God protects us as long as we are ordained to live. If I take a jump and die, it would merely mean that I am ordained to die like that, it would not mean that God has withdrawn his protection."

The argument of Hadrat Ali impressed the Jew. He said "All you are right, we must observe the law and then seek the protection of the Master. We certainly lose the right of His protection when we break the law." Thereupon the Jew was converted to Islam and for the rest of his life he remained a true Muslim.

Some of the counsels of Hadrat Ali with reference to God are:

(1) Fear God and you will have no cause to fear anyone else. Fear of God checks the soul from committing sins and restrains one from transgression. Shedding tears for the fear of God enlightens the heart and fortifies it against the repetition of sins. Fear of God purifies the heart.

(2) Resignation to God's will is the cure of the diseases of the heart. Resignation to the will of God makes the greatest affliction easy.

(3) Glorify God even for little blessings. If you are grateful to God for His blessings, He will increase them.

(4) The word of God is the medicine of heart. A believer is thankful to God in prosperity and patient in adversity. To repose ones trust in God is the believers, castle.

Hadrat Ali used to pray to God in the following terms.

> "O God, forgive my sins of which you know more than me. And if I commit these sins again, even then because of your munificence forgive me. If all the promises that I had made with myself to act according to your command have not been fulfilled, kindly pardon my lapse. Moreover if I sought your proximity through my tongue but my heart did not keep accord with my tongue even then forgive me. O God, forgive my acts of commission or omission, advertent or inadvertent."

In one of his sermons, Hadrat Ali counselled the people about the life in this world and the life in the world Hereafter in the following terms:

"O men of God' May God keep you happy, and shower His favours on you? You should prepare yourself for the long journey that awaits you. There are many difficulties that beset your path. Death is ever anxious to devour you. Renounce the riches of the world and catch hold of piety. Life in this world is short, whereas life after death will be everlasting. Buy those commodities here which will stand you in good stead in the other world. Do not demean yourself before God who is well acquainted with your innermost feelings. Do not allow your soul to be lost in this world before death may overtake you. O men' Cast a glance on this world from a wise man's point of view. She turns out her guests in a short pace of time. She harasses those with whom she fondles and prattles. Whatever part of life is wasted in idle pursuits can never be recalled. Its gratifications and enjoyments are soon changed into suffering and pain; its embellishment and decorations are changed into deformation and impoverishment. The days of this life are numbered. Death is inevitable and is bound to come soon. After having adorned your person with good deed, you should not pay any heed whether death catches you or you catch death. Many men buy clothes, which instead of being worn by them are used in their coffin. Many persons build houses which instead of becoming abodes become their graves. No one has lived forever in this world and no one has invented such a medicine which may make men immune from the clutches of death. Solomon the prophet reigned with great pomp and majesty but when his time came he had to depart leaving all such pomp and glory. The world was left without him and his places became a heap of ruins. Look to the case of those men who lived impregnable citadels on the top of mountains with the most powerful army and when their time came death ejected them from those fortified places and put them to eternal sleep in graves. One can hear the whisper of angels over their graves "Where are those stiff-necked people who boasted of their pelf and power and their crowns and thrones? Where are their royal robes? What became of those beauties whose radiance under veils dimmed the light of the sun? Where have gone those forts which were decorated with golden curtains, in front of which stood sentries for watch and ward? Do not they tell us how powerless they were? Have not the worms eaten those bodies, who a few days ago set a magnificent and sumptuous table with luxurious plates?. The vicissitudes of fortune have ruined their citadels, destroyed their royal robes and reduced to dust their crowns and thrones."

In another sermon, Hadrat Ali dwelt on the evils of the world as follows:

"Beware! The world stands on the threshold of decay and destruction. Its mouth sounds the farewell notes of annihilation. It is uncanny and uncharitable. With great rapidity it turns its back. Alas, the world drives its inhabitants into pitfalls of destruction Through the hands of death it drags its exasperated neighbours to annihilation. Its transparent water becomes bitter and its sparkling spring becomes opaque in the next world. It has nothing to offer except the leavings which stick to utensils after the meal or the wet piece of stone which is kept in the mouth to quench parching thirst. Whatever is in the world is superficial, mortal and perishable O followers of God'. Then get ready to leave this abode whose in-dweller are destined to taste death. Take heed lest the desires and lust should overwhelm you and this transitory life should appear a long one to you and its short sojourn be taken as a long one by you. By God, if you grumble and moan like the wretched camels of burden shed bitter tears like a pigeon and implore forgiveness of God like those monks who have renounced the world and having renounced your worldly goods and family, you come out to seek nearness to God so that. He may exalt your lot or forgive some of your sins which the angels have recorded in your book of deeds, all these things will have little value as compared with the reward which awaits you if you follow my instructions. By God, if for the love of God you melt your hearts away and for the love of His rewards and fear of His punishment your eyes shed blood instead of tears and you live in this condition till this world lasts, even then your indefatigable and untiring efforts can be of no match fo the numerous blessings which God has so kindly and bountifully bestowed upon you. You can never return the thanks of the Almighty Lord for the guidance. He has so mercifully shown to us."

In another sermon, Hadrat Ali talked about the world and the Hereafter in the following terms:

"The world has turned its face and given an indication of its impending end. The Hereafter is now becoming manifest. Beware, today is the day to activate your body, tomorrow is the day assigned for the race. Now either Paradise or. Hell lie ahead of you. Is there no one among you who should repent before his death and do some good deeds which would stand him in good stead in the Hereafter? You are living today in the worlds of hopes and desires, but beware that death lies in ambush. He who does good deeds before his death, such deeds would be a source of profit for him. His death will not harm in any way. He who falls into error before his death will be at loss and will come to grief. In the event of weal or woe you should act as one would act in the case of fear or terror. The truth is that there is no reward greater than Paradise and there is no punishment severer than Hell. Beware that whom the truth does not profit, falsehood will certainly harm him. He who is not guided is doomed to destruction. Beware that you have been given the command to march. The goods that you can carry with you on your march have also been indicated. I am worried about you in two things, firstly your subservience to your lust and secondly the excess of your longings March to the. Hereafter with such assets which can save you from punishment on the Doomsday."

In most of his sermons, Hadrat Ali has brought out the transitory character of the world in the following words:

> "All praise is for God. Do not despair of His mercy. His bounties are unlimited. There is no shame in His worship. He is God whose mercy is ever lasting and Whose bounties would never exhaust. Remember that the world is transitory in character and your life is a mere sojourn. The world is doomed to destruction. It is outwardly pleasant and attractive, but inwardly hollow. See that when you depart from this world you do so with good grace and carry with you assets which all stand you in good stead in the Hereafter. For this journey do not overload yourself with unnecessary paraphernalia. Do not covet anything beyond what is necessary. Keep in mind that the world is a tavern where no one can stay for long. Do not be enamoured of the world. . Its attracts are a trap Those who are lured by its charms get involved into an ordeal You should keep in mind that you will have to be called to account for what you do in the world For the wise, the world is a shadow

> which may appear at one mompnt and soon disappear. Fear God and face death with a stock of good deeds. Purchase everlasting things for things which are perishable. An arduous journey awaits you. Prepare yourself for it. Be ever ready to face death, for it may come at any moments. Be receptive to words of advice God Almighty has not created you in vain nor has He left you free to run amok. Death separates you from this world and Paradise or Hell in the Hereafter. Remember that your life is diminishing every moment. You should hasten cheerfully to your real destination While alone, purchase such assets which would be a source of profit to you in the Hereafter. You should overpower your lusts. Know that desires are deceptive and death lies in ambush. Satan is after you. It is the game of Satan that death should catch you unaware. When you have not amassed the assets necessary for the journey to eternity, against the manoeuvres of Satan, seek the protection of God.

Dwelling on the same theme, in the course of other sermons, Hadrat Ali said:

> "The world is a tavern where no one can stay for long. Such is the lure of the world that none can escape from being involved therein. The world is an ordeal and a trial. Whatever you get out of the world will be of no avail to you. It is only that which helps you for the Hereafter that can be a source of profit for you. For the wise, the world is merely a shadow which may disappear any moment thus manifesting its unreality."

> "O people, what should I say about the world which begins in grief and ends in destruction. Those who are rich and wealthy are involved in mischief and those

who are poor and needy are grieved and distressed. The world eludes him who seeks it. It runs after him who runs away from it. He who sees it as a place of trial is enlightened, he who is lured by its charm is blinded."

Hadrat Ali was a political thinker. In his writings in Nahj-ul-Balagha we come across many passages which project his political thought in the context of Islam. It is surprising that such thoughts expressed fifteen hundred years ago have an air of his modernity about them. One marvels at the profoundity of his thought.

State and Government: Hadrat Ali defined the State as "Community in action". He defined Government as an instrument of the State charged with the responsibility of fulfilling the purpose of the State. He conceived Islamic Ummah as an organic entity capable of possessing moral and spiritual qualities. He held that an individual cannot lead his life in isolation and has to live as a part of the Ummah safeguarding the "Haqooq-ul-Abad" (duties of individuals towards his fellow men). This can be done by developing a sense of group solidarity and loyalty and by each person striving to live in harmony with his fellow men without encroaching upon or usurping the rights of others. Hadrat Ali held that mankind with all its faults and vices would survive by a corporate sense of responsibility. As such good government should not be merely regulative; it should be reformative as well in its character and application.

The Caliph: Hadrat Ali held that the Caliph is the agent of the community charged with the responsibility to administer the affairs of the community in accordance with the injunctions of Islam. He should strive to follow in the footsteps of the Holy Prophet. He should be a pious and staunch Muslim who should follow the Shanah himself and should enforce it for others. He should be a man of knowledge and should not be ignorant. He should not be covetous or ambitious. He should be concerned more with Hereafter than the world. He should be sympathetic. He should not be cruel and should not oppress the people. He should have a firm hold on authority and should see that the functionaries of the State perform their duties honestly and efficiently. He should be just and should administer justice without fear or favour. He should promote the welfare of the people. He should enforce law and order with a strong hand. He should be a source of strength for the weak and a matter of terror for those who usurp the rights of others. He should defend the country against foreign aggression. He should maintain law and order within the country. He should keep a strict watch on the functionaries of the State. He should be sympathetic and should solve the problems of the people. The people should have easy access to him and he should command their confidence. He should regard government as a trail and should take steps to ensure that when weighed in the balance he is not found wanting.

The People: Hadrat Ali held that the people are the main power and they have the right to criticise the Government. The Government should work for the welfare of the people and should keep them satisfied. Hadrat Ali was particular that the minorities should be well cared for and their rights should be safeguarded. The minorities should have the freedom of worship and they should enjoy autonomy in the administration of their own affairs. Hadrat Ali held that it was the obligation of the State to look after the destitute and the distressed. He attached particular importance to the care of the widows and orphans.

Taxation: Hadrat Ali held that the people should be taxed according to their capacity. There should be no hardship or coercion in the collection of taxes. The system of taxation should be such that the people pay the taxes voluntarily as a religious obligation. The Collectors should bot indulge in any act which is not liked by the people. They should not collect anything beyond what is enjoined by law. Taxes should be remitted in the case of famine, failure of crops or any other calamity.

Functionaries of the State: Hadrat Ali held that only such persons should be appointed as the functionaries of the State who spoke the truth, however unpalatable it might be. The functionaries of the State should fear God and they should perform their duties with pious intensions, good faith and fear of God. They should be scrupulously honest. They should be paid reasonable remuneration so that they are not beguiled into monetary temptations. There should be a good system of espionage to watch the working of the functionaries of the State at various levels. Hadrat Ali held that good care should be taken of the soldiers. They should be respected and treated kindly. Only pious and holy men with fear of God should be appointed as Qadis and they should administer justice without fear or favour in accordance with the commandments of God. They should not be greedy and should not make errors in their judgements. The businessmen and traders should be protected and proper facilities should be provided for the development of trade and industry Hadrat Ali laid down that the Government was under an obligation to ensure that prices of commodities were kept at a reasonable level and the businessmen were not allowed to make exorbitant profit. The functionaries of the State had to take steps to ensure that there was no hoarding or black marketing. Hadrat Ali enjoined that public funds were to be administered as a trust. Liberal allowances were to be paid to the people. The State should avoid ostentation. Public funds should not be wasted. Only as much should be spent as was absolutely necessary.

Foreign Policy: Hadrat Ali held that in the matter of foreign policy, the State should take steps to ensure peace with other states. War should be avoided as far as possible. The Government should, however, remain alert and be prepared to meet any emergency. If war is resorted to it should be only in the cause of God and for the vindication of the truth Hadrat Ali held that in the case of war, let the first shot to be fired by the enemy. Bloodshed was to be avoided as far as possible. In the enemy land the fields were not to be harmed and the fruit trees were not to be cut. The aged and the women were not to be made the victims of vengeance.

Hadrat Ali was a great thinker. In his sermons, addresses and other writings, which have come down to us in the shape of his book Nahl-ul-Balagha, we come across many a gem of precious thoughts. Some of these thoughts characterised by great depth are given hereunder.

Friends of Allah: Friends of. Allah are those who look to its inward aspect when the ordinary people look to the outward aspect of the world and when the other people are engrossed in the affairs of the world they get anxious about the Hereafter.

Momins and Hypocrites: A Momin is he whose neck if placed under my sword, would not think ill of me. A hypocrite is he whom even if I load with gold and silver he would not think good of me.

Faqih: A Faqih is one who would not make the people despair of the mercy of God.

Justice and Mercy: The purpose of justice is to give a person what is duc to him. Mercy goes a step further and it gives a person something more than what is due to him.

The World and the Hereafter: He who seeks the world, death runs after him, he who seeks the Hereafter the world runs after him.

Momin and Infidel: He who tells of his want to a Momin is as if has requested God. He who seeks his want from an infidel is making a complaint against God.

Proximity to the Ruler: He who is in proximity to the ruler is like a person riding on a lion and there can be no knowing when the lion might overturn and devour him.

Haste: Haste is a kind of madness. One who does things in haste has to face shame and if he is not ashamed his madness is confirmed.

Faith and Faithlessness: Faith with the faithless is faithlessness before God and faithlessness with the faithless is faith.

Philosophy: If what the philosopher says is correct, it is a cure, if what he says is incorrect it is a disease.

Forgiveness: Forgiveness is the Zakat of success. If you wish to succeed in life, learn to forgive others.

Secret of Success: Success depends on self-confidence. Self-confidence depends on due deliberation. Deliberation depends on protecting ones secrets. He who cannot keep his secret cannot succeed.

Kinds of Patience: Patience is of two kinds, firstly patience at a thing which one does not like, and secondly patience at not getting a thing one desires.

Wealth and Poverty: Wealth provides one with the facilities of home country while travelling in a foreign land. Poverty make a person a stranger even in his home land.

Faith: Faith lies in preferring truth to falsehood even when the truth might lead to any harm and falsehood might lead to any advantage. An evidence of your faith is that what you say is in accordance with what you practise.

Momin: A Momin is he whose face wears a smiling look even though his heart is distressed.

Perfection: Perfection consists in three things: patience in affliction moderation in pursuit and offer of assistance to a supplicant.

Heresy: Heresy has four aspects namely concealment of truth, waging of war against truth, going astray from the path of truth and adoption of an inimical attitude to truth.

Seven Things of the Devil: There are seven things of the devil namely: excessive anger, excessive sneezing, excessive yawning, vomiting, bleeding of the nose, clandestine discourse and sleeping during devotional exercise.

Generosity: Generosity lies in affording relief to the needy without his asking for it. When the supplicant is assisted when he asks for it, that is liberality and munificence and not generosity.

Tauhid: Tauhid is a conviction of the heart which is above doubt.

Justice: Justice is determination against which there can be no accusation.

Broad-mindedness: Learning and good disposition go together and lead to broad-mindedness.

Wealth and Health: One cannot trust two things namely wealth and health. One does not know when they might forsake him.

Two Types of Subsistence: There are two types of subsistence, one after which you run and the other which runs after you.

Truth and Falsehood: There is distance of four fingers between truth and falsehood. Falsehood is that you say that you heard it from someone else. The truth is that you say that you saw it with your own eyes.

Things that are the Best: Resignation to the will of God is the best policy. Knowledge is the best inheritance. Good conduct is the best ornament. The best wealth is the suppression of desires. The middle course is the best course.

Things to which Nothing is Better: No honour is more respectable than sword. No religion is better than Islam. No citadel is stronger than piety. No one is better interceder than repentance. No treasure is richer than contentment.

Success and Failure: When you succeed do not feel proud. When you fail do not lose patience.

Persons Doomed to Ignominy: Two persons are deemed to ignominy, firstly he who creates dissensions and secondly he who levies false accusations.

Three Friends: Your three friends are: your friend, a friend of your friend and an enemy of your enemy.

Three Foes: Your three foes are: your foe, the foe of your friend and the friend of your foe.

Two Types of Men: There are two types of men in the world– one who sells himself to the world and the world destroys him, the other is the one who ransomed himself for the world and has released himself from its captivity.

Greetings and Favours: If somebody greets you, greet him in better terms. If somebody favours you, confer a greater favour on him.

Humiliation: Accept death, but do not accept humiliation.

Two Hungry Persons: There are two hungry persons whose hunger is never satisfied, firstly he who seeks knowledge and secondly he who seeks the world.

Miser: A miser lives in the world as an indigent and he will be called for in the Hereafter to give account as a capitalist.

Offshoots of Patience: Desires, fear and piety are the offshoots of patience.

Miserliness, Patience, Piety and Cowardice: Miserliness is dishonour. Patience is bravery. Piety is shield against hell. Cowardice is inferiority complex.

The Greatest and the Vilest: Wisdom is the greatest treasure. Folly is the greatest poverty. Of all thing pride, is the vilest. The greatest excellence is good disposition.

Companies to be Avoided: Avoid the company of a fool for he will harm you while trying to benefit you. Avoid the company of a liar for he will bring you near what is undesirable and remove you from what is desirable. Avoid the company of a miser for he would withhold from you what you stand in need of. Avoid the company of a libertine for he will sell you for a trifle.

Two Things to be Afraid of: Two things of which you should be afraid of are firstly giving way to your lust, and secondly harbouring high and far-fetched hopes.

The Worst Enemies: Before God two persons are the worst enemies, firstly the man who makes innovations, and secondly the man who creates dissensions.

Things that are Worse: There is no distress worse than ignorance. There is no enemy worse than self-adulation. There is no worse companion than bad conduct.

Hadrat Ali had the peculiar skill to explain things by giving appropriate similes In his various addresses and sermons we come across many instances of the brilliance of his expression in bringing home the truth through interesting examples.

The World: He likened the world to a serpent which was outwardly very soft skinned but poisonous from within.

Falsehood: Hadrat Ali held that like the feathers of a peacock, falsehood might look very attractive, but was as ugly as the feet of the peacock. Falsehood has no legs to stand upon.

The Unbelievers: Hadrat Ali compared the unbelievers to a bat which can see when it is dark, but which is blind and cannot see anything when it is daylight.

People who did not Respond to His Call: When Hadrat Ali exhorted the people of Iraq to respond to his call for war against Muāwiyah, they did not respond to his call. He said, "You are like a pregnant woman who undergoes the ordeal of childbirth, but gives birth to a dead child."

The Tree and the Fruit: When after the death of the Holy Prophet, the Quraish based their claim to the caliphate on the ground that they belonged to the same tree as the Holy Prophet, Hadrat Ali said, "It is strange that they look to the tree, but neglect its fruit."

People of Basra: When the people of Basra who had originally taken the oath of allegiance to him, but later chose to fight against him, Hadrat Ali said that these people were near the water but far from the sky.

People of the Age of Ignorance: Referring to the people of the age of ignorance in the pre-Islamic era, Hadrat Ali said that they were like an egg which is broken in the nest.

People of Kufa: Addressing the people of Kufa, Hadrat Ali said: "When I invite you to fight, your eyes begin to move in your sockets as if you are in the agony of death. You are like the camels whose herdsmen have disappeared and when these animals are collected on one side, they scatter on the other side."

Mughira b Shu'aba: Mughira was regarded by the Quraish as a wise man. When Mughira favoured Muawiyah, Hadrat Ali said, "Mughira has profited from Islam only to the extent seeking worldly end. He is obvious of the Hereafter."

People who Run after the World: About the people who run after the world, Hadrat Ali said: "Those people who run after the world are like beasts who fall at one another, with the strong oppressing the weak."

People who are not Deceived by the World: About the people who are not deceived by the world, Hadrat Ali said, "Those who have understood the deceptive character of the world do not feel distressed on death. They are like the people who migrate from a famine-struck land to a land of plenty."

Complaint against the Umayyads: During the caliphate of Hadrat Othman, Hadrat Ali had a complaint that the Umayyads were withholding from him what was due to him. He said, "The Umayyads are withholding what is due to me as the camelman, when milking the she-camel, withholds the milk from the young one of the camel"

Falsehood of Muawiyah: Referring to the falsehood of Muawiyah, Hadrat Ali said that falsehood had appeared in his case as the horns on the head of a young one of a goat.

Shedding of Sins through Prayer: In a sermon, Hadrat Ali said that through prayer the sins of a man are shed as a tree sheds it leaves.

Cleanliness and Prayers: In another sermon, Hadrat Ali said "Prayer is like a hot spring of water which flows at your door and provides you the wherewithal for cleanliness."

Crumbs after the Meals: In a sermon, Hadrat Ali said that the world had run its cause and nothing had been left of it except the crumbs after the meals.

People who did not Respond to His Call: In an address, Hadrat Ali compared the people who did not respond to his call to a camel who ran away from the herd shrieking with the pain of belly.

Heart of the People: In a sermon Hadrat Ali prayed for the heart of the people to melt at the mention of the Word of God as salt dissolves in the water.

Ignorant Persons: In an address, Hadrat Ali said that the ignorant persons were like a person riding on a beast of burden which could not see. He deplored that such ignorant persons dealt with the injunctions of Islam as air scatters the straw.

Ashas b Qais: Hadrat Ali said that among his companions. Ashas b Qais was what. Abdullah b. Abi Sahl was in the time of the Holy Prophet.

Patience and Faith: Hadrat Ali held that patience and faith bear the same relations as in the case of a human being the head bears to the body. There can be nobody without head, and there can be no faith without patience.

Disease and Sins: Hadrat Ali held that disease sheds sins as the tree sheds the dead leaves.

Death of the Virtuous: Hadrat Ali compared the death of the virtuous to the migration journey of the people from a famine-struck land to a land of plenty.

Days of Life: Hadrat Ali held that the days of life pass as the passing of clouds in the sky.

Devotion to the World: Hadrat Ali held that those who are devoted to the world are like barking dogs and ferocious animals who fall at one another and the strong devour the weak.

Seekers of the World: Hadrat Ali compared the men seeking the world to camels which are let loose and which roam about causing mischief.

Virtue of Silence: Hadrat Ali advocated the virtue of silence by advancing the simile that water can be preserved in a water skin only when its mouth is tied.

Thirsty Camels on a Water Pond: When the people flocked to him and urged him to accept their allegiance, Hadrat Ali compared them to thirsty camels who flock to the water pond when their strings are untied.

Caliphate of Hadrat Umar: When Hadrat. Abu Bakr died and still ignoring his claims, Hadrat Umar became the Caliph, Hadrat Ali held that the second Caliph was like a person riding a camel whose reins if tightened would injure the camel and if loosened would endanger the rider.

Umayyad Use of the Baitul Mal: Referring to the appropriation of the funds of the Baitul-Mal by Umayyads for personal ends during the caliphate of Hadrat Othman, Hadrat Ali held that tney ate away the public funds as the camel eats away the grass.

Withholding the Milk of the She-camel from its Young One: Hadrat Ali had the complaint that during the caliphate of Hadrat Othman the Umayyads withheld from him what was his right like the camelman who, while milking the she-camel, withholds its milk from its young one.

Handle of the Grinding Stone: When Hadrat. Abu Bakr became the Caliph, Hadrat Ali held that Hadrat. Abu Bakr had assumed the mantle of the caliphate forcibly while he knew that he (Hadrat Ali) was as essential for the caliphate as the handle is necessary for moving the grinding stone.

The Simile of a Sinner: Hadrat Ali held that a sinner is like a person riding on an animal over which he has no control and which is running fast to hurl him into precipice.

Drops of Rain: Hadrat Ali held that the injunctions of God descend like the drops of rain.

The Summer Clouds: When the people of Kufa did not respond to the call of Hadrat Ali to rise to meet the challenge of Muawiyah, Hadrat Ali said that he longed for warriors who in their action and speed should be like the summer clouds.

Goat and the Lion: Addressing the people of Kufa, Hadrat Ali said, "I want you to tread the path of the truth, but you run from it as the goat runs away on hearing the roar of a lion."

Taking the Thorn out of the Foot with a Thorn: On another occasion Hadrat Ali said that the people of Kufa were like a person who picked out the thorn from his foot with a thorn.

Solution of Salt in Water: With reference to the people of Kufa, Hadrat Ali prayed "O God melt their hearts as the salt is dissolved in water."

Bull with Crooked Horns: When Talha defected after taking the oath of allegiance to him, Hadrat Ali likened Talha to a bull with crooked horns.

Shaking of Plants: Referring to the piety of the Companions of the Holy Prophet, Hadrat Ali said that they shuddered at the mention of the. Hereafter as the plants shake when a strong wind blows.

Pregnant Woman Separating from the Child: Addressing the people of Kufa, Hadrat Ali said that they were not dependable and they were likely to leave him, as the pregnant woman on childbirth is separated from the child bred in her womb.

Household of the Holy Prophet: Hadrat Ali said that the simile of the household of the Holy Prophet was like stars which if one star sets another star rises.

Foaming Waves of the Sea: While addressing Hadrat Othman, Hadrat Ali said that treason was likely to wage like the foaming waves of the sea.

He Decried Flattery: Once a person flattered Hadrat Ali. Hadrat Ali said:

> "Do not flatter me. I am not what you say, but I am more than what you think of me in your heart."

He Denounced Praise: One day Hadrat Ali delivered a sermon which was most impressive and eloquent. Some one praised him for his sermon. He said:

"Do not praise me. That would mislead me and beguile me into vainglory. Remember that all praise is for God alone."

He would Carry his Own Burden: One day Hadrat Ali purchased some provisions in the market. It was a heavy load and he carried it himself. Many persons offered to carry the load for him. He refused the offer saying that everyone should carry his burden himself.

He did not Want the People to Follow in his Retinue: One day Hadrat Ali was riding a horse. Some people followed him and began to walk in his train. He asked them why they were following him. They said that they felt elated to walk in his retinue. He said:

"Go back to your business By walking behind me you will breed feelings of inferiority in yourselves and infect me with arrogance."

He Prayed for Patience to Bear Suffering: At the battle of Uhud, Hadrat Ali received over a hundred wounds. In spite of these wounds he continued fighting and said:

"May God grant me patience to bear this suffering. It is a favour of God that he gave me the courage to stand and fight and not to leave the battlefield."

His Complaint against his People: One night Hadrat Ali saw the Holy Prophet in a dream. He complained to the Holy Prophet that he had received much trouble from his people. The Holy Prophet said that he might invoke the curse of God on them. When it was day, he lifted his hands after the morning prayer and said:

"O God, give me a better people and give these people a worse ruler than me."

He Rode on a Mule instead of a Horse: When going to battle, Hadrat Ali used to ride on a mule instead of a horse. He was asked why he preferred a mule to a horse when the horse would carry him faster. He said that it was so he did not wish to fly from the battlefield.

He would Never Turn his Back to the Enemy: Hadrat Ali always wore the armour on the front part of his body. He was asked why he did not wear the armour on his back. He said that it was so because he did not want to turn his back to the enemy.

He would not Seek a Concession: Once Hadrat Ali went to the market to purchase some cloth. He went to a shop and a shop-keeper recognising him offered the cloth at a concessional rate. Hadrat Ali refused to make the purchase.

He Preferred his Slave to himself: Once Hadrat Ali went to the bazar to purchase some cloth for himself and his slave. One piece was purchased at a higher price and the other at a lower price. He gave the costlier piece of cloth to his slave and kept the cloth of inferior quality for himself.

He had no Ambition for the Caliphate: It is related that when on the way to Basra, Hadrat Ali and his troops were camping at Rabda, Ibn. Abbas came to see him. At that time Hadrat Ali was mending his shoe. Hadrat Ali asked Ibn. Abbas as to what would be the value of the shoe. Ibn. Abbas said that the old shoe had hardly any value and its value would at the most not exceed quarter of a dirham. Hadrat Ali thereupon said, "By God, this shoe is more valuable to me than the caliphate. I have no ambition to rule."

He Freed the Slave who did not Respond to his Call: Once Hadrat Ali called his slave, but the slave did not respond to his call. He called him thrice, but the slave kept silent. Thereafter,

Hadrat Ali went to the slave and said, "Did you not hear my call?". He said that he had listened to his call, but was at that time calling upon God Who had subjected him to the humiliation of slavery". Thereupon Hadrat Ali said, "I release you from slavery forthwith in the name of God. "

He Saw God with Inward Eyes: Once Hadrat Ali was asked whether he had seen God. He said that verily he had seen God because he could not worship Him without knowing Him. He was asked how he had seen Him and he said that. He had seen him with the inward eyes of the heart.

He Lost Consciousness while Praying: Once an arrow stuck in the feet of Hadrat Ali. It could not be taken out because of the intensity of the pain felt. When Hadrat Ali stood up in prayers, he was so much absorbed in the devotional exercise that the surgeon pulled out the arrow without Hadrat Ali feeling any pain.

He would not Pay the Enemy on its Own Coin: At the battlefield of Siffin, the forces of Muawiyah had the control over the source of water supply and they would not allow, thereto, the troops of Hadrat Ali. When the troops of Hadrat Ali overpowered the enemy and got control over the source of water supply, Hadrat Ali was advised that he should deny access of water to the enemy. He repudiated the advice saying that he would not pay the enemy in its own coin, but in the coin of Islam.

He Preferred his Men to Himself: During the water shortage in Siffin he refused to quench his own thirst saying that the water should be given to those of his men who were more thirsty than him

Two Wrongs cannot Make a Right: When, after the battle of Siffin, Muawiyah began harassing the people by making raids into the territory adjoining Syria, the Governor of Hadrat Ali,

Kameel b Ziyad, suggested that he should be authorised to lead retributive expeditions into Syria. Hadrat Ali turned down the suggestion saying, "Two wrongs cannot make a right. Let Muawiyah take pleasure in harassing innocent people I cannot resort to such measures."

He was Dispirited because he had no Guest: One day Hadrat Ali felt unusually dispirited and dejected. When asked about the reason for his unusual dejection he said that he was feeling dispirited because he had received no guest for a week.

He wore Dress of Coarse Cloth: Hadrat Ali always wore dress of coarse cloth. When asked why did he wear such shabby dress when he was the head of the State, he said that it was so because coarse cloth softened the heart while fine cloth hardened the heart.

He Wanted to Travel Light: The house of Hadrat Ali was bereft of the usual furniture. When asked why he deprived himself of such necessities when he was the ruler of a State he said, "This life is a journey and while on a journey one should travel light. I have booked my luggage for the destination—the Hereafter."

He would not Break Open the Lock of the Shop of God: Once. Aqueel, a brother of Hadrat Ali, asked him to provide some relief for him as he was feeling sore. Hadrat Ali said that when he got his usual allowance from the Bartul Mal, he would give something out of it to him. That did not satisfy Aqueel. Hadrat Ali thereupon said, "Then you may break open the locks of the shops in the market. Aqueel said, "Do you want me to become a thief. " Hadrat Ali retorted "Then do you want me to break open the lock of the shop of God and become a brigand instead of the custodian of the BaituI Mal."

He was not Afraid of Death: In the battle of Siffin, Hadrat Ali penetrated into the front ranks of the Syrian forces without any protective armour. One after another his assailants fell before the onslaught of his sword. His son Imam Hasan objected to such neglect to protect himself. Hadrat Ali said. "It is immaterial to me whether I fall to death or death falls on me. I love death as much as a suckling loves the milk of its mother."

He did not Care for the Booty: In a battle Hadrat Ali killed a wealthy Quraish chief Umar b Uqba, but contrary to the Arab custom he did not mutilate his body, nor took off his costly coat of mail. When asked why he had not taken his valuable coat of mail, Hadrat Ali said, "The lion who enters the battlefield either kills himself or is killed. He does not brother about the booty."

He would not Own the Treasure in the Land that He had Purchased: Once Hadrat Ali purchased a plot of land from a person in Medina. When the plot was dug a treasure was found therein. Hadrat Ali would not accept the treasure as it did not form a part of his transaction with the original owner. He offered the treasure to the original owner, but he too did not accept it. Thereupon Hadrat Ali distributed the entire treasure in charity.

He undertook to Clear the Debt of a Dead Muslim: Once the Holy Prophet attended the funeral of a dead Muslim. Before leading the funeral prayer, the Holy Prophet enquired whether the dead man had to clear any debt. He was informed that the dead man had to pay the debt of a dinar. The Holy Prophet said that before he could lead the funeral prayer someone should undertake the responsibility of clearing the debt of the dead Muslim. It was Hadrat Ali who stepped forward to undertake the responsibility for clearing the debt.

He would not Accept the Allegiance from whom he had Released: Marwan, a cousin of Muawiyah, was a bitter enemy of Hadrat Ali. He had played a great part in inciting revolt against the caliphate of Hadrat Ali. He was taken captive in the battle of the Camel at Basra and when brought before Hadrat Ali he asked for mercy. Hadrat Ali released him unconditionally. Thereupon, Marwan offered to pay allegiance to him, but Hadrat Ali said, "I did not want his allegiance I released him for the sake of God and not for securing allegiance to me."

He did not Believe in the Prognostications of the Astrologer: When Hadrat Ali led his troops against the Kharijites at the battle of Nahrawan, an astrologer advised him not to proceed to battle as the time was not propitious. Hadrat Ali refused to act on the advice saying, all knowledge of the unknown belongs to God I cannot accept any person as a partner in the knowledge of God."

He would Take no Precaution to Protect Himself: During the last days of his life, when Hadrat Ali was asked to take protective measures against any murderous attack, he said, "The shield of God is around my body, and nobody can harm me against the will of God. And if God wills me to be martyred, no protective measures will avail."

People Stood in the Way of his Right: At Basra, someone said to Hadrat Ali that he was ambitious for the caliphate Hadrat Ali said, "I am not ambitious, what has happened is that there are people who stand in the way of my right. To strive for the right is no ambition."

Spacious House: At Basra, Hadrat Ali went to the house of one of his companions A ala b Ziyad. He had constructed a spacious house. Hadrat Ali was critical of the spaciousness of the house. He said, "A'ala what have you gained by constructing a spacious house in this world. You should have built a spacious house for yourself in the world Hereafter."

Renunciation, not the Way of Islam: It was complained to Hadrat Ali that one of his Companions. Ibne Ziyad was undergoing devotional exercise to such an extent that he had neglected and disregarded his obligations to his wife and children. Hadrat Ali reprimanded him and said that renunciation was not the way of Islam. He asked him to maintain a proper balance between his duties to God and his duties to the people.

Hosting Dinners: When it was brought to the notice of Hadrat Ali that one of his Governors had hosted a big dinner Hadrat Ali wrote him a letter expressing his disapproval and said "What have you gained by hosting such dinner where the wealthy are fed extravagantly and the poor are turned out."

He could Still Wield the Sword: Writing to Muawiyah, Hadrat Ali said in one of his letters, "I wield the same sword with which I severed the head of your maternal grandfather, maternal uncle and brother with the same stroke."

11

Perfect Lesson

Success is always one of the greatest criteria of truth; and it is not so with the vulgar alone. Even in the early days of Christianity, the good Pharisee said, "Let them alone; if these men be false, they will come to nought, or else you yourselves shall perish." If Constantine had not seen or fancied he had seen the notable cross in the heavens; if he had not marched to success under its auspices; if it had not led him on to victory and to the throne, we can hardly conceive what would have been the fate of Christianity. What the victory of Bedr was for Islam, the victory of the Milvian Bridge was for Christianity. It thenceforth ruled from the throne of the Caesares.

For the Moslems, the victory of Bedr was indeed most auspicious. It was not surprising that they, like the Israelites or Christians of yore, saw the hand of Providence in their success over the Idolaters. Had the Moslems failed, we can imagine what their fate would have been—a universal massacre.

Whilst Mohammed was engaged in this expedition, he lost one of his favourite daughters, Rukaiya married to Othman, who had only recently returned from the Abyssinian exile. But the fury and the desire for revenge with which the Idolaters were burning did not allow him time to indulge in domestic sorrow. As soon as all the Koreishite prisoners had returned home, Abu Sufian issued forth from Mecca with two hundred well-equipped horsemen, vowing solemnly never to return until he had avenged himself on Mohammed and his followers. Scouring the country to within a few miles of Medina, he came down with a fell swoop on the unprepared Moslems slaying the people, ravaging the fields, and burning the date-groves which furnished the staple food of the Arabs. The Meccans had provided themselves with sacks of meal for the foray. As soon, however, as the Moslems sallied forth from Medina to avenge the murders, the Meccans turned bridle and fled, dropping the sacks in order to lighten their horses; whence this affair was derisively called by the Moslems, *Ghazwat-us-sawik*, 'The battle of the meal-sacks."

It was on this occasion, according to the authorites of Washington Irving, that the Prophet gave another example of the extraordinary nobleness of his heart. He was one day sleeping alone at the foot of a tree, at a distance from his camp, when he was awakened by a noise, and beheld Durthur, a hostile warrior, standing over him with a drawn sword. "Oh Mohammed," cried he, "who is there now to save thee?" "God!" replied the Prophet. Struck with awe, Durthur let fall his sword, which was instantly seized upon by Mohammed. Brandishing the weapon, he exclaimed in turn, "Who is there now to save thee, oh Durthur?" "Alas, no one!" replied the soldier, "Then learn from me to be merciful." So saying, he returned the sword. The heart of the stern warrior was overcome; and in after years he proved one of the stanchest adherents of the Prophet.

But this skirmish between the Idolaters and the Moslems, like others which followed it, proved only a prelude to the great drama which was about to be enacted.

The Idolaters were burning for revenge. They made formidable preparations for another war upon the Moslems. Their emissaries succeeded in obtaining the assistance of the tribes of Tihama and

Kinana. Their united forces soon amounted to three thousand well-equipped soldiers (of whom seven hundred were tough warriors), animated with but one desire, that of revenge. This army was as formidable to the petty tribes of Arabia, as the multi-tudinous hordes of Xerxes to the Grecian states. Marching under the command of the relentless Abu Sufian, and meeting with no opposition from any side, they took up a well-chosen position to the northeast of Medina, where only the hill of Ohod and a valley separated them from the devoted city. From this safe vantage-ground they ravaged the fields and fruit -groves of the Medinites.

Grave Experiences

Forced by the enthusiasm of his followers, and by their fury at the destruction of their property, Mohammed marched out of Medina with a thousand men. The ill-concealed enmity of the Jews led to the defection of Abdullah ibn Ubbay, the leader of the Munnafiqin, (the Hypocrites), with three hundred of his followers. This desertion reduced the strength of Mohammed's small force to seven hundred men, who only possessed two horses amongst them. But still this gallant band advanced steadily on. Marching quietly through groves of fruit-trees, they soon gained the hill of Ohod. They passed the night in a defile; and in the morning, after offering prayers as they stood in arms, they debouched into the plain. Mohammed now took up his position immediately under the hill. Posting a few archers on a height behind the troops, he gave them strict injunctions not to abandon their place whatever happened, but to harass the cavelry of the enemy, and protect the flanks of the Moslems. The Idolaters, confident in their numbers, marched down into the plain with their idols in the centre of their army, and the wives of the chiefs chanting their war-songs and beating their timbrels. The first onslaught of the Koreish was fearful, but the Moslems repulsed them bravely. These latter, under Hamza, seeing their confusion, dashed into their midst, dealing blows in all sides. Victory had almost declared for the Moslems, when the archers, forgetting the injunction of Mohammed, and seeing the enemy in flight, dispersed in search of plunder. Khalid Ben Walid, one of the Koreish, at once perceived their error, and rallying the horse, fell on the rear of the Moslems. The infantry of the Koreish also turned, and the troops of the Prophet, taken both in rear and front, had to renew the battle at fearful odds. Some of the bravest chiefs in the Moslem army fell fighting. The intrepid Hamza, with several others, was killed; Ali, who had chivalrously answered the first call of defiance (Rajz) of the Idolaters,' and Omar and Abu Bakr were severely wounded. The efforts of the Idolaters were, however, principally directed toward Mohammed, who surrounded by a few disciples, and cut off from the main body of his people, became now the chief object of their fiercest assaults. His friends fell fast around him. Though bleeding from every wound, he did not forget their loving hearts, and blessed the hand that tried to stanch the blood which flowed from his forehead. But rescue was nigh. The brave warriors who under Ali had been fighting in the centre with the energy of despair, succeeded in retreating to a point on the hill, where they were secure from the attacks of the enemy, but full of consternation at the loss, as they supposed, of their great Master. Seeing, however, their brethren still fighting in another part of the field, they rushed down into the midst of the Idolaters. Penetrating to the place where the small group of Moslems yet defended the Prophet, and finding that he still lived, they succeeded, after great exertions, in retreating with him to the heights of Mount Ohod, where they breathed again. Ali fetched water in his shield from the hollow of a rock. With this he bathed Mohammed's face and wounds, and with his companions offered up the midday prayers sitting.

The Koreish were too much exhausted to follow up their advantage, either by attacking Medina or driving the Moslems from the heights of Ohod. They retreated from the Medinite territories, after barbarously mutilating their slain enemies. The wife of Abu Sufian, Hind the daughter of Otba, with the other Koreishite women of the highest rank, showed the greatest ferocity in this savage work of vengeance, tearing out and devouring the heart of Hamza, and making bracelets and necklaces of the ears and noses of the dead.

The inhuman barbarities practised on the slain created in the bosom of the Moslems a feeling of bitter exasperation. Even Mohammed was at first so moved by grief and indignation as to declare that the dead of the Koreish should be treated in like manner as soon as a victory was gained over them. But his pitiful heart rebelled at his own thoughts, and in calmer moments he uttered the inspired words, "Bear wrong patiently; verily best it will be for the patiently-enduring." And from that day the horrible practice of mutilation which prevailed among all the nations of antiquity was inexorably forbidden to the Moslems.

Shortly after his return to Medina,Muhammed collected his people together to pursue the retreatting enemy, probably to show that the Moslems were yet too strong to be attacked with impunity. Abu Suflan, hearing of this, hastened back to Mecca, having first murdered two Medinites whom he met. He, however, sent a message to the Prophet, saying that he would soon return to exterminate him and his people. The Prophet's reply was characteristic, "We put our trust in God."

The moral effect of this disastrous battle was at once shown by the forays which the neighbouring nomads prepared to make on the Medinite territories. Most of them, however, were repressed by the energetic action of Mohammed, though some of the hostile tribes succeeded in enticing Moslem missionaries into their midst, under the pretence of embracing Islam, and then massacred them. On one such occasion, seventy Moslems were treacherously murdered near a brook called Bir-Mauna, within the territories of two tribes, the Bani-Amir and the Bani-Sulaim, chiefly through the instrumentality of the latter. One of the two survivors of this scene of perfidious slaughter escaped towards Medina. Meeting two unarmed Arabs on the way, and mistaking them for enemies, he killed them. These Arabs belonged to the tribe of Bani-Amir, and were travelling under a safe-conduct of the Prophet, which circumstance, however, was unknown to the fugitive Moslem. When he arrived at Medina and told his story, the heart of the Prophet was filled with grief, and he exclaimed. "Those two men had my safe-conduct; why did thou kill them?" "I did not know, O Apostle of God," was the man's reply.

Bani-Amir sent to Mohammed for redress and compensation (Diat) for their murdered tribesmen. Mohammed knew that it was the duty of his people and those who had accepted the charter, to pay the compensation-money. The Jewish tribes of the Bani-Nadhir, Bani-Kuraizha, and others, were thus bound equally with the Moslems to contribute towards this payment.Mohammed, with a few chosen companions proceeded first to Bani-Nadhir, and required from them their quota. They seemingly at once agreed to this demand, and requested him to wait with them a while. Whilst sitting with his back to the wall of a house, he observed sinister movements amongst the inhabitants which led him at once to divine their intention of murdering him.

To explain, however, the hostility of the Jews, we must retrace our steps. We have seen with what bitter animosity they dogged Mohammed's footsteps, from the moment of his arrival at Medina. They tried to sow disaffection among his people. They libelled him and his followers. "They mispronounced his Koranic words—'twisting their tongues'—so as to give them an offensive meaning. Their 'look down upon us, sounded like 'O our wicked one.' For 'forgiveness,' they said 'sin;' for 'peace upon thee,'' contempt upon thee,' and the like." But this was not all. By their superior education and intelligence, by their union with the party of the Munafikin (the 'Hypocrites'), and by the general unanimity which prevailed among them (so different from the disunion of the Arabs), the Jews formed a most dangerous element within the federated state which had risen under the rule of the great Teacher of Islam. Among unadvanced nations, poets occupy the position and exercise the influence of the Press in modern times. the Jewish poets by their superior culture naturally exercised a vast influence among the Medinites; and this influence was chiefly directed towards sowing sedition among the Moslems, and widening the breach between them and the opposing faction. The defeat of the Idolaters at Bedr was felt as deeply by the Jews as by the Meccans. Immediately after this battle, a distinguished member of their race, called Kab, the son of Ashraf, belonging to the tribe of Nadhir, publicly deploring the ill-success of the Idolaters, proceeded towards Mecca. Finding the people there filled with consternation and grief, he spared no exertion to revive their courage. By ill satires against the Prophet and his disciples, by his elegies on the Meccans who had fallen at Bedr, he succeeded in exciting the Koreish to that frenzy of vengeance which found a vent on the plains of Ohod. Having attained his object, he retraced his steps homewards. His acts were openly directed against the commonwealth of which he was a member. He belonged to a tribe which had entered into the compact with the Moslems, and pledged itself for the internal as well as external safety of the State. On the arrival of this traitor in Medina, he was executed. Another Jew of the name of Abu Rafe Sellam, belonging to the Bani-Nadhir, who had tried to stir up the neighbouring tribes against the Moslems, was also executed. The fate of these two traitors, and the expulsion of their brethren the Bani-Kainuka from the Medinite territories, had given rise to a bitter feeling of animosity among the Nadhir against the Prophet. The circumstances connected with the banishment of the Kainuka are so romantic as to be worth relating in this sketch of the Prophet's career. Whilst the other Jewish tribes were chiefly agricultural, the Bani-Kainuka hardly possessed a single field or date-plantation. They were for the most part artisans employed in handicraft of all kinds. Seditious and unruly, always ready for a broil, like their coreligionists of Alexandria, these Bani-Kainuka were also noted for the extreme laxity of their morals. One day in Shawwal, 2 A.H. (February, 624 A.C.), a young girl from the country came to their bazaar or market (Suk) to sell milk. The Jewish youths, outraging every principle of honour and hospitality, insulted her grossly. A Moslem passer-by took the part of the girl; and in the fray which ensued, the author of the outrage was killed, whereupon the entire body of the Jews present rose, and slaughtered the Moslem. A wild scene then followed. The Moslems, enraged at the murder of their compatriot, flew to arms; blood flowed fast, and many were killed on both sides. At the first news of the riots, Mohammed hastened to the spot, and by his presence succeeded in restraining the fury of his followers. He at once perceived what the end would be of these seditions and disorders if allowed to take their course. Medina would be turned into an amphitheatre, in which members of hostile factions might murder one another with impunity. The Jews had openly and knowingly infringed the terms of their compact. It was necessary to put a stop to this with a firm hand, or farewell to all hope of peace and security. Consequently Mohammed proceeded at once to the quarter of the Bani-Kainuka and required them to enter definitely into the Moslem commonwealth by embracing Islam or to vacate Medina. The reply of the Jews was couched in the most offensive terms. "O Mohammed, do not be elated with thy victory over thy people (the Koreish). Thou hast had an affair with men ignorant of the art of war. If thou art desirous of having any dealings with us, we shall show thee that we are men." They then shut themselves up in their fortress and set Mohammed's authority at defiance. But their reduction was an absolute duty; and siege was accordingly laid to their strongholds without loss of time. After fifteen days they surrendered. At first it was intended to inflict some severe punishment on them, but the clemency of Mohammed's nature overcame the dictates of justice, and the Bani-Kainuka were simply banished.

All these circumstances were rankling within the breasts of the Bani-Nadhir. They only waited for a favourable opportunity to rid themselves of Mohammed, and, therefore, looked upon his arrival amongst them as providential. But their sinister designs, as we have before said, did not escape the eagle eye of the Prophet. He immediately left the place without raising the suspicions of the Jews, and thus saved himself and his disciples from almost certain destruction.

Bani-Nadhir had now placed themselves in exactly the same position as the Bani-Kainuka had previously done. They had by their own act placed themselves outside the pale of the charter; and, therefore, on his arrival at Medina, Mohammed sent them a message of the same import as that which was sent to the Kainuka.

Relying on the support of the Munafikm and Abdullah-ibn-Ubbay, the Bani-Nadhir returned a defiant answer. Disappointed, however, in the promised assistance of Abdullah and of their brethren, the Bani-Kuraizha, after a siege of fifteen days they sued for terms. The previous offer was renewed, and they agreed to evacuate their territories. They were allowed to take all their moveable property with them, with the exception of arms. In order to prevent the Moslems from occupying their dwellings, they destroyed these before leaving.

Their land, warlike materials, etc., which they could not carry away, were distributed by the Prophet, with the consent and warm approbation of the Ansar, among the Muhajerin, who, up to the present time, had been entirely dependent for support on the generous munificence of the Medinites. Notwithstanding the strong brotherly love which existed between the "Refugees" and the "Auxiliaries," Mohammed knew that the assistance of the Medinites afforded but a precarious means of subsistence. He accordingly assembled the principal men from among the Ansar, and asked them whether they would allow him to distribute among their poor brethren who had followed him from Mecca, the goods left behind by the Jews. With one voice they answered, "Give to our brothers the goods of the Jews; assign to them even a portion of ours; we willingly consent." Upon this, the Prophet divided the property among the Muhajerin and two of the Ansar who were extremely poor.

The expulsion of the Bani-Nadhir took place in the month of Rabi I. of the 4th year. The remaining portion of this year and the early part of the next were passed in the repression of various spasmodic efforts on the part of the nomad tribes to harass the Moslems, and in inflicting punishments for murderous forays on the Medinite territories.

Meanwhile the enemies of the Prophet were not idle. Far and wide the Idolater had sent their emissaries to stir up the tribes against the Moslems. The Jews were the most active in these efforts.

Some of the Bani-Nadhir had remained behind with their brethren near Khaibar, and there, fired with the hope of vengeance, had set themselves to work to form another league against the Moslems. Their efforts were successful beyond their utmost hopes. A formidable coalition was soon formed; and an army consisting of ten thousand well-appointed men marched upon Medina, under the command of the restless Abu Sufian. Meeting no opposition on their way, they soon encamped within a few miles of Medina, on its most vulnerable side towards Ohod. To oppose this host, the Moslems could only muster a body of three thousand men. Forced thus by their inferiority in numbers, as well as by the factious opposition of the "Hypocrites" within the city, to remain on the defensive, they dug a deep trench round the unprotected quarters of Medina; and, leaving their women and children for safety in their fortified houses, they encamped outside the city with the moat in front of them. In the meantime, they relied for the safety of another side, if not upon the active assistance, at least upon the neutrality of the Bani Kuraizha, who possessed several fortresses at a short distance towards the south-east, and were bound by the Compact, to which we have so often referred, to assist the Moslems against every assailant. These Jews, however, were persuaded by the Idolaters to violate their pledged faith and to join the Koreish. As soon as the news of their defection reached Mohammed, he deputed "the two Sads," Sad-ibn-Muadz and Sad-ibn-Ubada, to entreat them to return to their duty. The reply was defiant and sullen: "Who is Mohammed: and who is the Apostle of God that we should obey him? There is no bond or compact between us and him."

As these Jews were well acquainted with the locality, and could materially assist the besiegers by showing them the weak points of the city, the consternation among the Moslems became great, whilst the disaffected body within the walls increased the elements of danger.

The Idolaters and the Jews, failing in all their attempts to draw the Moslems into the open field, or to surprise the city under the direction of Jewish guides, determined upon a regular assault.

The siege had already lasted twenty days. The restless tribes of the desert, who had made common cause with the Koreish and their Jewish allies, and who had expected an easy prey, were becoming weary of this protracted campaign. Great efforts were made at this critical moment by the leaders of the beleaguering host to cross the trench and fall upon the small Moslem force. Every attempt was, however, repulsed by untiring vigilance on the part of Mohammed. The elements now seemed to combine against the besieging army; their horses were perishing fast and provisions were becoming scanty. Disunion was rife in their midst, and the far-seeing chief of the Moslems, with matchless prudence, tormented it into actual division. Suddenly this vast coalition, which had seemed to menace the Moslems with inevitable destruction, vanished into thin air. In the darkness of night, amidst a storm of wind and rain,—their tents overthrown, their lights put out,—Abu Sufian and the majority of his formidable army fled; the rest took refuge with the Bani-Kuraizha. Mohammed had in the night foretold to his followers the dispersion of their enemies. Day-break saw his prognostications fulfilled, and the Moslems returned in joy to the city.

Prevalence of Truth

But the victory was hardly achieved in the opinion of the Moslems, as long as the Bani Kuraizha remained so near and in such dangerous proximity to the city of Islam. They had proved themselves traitors in spite of their sworn alliance, and had at one time almost surprised Medina from their side, an event which would have involved the general massacre of every soul in the place. The Moslems, therefore, thought it their wisest policy to strike a blow before the Jews could renew their machinations. Under the guidance of Mohammed, they immediately marched upon the Jewish fortresses, and after a siege of twenty-five days, the Bani Kuraizha offered to surrender on the terms granted to the Bani Nadhir. This was refused, and they were required to surrender at discretion. Relying on the intercession of their old allies, the Aus, and on the condition that their punishment should be left to the judgment of the Ausite chief, Sad-ibn-Muadz, they submitted at discretion. Unhappily, this man, infuriated by the treacherous conduct of Bani-Kuraizha, and their untiring hostility to the new faith, passed a sentence of unusual severity upon them. He ordered that the fighting men should be put to death, and that the women and children, with all their belongings, should become the property of the Moslems. This deplorable sentence was inexorably carried into execution.

The formidable coalition formed by the Jews and the Idolaters to compass the destruction of the new commonwealth of Medina, had utterly failed, well might the Moslems say miraculously. But the surrounding tribes of the desert, wild and fierce, were committing depredations, accompanied with murders on the Medinite territories; and the existence of the state required the employment of the sternest measures for their repression. Several expeditions were dispatched against these marauders, but the slippery sons of the desert generally evaded the approach of the Moslems. The Bani-Uhyan, who had requested Mohammed to send a few of his disciples among them to teach the precepts of Islam, and who, on the arrival of the missionaries, to the number of six, had killed three of them, and sold the surviving three to the Meccans,—had, up to this period, remained unpunished. But the time had come when this crime should be avenged. In the month of Jamadi I. of this year, a body of troops under the personal command of the Prophet, marched against the Bani-Lihyan. The marauder's, however, receiving timely notice of the Prophet's approach, fled into the mountains, and the Moslems returned to Medina without having accomplished their purpose.

A few days had only elapsed, when a chief of the Bani-Fezara, a branch of the nomad horde of Ghatafan, [Khail-i-Ghatafan] suddenly fell upon the open suburbs of the city, and drove off an enormous herd of camels, murdering the man who had charge of them, and carrying off his wife. The Moslems were immediately on their track, and a few of the animals were recovered; but the

Bedouins escaped into the desert with the largest portion of their booty.

The human mind always attaches an idea of sublime grandeur to the character of a man who, whilst possessing the power of returning evil for evil, not only preaches but practises the divine principle of forgiveness. Mohammed, as the Chief of the State and guardian of the life and liberties of his people, in the exercise of justice sternly punished every individual guilty of crime.Mohammed, the Prophet, the Teacher, the Exalter of the human race, was gentle and kind and merciful, even to his greatest enemies. In him were combined the highest attributes that the mind of man can conceive, Justice and Mercy.

A chief of the tribe of Hanafa, named Thumama, son of Uthal, was taken prisoner by the Moslems in one of their expeditions against the unruly Arabs of the desert. He was brought to Medina, where he was so affected by the kindness of the Prophet that from an enemy he soon became a most devoted follower. Returning to his people, he stopped the transport to Mecca of provisions from Yemama, where the Bani-Hanafa were domiciled. The Meccans drew the greatest part of the necessaries of life from Yemama, and this stoppage by Thumama reduced them to the saddest straits. Failing to move the Hanafites, they at last addressed themselves to Mohammed, and besought him, by every tie, to intercede for them. The Prophet's heart was touched with pity, and he at once requested Thumama to allow the Meccans to have whatever they wanted, and, at his word, the convoys were again permitted to reach Mecca.

A tribe of Christian Bedouins (the Bani-Kalb) settled about Dumat-ul-jaiidal, had, in their depredations, appeared on the Medinite territories. An expedition was now dispatched to summon them to embrace Islam, and forego their lawless practices. Whilst delivering his injunctions to the captain who headed this small force, Mohammed peremptorily enjoined him, "in no case shalt thou use deceit or perfidy, nor shalt thou kill any child."

In the month of Shaban of this year, (November, December, 627,) an expedition was directed against the Bani-Mustalik. These people had, up to this time, been on friendly terms with the Moslems. But recently, instigated by their chief Harith, the son of Abu Dhirar, they had thrown off their allegiance, and committed forays on the suburbs of Medina. The expedition was entirely successful, and several prisoners were taken, amongst whom was a daughter of Harith, called Juwairiya.

Six years had now passed since the exiles of Mecca had left their homes and their country for the sake of their faith, and of him who had infused into them a new consciousness, such as they had never felt before, awakening in them the spirit of union, love, and brotherhood. People flocked from every part of Arabia, to listen to the words of the wondrous man who had achieved all this; to ask his counsel in all the affairs of everyday life, even as the sons of Israel consulted of old, that grand seer, Samuel,—or, perhaps, only to see him and talk to him.

But the hearts of these exiles still yearned sadly for the place of their birth. Driven from their homes, they had found refuge in a rival city; expelled from the precincts of the sacred Kaaba, which formed the glorious centre of all their associations—the one spot round which gathered the history of their nation,—for six years had they been denied the pilgrimage of the holy shrine, a custom round which Time, with its hoary traditions, had cast the halo of sanctity. The Teacher himself longed to see the place of his nativity with as great a yearning. The temple of the Kaaba belonged to the whole Arab nation. The Koreish were merely the custodians of this shrine, and were not authorised by the public law of the country to interdict the approach even of an enemy, if he presented himself without any hostile design, and with the avowed object of fulfilling a religious duty.

The season of the pilgrimage had approached; the Prophet accordingly announced his intention of visiting the Holy Places. At once a thousand voices responded to the call. Preparations were rapidly made, and, accompanied by seven hundred Moslems, Ansar and Muhajerin, all perfectly unarmed, he set out on the pilgrimage. The animosity of the Koreish, however, was not yet extinguished. They posted themelsves, with a large army, some miles in advance of Mecca, to bar the way, but soon after fell back on the city, in order to keep every point of access closed to the Moslems. They swore solemnly not to allow the followers of the Prophet to enter the shrine, and maltreated the envoy who was sent to them to solicit permission to visit the Holy Places. A body of the Meccans went round the Prophet's encampment with the avowed object of killing any unwary Moslem who might leave the camp. They even attacked the Prophet with stones and arrows. Finding the Idolaters immoveable, and wishful himself to end the state of warfare between the Moslemes and the Koreish, Mohammed expressed himself willing to agree to any terms the Meccans might feel inclined to impose. After much difficulty a treaty was concluded, by which it was agreed that all hostilities should cease for ten years; that any one coming from the Koreish to the Prophet without the permission of his guardian or chief, should be re-delivered to the Idolaters; that any individual from among the Moslems going over to the Meccans, should not be surrendered; that any tribe desirous of entering into alliance, either with the Koreish or with the Moslems, should be at liberty to do so without hindrance; that the Moslems should retrace their steps on this occasion, without advancing further; that they should be permitted, in the following year, to visit Mecca, and to remain there for three days with their travelling arms, namely, their scimitars in sheaths.

Best Model

The unexampled moderation and magnanimity displayed by Mohammed in concluding this treaty caused some discontent among the more impulsive of his followers, in whose hearts the injuries and cruelties inflicted by the Koreish yet rankled. In virtue of the third stipulation of the treaty, by which the Moslems bound themselves to surrender every Idolater who came over to their cause without the permission of their patron or chief—the Koreish demanded the surrender of several of the Prophet's disciples, and their demand was immediately compiled with by Mohammed, in spite of the murmurs of some of the Moslems.

On his return to Medina, Mohammed, in pursuance of the Catholic wish by which he was inspired, that his religion should embrace all Humanity within its comprehensive bosom, dispatched several envoys to invite the neighbouring sovereigns and nations, immersed in absolute moral darkness, to adopt Islam, and to drink of the cup of life offered to them by the Prophet of Arabia.

Two of the most noted of these embassies were to Heraclius the Emperor of Byzantium, and to Khusru Parviz, the Kesra of Persia. Khusru was then in the first flush of his mighty victories over the Romans. When he received Mohammed's letter he found his name placed after that of the Prophet. Enraged at the insult, the great King tore the letter into pieces. When the news of this contemptuous treatment was brought to the Prophet, he quietly replied, 'Thus will the empire of Kesra be torn to pieces."The fulfilment of the prophecy is engraved on the pages of history. Heraclius, more politic, or more reverential, treated the messenger with greater respect.

The hand of an assassin dashed all these expectations to the ground. The accession of the Ommiades, through treachery and intrigue, to the office which the virtues of the Khulafai-rashidin had sanctified, was a severe blow to the progress of knowledge and liberalism in the Islamic world. Their stormy reigns, harassed by fearful wars, left the nation little leisure to devote to the gentler pursuits of science; and to this, among the sovereigns, was joined a characteristic idolatry of the past. During the comparatively long rule of a century, the House of Ommiya produced only one man devoted to the cultivation of letters and this man was Abu Hashem Khalid ben Yezid, "the philosopher of the Merwanian family," as he has been called, who was set aside from the succession on account of his learning.

The jealous suspicion, and the untiring enimosity of the children of Hind and Abu-Sufian had obliged the descendants of the Prophet to take refuge in solitude and humble privacy."In the night of misery and unhappiness" they followed truly and faithfully the precepts of their ancestor, and found consolation in intellectual pursuits, and in that introspection which distinguishes noble hearts. Their ardent love of knowledge, their passionate devotion to the cause of humanity—(their spirit looking upwards far above the literalness of common interpretations of the Law)—their recognition of the all embracing Soul of the universe brought into strong relief all the spirituality and expansiveness of Islam. Their adherents, under the influence of a deep-seated feeling of hatred, were often induced to make use of their names in their own revolts against the usurping race. But the noblest of the Ommiades recognised in the fullness of gratitude their true worth when he wished to cast his diadem at their feet.

Surrounded by men whose love, devotion and sympathy with their patience, had gathered round them, they were naturally influenced in a greater or less degree by the varied ideas of their followers. Yet their philosophy never sings to that war of words without life and without earnestness, which characterised the schools of Athens, of Alexandria, or of Baghdad under the later Abbassides.

With the rise of the house of Abbas, another era commences. Its members had drunk at the same fountain-head with the children of Fatima, and the lessons they had learnt in the common school of affliction, did not lose efficacy when they attained the caliphate. Abu-la- Abbas Saffah (the Relentless) was as remarkale for his devotion to letters as for his warlike qualities. Mansur, Hadi and Mehdi were not only warm patrons of the learned who flocked to their courts from all parts of the world, but were themselves assiduous cultivators of every branch of knowledge.

Particular epochs in the history of the world always stand out as the brightest portions of a nation's life. Athens had her

Periclean age; Rome her Augustan era; so too had the Islamc world her period of glory; and we may with justice look upon the reigns of Harun and Abdullah al-Mamun as an epoch of equal, if not of superior greatness and magnificence. Under these two caliphs, the Moslems come distinctly before the world to fulfil the high purpose for which providence has designed them. The Saracenic race, by their elastic genius as well as by their central position—with the hoarded treasures of dying Greece and Rome on one side and of Persia on the other—and India and China far away sleeping the sleep of ages—were pre-eminently fitted to become the teachers of humanity. Under the inspiring influences of the great Prophet, who gave them a code and a nationality, and assisted by their sovereigns the Saracens caught up the lessons of wisdom from the East and the West, combined them with the teaching of the Master and "started from soldiers into scholars."

City of Knowledge

Under the Ommiades, we see the Moslems passing through a period of probation to prepare them for the glorious task they were called upon to undertake. Under the Abbassides we see in them the repositaries of the knowledge of the world. Every part of the globe is ransacked by the agents of the Caliphs for the hoarded literary treasures of antiquity; these are brought to the capital, "the garden of justice," and laid open before an admiring and appreciating public. Schools and academies spring up on every side; the great philosophers of the ancient world are studied along with the Koran. Galen, Dioscorides, Themistius, Aristotle, Plato are reverenced—even more than they ever were among their own people. The sovereigns themselves assist in literary meetings and philosophical disquisitions. For the first time in the history of humanity, a religious and autocratic government is observed to ally itself with philosophy, preparing and partaking in its triumphs.

Every city in the empire sought to outrival the other in the cultivation of the arts and sciences. Every governor and provincial chief tried to emulate the sovereign. From every part of the globe students and scholars flocked to Cordova, to Baghdad, and to Cairo, to listen to the words of the saracenic sages. Men who became in after life the heads of the Christian Church, drank at the fountain of Mohammed. And when the house of Abbas lost its hold on the Empire of the East, the chiefs who sprang up to occupy their place, endeavoured to rival the Caliphs in their partonge of science and learning. The Buyide, the Samanide, the Ghaznavide in the East, the Fatimite and the Ayubite in the West, the Moorish sovereigns in Spain, outvied each other in the cultivation of arts and letters. From the shores of the Atlantic eastward to the Indian Ocean, far away even to the Pacific, resounded the voice of philosophy and learning, under Moslem guidance and Moslem inspiration. This glorious period lasted till the close of the 15th and the commencement of the 16th century of the Christian era. Then forgetting the precepts of the Master, the Moslems sank to the level of the barbarous hordes who flooded Moslem Asia, and the polytheistic races of conquered lands, and thus adopted a hardness of heart, a literalness of faith, and an abject superstitious turn of mind, entirely contrary to the teachings of Mohammed.

The high position assigned by the Prophet to science and philosophy, and the devotion of his early descendants to every branch of intellectual pursuit had led to the rapid development of intellectual liberty among the Moslems.

One of the most distinguishing characteristics of the Koran is the curious, and to a superficial observer inconsistent manner, in which it combines the existence of a Divine Will—(which not only orders all things, but which acts directly upon men and addresses itself to the springs of thought in them)—with the assertion of a Free Agency in man and the liberty of intellect. It seems inconsistent at first sign that man should be judged by his works—a doctrine which forms the foundation of Islamic morality—if all his actions are ruled by an all powerful Will. The earnest faith of Mohammed in an active, ever-living principle, joined to his trust in the progress of man, supplies a key to this mystery. To

Mohammed the fundamental laws of Truth and Nature, which seem innate in the moral Consciousness of Humanity—are the essence of Divine ordinance. They are as much laws, in the strictest sense of the word, as the laws which regulate the movements of the celestial bodies. But the will of God is not an arbitrary will; it is an educating will, to be as humbly obeyed by the scholar in his walks of learning, as by the devotee in his cell. One hour's contemplation of the words of the Creator, one hour's conscientious study of the principles which regulate the phenomena of the creation, is more acceptable to God than seventy years of devotion and prayer.

Justice for All

Islam allowed its followers take varied shape at different times and in different individuals. The divisions in the Church of Mohammed, which pass under the name of schisms, have originated almost exclusively from political causes and tribal or clan-jealousies, though of course some degree of religious rancour added betterness to the feelings of partizanship.

The Moslem doctors, as found of dogmatising and as wedded to the past as their rival brothers of the West, have from the earliest times divided the dogmas of their religion into fundamental and nonfundamental. The former include the points of faith which the believer is bound to accept, such as belief in the existence of a Deity, a sense of future accountability, etc.; the latter specify the duties which emanate from such beliefs. These fundamental dogmas—perhaps properly so called, as they furnish the chief basis for the construction of every system of positive morality,—were early dissociated from true philosophy and relegated to the domians of dogmatic theology; they now furnished the principal battleground for the revived Rationalism in Islam. One section held that all these fundamental points of faith were as much within the cognizance of reason as the duties arising from them; another as strongly asserted that its province was confined to the non-fundamental points, whilst others held intermediate notions.

On the question of free will and predestination, three men, named Mabad al Johni, Gilan of Damascus, and Eunas al Aswari had already broken away from the tradition of the past and acknowledged the absolute free-agency of man.This Bidator heresy, as the orthodox Shahrastani calls it, was occasioned by the decided predestinarianism of Jahm ben Safwan, who in the absolute denial of free will to man almost rivalled Calvin, and whose opinions found much favour with the moody bigots who occupied the office of Caliphs. Immediately after came Wasil ben Ata, a disciple of Imam Hassan al-basri (of Bassora). The master himself was educated in the school of the early descendants of the Prophet, "philosophers of the family of Mohammed", as they have been so nobly designated, and the liberality of his views was naturally in remarkable contrast to those of his age. Wasil had imbibed knowlege from the same source, but he soon separated from Hassan on a question of religious dogma, which shewed his impulsive nature, and founded a school of his own. His disciples have from his time been called Mutazala, Separatists or Seceders. He soon formulated the principles which constituted the bases of his difference from the other existing schools. His impulsiveness often led him, like Luther, to overstep the bounds of reason in his antagonism against intellectual tyranny; yet the general rationalism which distinguished his school from every other brought the strongest and most liberal minds to his side.Under their influence, the principles of logic and philosophy were brought to bear on the precepts of religion, thus giving rise to an especial science—the science of theological philosophy.

The Mutazaias unanimously hold," says Shahrastani, "that God is Eternal; and that Eternity is the peculiar property of His essence; but they deny the existence of any eternal attributes (as distinct from His nature). For they say, He is Omniscient as to His nature; Living as to His nature; Almighty as to His nature; but not through any knowledge, power or life existing in Him as eternal attributes, for knowledge, power and life are part of His essence. Otherwise, if they are to be looked upon as eternal attributes of the Deity, it will give rise to a multiplicity of eternal entities."

They maintain that the knowledge of God is as much within the province of reason as that of any other Entity that He cannot be beheld with the corporeal sight, and with the exception of Himself everything else is liable to change or to suffer extinction. They also maintain that Justice is the animating principle of human actions; Justice according to them being the dictates of reason and the concordance of the ultimate result of the conduct of man with such dictates. Again, they hold that there is no eternal law as regards human action; that the divine ordinances which regulate the conduct of men are the results of growth and development; that God has commanded and forbidden, promised or threatened by a law which grew gradually. At the same time they say, that he who works righteousness merits rewards, and he who works evil deserves punishment; and this, they say, is consonant with reason. The Mutazalas also say that all knowledge is attained through reason, and must necessarily be so obtained. They hold that the congnition of good and evil is also within the province of reason; that nothing is known to be wrong or right until reason has enlightened us as to the distinction; and that thankfulness for the blessings of the Benefactor is made obligatory by reason, even before the promulgation of any law on the subject."

The Mutazalas unanimously maintain that man has perfect freedom; he is the author of his actions both good and evil, and deserves reward and punishment hereafter accordingly.

The Sifatiyas (the Attributists) who represent the old Patristic notions in the most stereotyped form, are the direct antitheses of the Mutazalas. The Ashariyas (an off shoot of the Sifatite schools, followers of Abu-1-Hassan Ali-al-Ashari), with slight variations uphold the doctrines of the parent stock; maintaining that God possesses eternal attributes, that we cannot arrive at the knowledge of His existence by reason; that reason cannot enable us to diṣtinguish right from wrong; that the Divine ordinances are eternal; that God can be beheld; and that man has power over his eivl deeds alone, all good actions coming from God.The Jabariyas, however, deny every freedom to man, holding that all human actions are the result of Divine will.

Against these anthropomorphic doctrines, as the Mutazalas with truth designated them, then efforts were mainly directed; and naturally they called themselves the upholders of the unity and justice of God. The Mutazalas are thus, decided Rationalists, on account of the great predominance they allow of man; they are Utilitarians, in adopting the doctrine of general usefulness and the promotion of the happiness of the many, as the criterion of right and wrong; they are Evolutionists, in regarding every law that regulates the mutual relations of human beings, as the result and product of a process of development. In their ideas of the long antiquity of man on earth, they occupy a vantage ground in relation to the natural philosophers of the modem world. That grand collection of Mutazalite ideas—which passes under the name of Tuhfat-ul-Akhwan-us-Safa,—""gifts of the Brothers of Purity,"—in the purity of its sentiments, its fervent love of humanity, its earnest faith in the progress of man, and in its universal charity embracing even the brute creation in its fold, is a masterpiece of its kind.

Their doctrines were adopted by Abdullah-al-Mamun, the grandest and most liberal-minded of the Saracenic sovereigns, and one of the most far seeing monarchs of any age. The aim of his life, and also of that of his two successors, Motassem and Vathek, was to infuse this rationalistic spirit which animated them and a portion of their subjects, into the whole Moslem world. Unfortunately for Islam it was found, as a Westem historian remarks, that the Jurists of Baghdad were more powerful than the Caliphs; and the triumph of patristicism under Mutawwakil, was one of the chief causes of the downfall of the Caliphate.

Generally, the Shias tend towards the Mutazalite doctrines; the Sunnites towards those of the Sifatiyas, but the extremes, as everywhere, merge into each other.

The Shias of the Moderate Mutazalite school are divided into the Usuli and the Akhbari, namely (1) those who adhere to certain principles of interpretation as laid down by the Mujtahids (heads of the schools), whilst repudiating all traditions not received from certain established and recognised sources; and (2) those who deny entirely the influence of authority on matters of opinion (except in so far as it may tend to direct individual judgment into a healthy channel.)

The Sunnites are divided by Shahrastani into the Ahl-ul-hadis, "people of tradition" and the ahl-ur-Rai, "people of reason or judgment." the Shafeites, the Malekites, and the Hanbalites have been classed in the former, the Hanefites in the latter division. These schools take their name from four great jurisconsults of the (Sunnite) Moslem world. The Shafeites, the Malekites, and the Hanbalites are strict Sifatiyas and exceedingly anthropomorphic in their views regarding the attributes of the Deity, and unswervingly adhere to every principle and tradition of the past. The Hanifites, admitting the traditions, leave the interpretation to individual judgment and analogy. Thus the Shiite Akhbari and the Sunnite Hanifi meet on common grounds.

Mystic Attitudes

The wonderful mysticism which forms the life and soul of modem Persian literature, owes its distinct origin to the esoteric significance attached by an important section of the Moslems to the words of the Koran. The elevated feeling of divine pervasion with which Mohammed often spoke: the depth of fervent and ecstatic rapture which characterised his devotion, constituted the chief basis on which Moslem mysticism was founded. During the lifetime of the Prophet, when the performance of duties was regarded before speculation, there was little scope for the full development of the contemplative and mystical element in Islam.

This mystical and contemplative element has existed in all religions, and among every people. As our battles, moral and physical, grow fewer, we look upon this character— the character of quiet contemplation—as the true type of humanity. But yet it will vary with the peculiarities of the individual and the race, and according to their tendency to confound the abstract with the concrete. The Hindu looks to the absorption of the special in the Infinite, as the culmination of happiness; and to attain this end, he remains immovable in one spot, and resigns himself to complete apathy. The sense of infinity makes it difficult for him to distinguish between the priest and the God, or himself and the God, objectively; and eventually between the Deity and the different forms of nature in which he is supposed to be manifested. Gradually this train of contemplation leads to the formal conclusion, as appears from the Bhagavad Gita, that Creator and Creation are identical. We see thus how curiously pantheism approaches in its extreme manifestation to fetishism, which preceded every other idea of the Divinity. In its infancy the human mind knows no spiritual sentiment by one of unmixed terror. The primeval forests which the hand of man has not yet touched, the stupendous mountains looming in the distance, the darkeness of the night, with the grim weild shapes which hover over it; the howlings of the wind through the forest tops, all inspire fear and awe in the infant mind of man. He worships every material object he sees more powerful or more awestriking than himself or his immediate surroundings. Gradually he comes to attach an ideality to all these objects of Nature and things these idealities worthy of adoration. In process of time all these separate idealities merge in one universal all-embracing ideality. Fetishism is only the first step to Monotheism and Pantheism, and each of these merges into one another in their extremes. The early Zoroastrian was very little of the pantheist. Zervanism was a growth of later ages.

Neoplatonism, itself the child of Eastern thought, had impressed its character on Christianity, and probably given rise to the Eucharistic idea. With the exception of Johannes Scotus, the mystics of Europe during the middle ages fought only on this ground. Mysticism properly so-called, with its higher yearning after the Infinite, was ushered in by the Moslems, as we shall hereafter see.

The idea among the nobler minds, that there was a deeper and more inward sense in the words of the Koran, arose not from the wish to escape from the rigour of texts and dogmas, but from a profound conviction that those words meant more, not less than the popular expounders supposed them to mean.

This conviction, combined with a deep feeling of Divine Pervasion—a feeling originating from and in perfect accordance with the teachings of the Koran, and the instructions of the Prophet—led to the development among the Moslems of that contemplative or idealistic philosophy which has received the name of Sufiism, the spread of which, among the Western Mohammedans, was probably assisted by the prevalence of Platonic ideas. The celebrated Imam (abu Hamid Mohammed) al-Gazzali in the East, and Ibn Tufail in the West, were the two greatest representatives of idealistic philosophy among the Moslems. The former, dissatisfied with every philosophical system which based knowledge on experience or reason, had taken refuge in Sufiism. From that moment, the destruction of philosophers became the chief object of his life. He directed his attacks chiefly against Abu Ali Ibn Sina (Avicenna) and his peripatetism.' Al-Gazzali's influence served greatly to promote the diffusion of Sufiism among the Eastern Moslems and he has been justly called the Plato of the Mohammedans. A noble train followed in his footsteps. Idealistic philosophy was embraced by the greatest intellects of the Mohammedan East. The Moulana Jelal-ud-din of Rum (Turkey), whose Masnavi is adored by the Sufi, Sanai whom Jelal-ud-din himself has called his superior, Farid-ud-din Attar Shams-ud-din Haflz, Khakani, the moralist Sadi, the romancer Nizami,—all belonged to this school; and some of the Sufis even lay claim to the Homer of Persia, Firdousi, as one of their school.

Their arguments, however, for thus claiming the greatest poet of Iran, and one of the greatest of the world, are based on but slender foundation.His mind was of a sterner type; and, as a natural consequence, the idealism which pervades his writings is different from the vague mysticism of the Sufi school. For certain poetic minds mysticism has immense charm. But for intellects cast in the mould of stem reason, it is too dreamy ever to become a favourite doctrine. Hence the aversion of Abu Ali Ibn Sina (Avicenna), and of Khwaja Nasir-ud-din of Tus,—the greatest Moslem astronomer of the 13th century—to Sufiism.

The Sufis base the practice of morality entirely on Love, and abhor the idea of fear as the origin of duties. One of them, on being asked, who were bad, answered, those who serve God out of fear of punishment or hope of reward from what motive then do you serve God?' asked the interrogator. Out of Love to Him' said the Sufi, basing his reply on the mystic tradition handed down from Mohammed, that God divided Love into a hundred parts, ninetynine of which He reserved for Himself, and allotted one to mankind; and that all the love which exists in the world is due to that one part; that through that alone human beings love each other; and that man is nearest to God when his soul is wrapt in the devotions of Universal Love.

The pure, we may say the exalted side of this beautiful idealism, entirely founded on the teachings of Mohammed, has furnished glorious themes to the poets of Islam. The idylls of that Universal Divine Love, which pervades Nature from the lowest type of creation to the highest, sung in sweet strains and rapturous words by Jelal-ud-din, Sanai and Attar are regarded by the Sufis with a veneration only less than that entertained for the Koran, and sometimes with an equal feeling of respect.

Sufiism in the Mohammedan world,—like its counterpart in Christendom,—has, in its practical operation, however, been productive of many mischievous results. In perfectly well-attuned minds, mysticism takes the form of a noble type of idealistic philosophy; but the generality of mindkind are more likely to unhinge their brains by busying themselves with the mysteries of the Divine Essence, and our relation to it. Every ignorant and idle specimen of humanity who, despising real knowledge, abandoned the fields of true philosophy, and betook himself to the domains of mysticism, would thus set himself up as one of the Ahl-i-marfat, "people of knowledge." And that this actually occurred in the time of Gazzali, we see by his bitter complaint, that things had come to such a pass that husbandmen were leaving their tillage and claiming the privileges of "the advanced." In fact, the greatest objection to vulgar mysticism, whether in Islam or in Christendum, is that, being in itself no religion, wherever it prevails it unsettles the mind and weakens the foundations of morality; indeed, it brings about a state of things which is every day visible in the naturalistic pantheism of India.

Yet the benefits, conferred by the nobler type of idealistic philosophy are too great to be ignored; and the Idealism of Abu Ali Ibn Sina (Avicenna) and Ibne Rushd (Averroes) has done more to develope in Europe the conception of Universal divinity than all the dreamy ideals of succeeding thinkers. Christian Europe owes its outburst of subjective pantheism, and its consequent emancipation from the intense materialism of the Church teachings, from the bondage of degrading superstitions—to the engrafting of Moslem mysticism, Moslem idealism, on the Eruopean mind. Western Christianity, we may say Christianity apart from the Platonism with which it was pregnant during the first five centuries, is of the most material character. It does not recognise a God apart from human conceptions; its deity is intensely anthropomorphic and personal. The pantheistic writings which flowed from the school of Averroes, reviving the old stoical notions of a soul of nature, directed attention to the great problem of the connection between the worlds of matter and of mind. The conception of an all pervading spirit which sleeps in the stone, dreams in the animal, and wakes in the man, "the belief that the hidden vital principle which produces the varied form of organisation is but the thrill of the Divine Essence that is present in them all"—this belief reappeared in Christianity as a faint echo of the deep mysticism which pervades Islam.

The Prophet (PBUH) had hardly settled comfortably in Medina that the Makkan enemies had started harassing him and those embracing Islam at his hands with continual conspiracies, invasions and battles.

The important events of this period are being related here briefly and at least one incident of each year of Hijrah revealing many things about the blessed life of the Prophet (PBUH), in whose light, the Ummah can set it, house in order and individuals can succeed in their moral upliftment if they are sincerely bent on it, for that is not (at all) difficult for Allah. (Q: XXXV: 17)

Submission to Almighty

The site where the mosque was to be built was denoted providentially by the camel sitting suddenly without human intervention, while the Prophet (PBUH) was on the move to Medina.

The land belonged to two orphans under the patronage and training of As'ad bin Zararah, the Prophet's (PBUH) herald. As'ad had a place here reserved for prayers by As'ad. When the Prophet approved of this piece of land for the construction of the mosque and wanted to purchase it the orphan owners refused to take it, and the Banu Al-Najjar tribe sought permission to purchase it and present it for the mosque. The Prophet (PBUH) rejected both offers. He had ten dinars, the stipulated price of land, paid by Abu Bakr (R). The ground was then levelled and construction started. In this construction work, the Prophet himself gave a helping hand in the movement of building materials, stones and bricks to the construction site with these words on his lips:

"O Allah! Life is after all is that hereafter. Forgive the Ansars (the helpers) and the Muhajirs (the migrants)."

The companions were also engaged in the transport of bricks and mortar for constructions chanting at the same time:

"The Prophet may toil and we remain sitting comfortably. That would be the greatest misguidance."

The walls were raised three yards about ten feet high, a construction of unburnt bricks and date palm trunks were used as pillars and the same as support for roof. The roof covering consisted of date palm leaves and mud offering shade from the sun but badly lacking during rains, making the unpaved (Kachcha) floor of the mosque muddy. But these true believers prostrated on it. Even pebbles spread over it failed to make it any better and cleaner.

'Abd-Allah was one of the most learned men of the Jews. His ancestry has been traced to the Israeli prophet Joseph (son of Jacob). He happened to hear the Prophet (PBUH) preaching. He was so enamoured of his speech that he retained some phrases:

1. O ye people! Spread salam. (prayerful greetings of invoking peace for every one acquainted or stranger).

2. Feed the hungry mouths.

3. Treat your kinsmen kindly and generally.

4. And offer prayers when other people are asleep.

On hearing these heart-shivering words, his heart had become filled with the light of Faith and Belief. When he pondered over the life of the Prophet he found them in perfect conformation with the prophesies of the books of the former prophets. He came to the Prophet (PBUH) and putting tough questions that a prophet only could answer and getting correct answers he announced. "O Apostle of Allah! I have come to believe in you but I would like that you should call people of my community and ask them about their opinion of me. The Prophet called the elders the Judaic community of Medina. Abd-Allah Ibn Salam went in hiding when they came. The Prophet (PBUH) asked them: What do you think of Abd-Allah Ibn Salam? All of them admitted that he was a learned man, son of a learned man and gentle man, and better than all of us. At this juncture, Abd-Allah bin Salam came out of hiding, reciting Kalimah La Ilaha Ill-Allah (the epitome of Islam), before them. When they saw that he had become a Muslim, they at once changed their opinion, calling him ignorant son of the ignorant, low born son of a lowborn and worst among us all.

Allah left no plea for the Jews with the Islam of Abd-Allah bin Salam.

After 'Abd-Allah Ibn Salam, Abu Qais Sarmah bin Abi Anas also embraced Islam. This Christian monk was an eloquent poet, preacher and learned in Metaphysics.

Through the Islam of this righteous person, Allah left no plea for the entire Christian community.

In the 1st year of Hijrah, two more units (raka'ts) were appended to the obligatory prayers. Only two rak'ats for the journeys were maintained (Qasr or halving of the moral). In this way Zuhr 'Asr and 'Isha became four rak'ats normally. During the period of stay in Mecca it was only two rak'ats.

When we consider the precarious position of a person after embracing Islam in Mecca where he became alienated in the family, relatives and friends and lonely in a crowd except for the small group of Muslims he was sick at heart and desired migration to a more congenial atmosphere, Allah in His Infinite Mercy regarded him a stranger or way-farer in the alien land of Mecca and he became a full fledged regular, permanent resident of Medina.

Prayer is that element of obligatory duties to Allah which is of prime importance and after two units of supererogatory prayer immediately on embracing Islam to the call for the next prayer he must respond positively, joining the congregation. A muslim child at the age of seven should start praying for early training (breaking to use a term of horse training or to habituate him to obedience in the ethical terminology). At ten, it is obligatory though not according to Jurists who recognize the age of majority or becoming adult for all obligations. It is obligatory to the end of his days, never relinquishing under any conditions, health or illness, joy or grief, staying at home or on a journey and fear and hazards, in the torrid zone of scorching sun or in the Frigid zone of perpetual snow and ice.

1. Persistently adhering to the worship of Allah throughout one's life is the manifestation of the perfection of patient perseverance. To observe strict punctuality in the five times daily prayer is the best training in recognizing the value of time, the greatest asset of man —life itself is after all respite from death an appointed hour or time at one's disposal. To keep one's body, clothes and house clean, free from filth and pollution is the best way of maintenance of good health. And lastly to keep one's body and mind under control before the grandeur and Majesty of Allah is the best source of light for spiritual luminosity.

2. The punctuality in prayer trains man in going to sleep early and waking up early, and the way its timings bring every other time-table subordinate to it, also shows how unbridled lusts and longings can be appropriately curbed and kept under control decently.

3. Attending congregational prayers at the mosque with punctuality is the soul of culture and progress. It is also the cleanest and most decent way of unity, integrity and exchange of ideas. A perfectly ignorant person can propagate his knowledge of the Word of God and the Sunnah of the Prophet.

4. Those who give up praying or become careless in the punctuality of congregations, remain deprived of these moral excellences. And it is apparent enough that the condition of the individuals of a community devoid of such fine traits of character, will not be enviable.

Allah, the Exalted says:

> Prayer restrains from shameful and evil deeds. And remembrance of Allah is the greatest (thing in life).
>
> — Al Quran XXIX: 45

Islamic Brotherhood

Allah, the Mighty and Majestic has made one Muslim another Muslim's brother. He says:

> So that by His Grace ye became brethren, and ye were on the brink of the Pit of Fire And He saved you from it.
>
> — Al Quran III: 103

1. This fraternity had the effect of making the community a monolithic structure. If a member of this fraternity entered a pact with an antagonistic party or community, the entire community of that individual followed that pact.

   If a Muslim went to some far-off land the entire nation was anxious to learn about his well-being. And if he became the victim of some tyrant's tyranny, the nation as a whole regarded it as its essential duty to take revenge.

   Every Muslim considered it his bounded duty to meet the needs of every orphan, widow and student as he would have met the needs of his own progeny, his real brother's progeny and his widow.

2. Much above this brotherhood which the Prophet (PBUH) established in Mecca between the Makkans and in Medina between the Ansar and the Muhajirs, as also between the Madinites. That between the Muhajirs and Ansar is generally known to people.

The mutual relationships of this brotherhood had the effect so far that a brother was offered a share in the inheritance of his brother. And soon after the formal fraternisation a richer brother used to make his brother the sharer of half of his riches, and movable and immovable property. Historians have left for us on record the names of these brothers with firmly established fraternity.

This system, as we find it today, came into existence in 2 A.H. The necessity for it arose when it was realized that the Muslims in a locality or a section thereof should come together to pray at a given (fixed) time. What needed consultation here was the method to be adopted for calling people. Somebody was of opinion that a fire be lit at a high place (to be visible from a distance), as prevalent among the Magians. Another suggested blowing a horn (a practice of the Jews). Yet another suggestion was in favour of ringing bells the method adopted by the Christians). The Prophet (PBUH) did not approve of any of the above means of giving a call to the believers. The next day 'Abd-Allah bin Zaid Ansari (R) and 'Umar Faruq (R) coming to the Prophet one after the other stated that they had heard these words in their dreams that we find today in the Azan. The Prophet (PBUH) declared calling these words loudly, the way of the Islamic Shariah. These words adequately fulfill the aim of the Prophet (PBUH) that had remained before him in legislating the Islamic principles. (Azan is in perfect accord with the Islamic ideology, covering the entire call to Islam, prophethood, worship etc.).

Azan is that simple and easy method of information which is befitting a universal Faith. It is really the propagation and declaration of Islamic principles. It was by using this instrument that the Muslims conveyed their principles to all the residents of every human settlement informing them of the only easy road to salvation. Distribution of small brochures and tracts and words of Nagar kirtans could never achieve this objective. Azan is proof of the fact that Islam rejected the idea of preferring couch shells and metals to human voice. And this too points to the prevention of idol worship and corroboration of the Unitarity of Allah.

Salman Farsi embraced Islam in 2 A.H. He was a resident of Asfahan and in his ancestral faith piebald horse was worshipped.

He came out of his homeland in search of the True Faith. During the course of his wanderings, he was caught and sold as slave. After trials with ten different religions, he had become a member of the Judaic community. The Jew with whom he lived often talked of the traits of an expected prophet (the promised messiah).

Salman (R) on the first sight of the Prophet (PBUH) recognized him on the basis of those signs and impressions which his Jewish master often related in his presence and entered the fold of Islam as the first fruit of Persia (now Iran).

It was the usual practice of the Prophet to turn to the People of the Book in those matters in which no instructions had been received upto certain time from Allah, the Exalted.

Prayer had been made obligatory in the beginning of prophethood. But no divine injunctions had been received pertaining to the direction to turn to in prayers. Therefore, during his thirteen years stay in Mecca he kept turning to Bait-al-Maqdis, the Qibia of the Judaic community. The practice continued even in Medina. But in the second year of Hijrah (17 months after migration) Allah revealed the injunction ordaining the change of Qiblah. This change was heart-warming to the Apostle of Allah (PBUH) since he from the depths of his heart desired that the Qiblah of Muslims should be the mosque built by Ibrahim (PBUH), called Ka'bah due to the building's cubical appearance and having been built solely for the worship of Allah and its greatness, dignity and honour for that reason, it has also been called Bait-Allah and Masjid-al-Haram (the sacred mosque) in the Quran.

In the detailed instructions in the Quran on this issue, it was also pointed out that:

1. Allah is free from all infirmities has similar association with all directions and not limited to any particular quarter or side:

   To Allah belong the East and the West: withersoever you turn, there is Allah's face.

   —Al Quran II: 115

2. And that taking to any side has been the custom of groups of people in every age.

   To each is a goal to which Allah turns him, then strive together (as in a race) towards all that is good. Wheresoever ye are, Allah will bring you together.

   —Al Quran II 148

3. And also that turning to a particular direction has nothing to do with the worship as such.

   It is not righteousness that ye turn your face towards East or West.

   —Al Quran II: 177

And again, that the major purpose of appointing is that for the followers of the Apostle there may be a distinct sign.

(Appointment of Qiblah was) only to those who followed the Messenger from those who would turn on their heels, (from the Faith)

That was the reason why, so long as the Prophet stayed at Mecca, Bait-al-Maqdis remained the Qiblah of the Muslims, for the pagans of Mecca had sent respect for Bait-al-Maqdis. And as for Ka'bah they had themselves desecrated it by turning it into a big centre of idol worship. Therefore, while at Mecca, the sign of discarding paganism and embracing Islam was to turn to Bait-al-Maqdis when praying.

When the Prophet came to Medina, mostly the Jews and Christians were living there. They had no respect for the Sacred Mosque of Mecca. But Bait-al-Maqdis they regarded as Bait-e-Eil or Haikal (Synagogue). So in Medina, discarding ancestral religion and entering the fold of Islam meant turning to the Masjid-e-Haram when praying — a remarkable sign of converts to Islam.

In obedience to the divine injunction, this became the Qiblah of Muslims for ever— to the end of days. And the reason behind it has been stated by Allah Himself in the Quran:

> The first house (of worship) appointed for men was that of Bakka: full of blessing and of guidance for all the worlds. (Q. III: 96)

Since it enjoys precedence in point of time and historical magnificence, it was in the fitness of things to make it Qibla:

> And remember Abraham and Isma'il raised the foundations of the house (with this prayer): Our Lord! Accept this (service) from us: for Thou art the All-Hearing, All-Knowing: (Q. II: 127)

Secondly, Abraham who is the founder of this mosque is the common ancestor of the Jews, Christians and Muslims. Therefore, the declaration of this mosque being appointed as the Qibla of the Muslim Community was a message to all the three largest communities of the world to come together and uniting enter Islam the realm of peace whole-heartedly.

I am dead sure no one can deny the precedence and historical greatness of Ka'bah. The Jews and the Christian have concensus on it that the foundation of Jerusalem was laid by Da'ud (David) (PBUH) and Sulaiman (Solomon) (PBUH) built it. So we can see that Ka'bah was built about 921 years before that of Jerusalem and one thousand nine hundred and twenty one years before 'Isa (PBUH). Mr R.C. Dutta in his book on history "Ancient civilization of India, on the basis of several evidence has concluded that the first phase of Indian civilization, the vedic age, was 1400 to 2, 000 years before Christ. He has also written that there was no temple in that period of history. That virtually proves that at the time of the building of Ka'bah, there was no temple even in Arya Vasat.

A careful study of Bible shows that Allah had foretold that the mosque that will be last appointed as Qiblah will be superior to the former.

It is really a great beneficence of Allah that He made His House in bakka valley our Qiblah and not Jerusalem. For, a Faith like Islam about which Allah has declared:

> .... and the Religion of Truth, to make it prevail over all religion (Q. XLVIII: 28)

This house ought to have been the Qiblah and not that which every unbelieving victor demolished and desecrated it, by making it a place of filth, enslaving the inmates, incarcerating and banishing them.

In Psalms, verses 4 and 5 Allah has congratulated (blessed) those living close to His House, has had the benevolent effect during several millennia since its, coming into existence it has never grown into the possession of any alien nation nor the nation defending, it has ever been dominated and enslaved.

Rights of the Poor

The most difficult problem facing the Economists and Politicians is how to strike a healthy balance between the members of a community in the matter of wealth and poverty.

From the days of the world famous Greek philosopher, Solon to our own days no one could solve this knotty problem.

In Europe, Nihilists aimed at common equal rights of the citizens of a state over the wealth of their country without distinctions.

The Socialists demand total abolition of private ownership of the means of earning wealth and handed over to the people.

Nationalists, on the other hand, are in favour of taking away landed property, both agricultural and residential from the possession of individuals and managed and controlled by the people.

(The author belongs to an age when these concepts had not taken a definite shape. He has a vague idea, erroneous mostly of the strong reaction of socialism in various forms against the cursed capitalism. Prominent among reactionaries, Marx and Engels were really concerned about the exploitation of the helpless suffering masses by the bourgeoisie, but failed to find a way out, being ignorant of the heavenly guidance which alone could help him, keeping him on the right path. Earlier the same movement, mazdaism, in Iran, had miserably failed).

To take away the right of possession of property by the individuals is impossible, being in-born in man and ineradicable. That is why the Quran had much earlier given the decision:

> Allah has bestowed his gifts of sustenance more freely on some of you than on others: those more favoured are not going to throw back their gifts to those whom their right hands possess so as to be equal in that respect.
>
> —Al Quran XVI: 71

1. Islam, which intends to make the Muslims the most superior cultured nation of the world, paid attention to this problem and decided it for ever. And this solution of this most intricate problem is known as obligation of Zakat.

2. Payment of Zakat was made obligatory for Muslim in 2 A.H. The Prophet was by nature kind-hearted and sympathetic and mercifully inclined to the poor and the suffering humanity and from the first day the Muslims were persuaded to come to the aid of the needy and the destitutes. Their sympathy was made the ally and friend of the poor, and Muslims had actually been doing a lot to ameliorate the distress of the under dog. However, there was no code of conduct and definite rules in this field, in the form of law and regulations to be strictly observed without fail. And whatever the affluent section of society did in this sphere of life was the dictate of their own conscience, generosity and kind-heartedness.

Allah, the Exalted, Most Merciful made Zakat obligatory as the third item of obligatory duties of a believer after belief and prayers. Zakat is, in fact, the promotion and regularization of the inborn trait of man's natural sympathy for his own species.

One great benefit of paying Zakat is that love of manner cannot suppress human moral sense, and he remains free from the evils of miserliness and with holding circulation of wealth, since he regards the depressed and the deprived sections of the society a part the community. And that is why even accumulation of immense wealth cannot make him haughty and puffed up in his own element of the haves.

And also, there is this benefit that a large majority of the disadvantaged section of society comes to nurse a feeling of affinity and love for him (the advantaged) and sympathy and well-wishing with his opulence, since they come to regard a portion of it as their fixed certain share. So to say, the wealth of a Muslim wealthy person becomes the capital of a Joint stock company holding shares of all classes, high and low and benefiting them unreservedly.

The community derives this great benefit, a blessing in disguise that this spending on the poor banishes the evil custom of begging, a degradation of humanity in any society.

Islam has appointed the right of the indigent in the wealth of the affluent in the name of Zakat payable in types of wealth of assured growth which is not abhorrent. Among these growing and multiplying sources of wealth are trade, agriculture, industries, animal breeding, mining and treasure groves.

Now let us see who are those entitled to receive the cash and kind realized as Zakat (by the state or any to her agency in the absence of the Islamic state). The Quran says:

> Alms are for the poor and the needy, and those employed to administer the (funds) for those whose hearts have been recently reconciled (to Truth); for those in bondage and in debt; in the cause of Allah and for the way-farer;
>
> —Al Quran IX: 60

These eight items on which Zakat has been divided shows how was the Zakat made obligatory, the needs of the country, community, and the individuals (both specific and personal) have been beautifully met.

The fifth item of this division is freeing those in bondage. Those well-versed in history know it well enough that slavery was in vogue in all the civilized countires of the world for millennia, China, India, Egypt. Roman empire and Iran. The kind-hearted Messiah, 'Isa (PBUH) did not say a word about it in his period of ministry. But Saint Paul has strengthened it. He says: "Servants, be obedient to them that are your masters according to the flesh, with fear and trembling, in singleness of your heart, as unto Christ."

—The Epistle of Paul to Ehesians 6: 5

And there are so many examples of her Christian attitude towards slaves.

It was Islam and Islam alone that for the first time in the history of mankind that raised a voice in support of the slaves, and various stages of their Redemption.

First, it pointed out and regularized a principle for the freedom of the slaves under the outlets for spending one's substance:

> For those who ask and for the ransom of slaves:
> (Q II: 177)

Secondly, freedom of slaves was pointed out as a means of salvation:

> But he had not made haste on the path that is steep. And what will explain to thee the path that is steep? (It is) freeing the bondman. — Al Quran XC: 11, 12, 13

Thirdly, for some faults freeing slaves has been appointed as a penalty or expiation. For example in case of unintentional murder, in its three different forms:

(a) The murdered person was a Muslim

(b) The murdered a Muslim but an individual of the enemy tribe

(c) The murdered a non-Muslim but from a tribe under a pact

Freeing a slave in all the three cases a, b and c.

(d) Expiation for a serious vow of penance or abstention, is freeing a slave: Give a slave his freedom (Q. V: 89)

(e) Expiation for Zihar (equating one consort with his mother or some other prohibited woman) is to free a slave. (Q. LVIII: 3)

(f) Expiation for intentional breaking of a fast in Ramadan is freeing a slave. (Tradition of the Prophet)

(g) Severe thrashing of a slave by his masters causing injury makes him liable to free a slave as expiation for his sinful act.

And finally, after all these items, the eight portion of the Islamic state's income (budget) has been reserved for this purpose.

In the nineteenth century, England spent hundreds of thousands pounds on the freedom movement of the slaves which no other European power ever did, and it goes to their credit. But compared with Islam under which one eighth of the states total income was reserved for this noble work had been in vogue centuries earlier. Is there yet a person courageous enough to deny the superiority of Islam in this respect?

One should also ponder over the 6th item of the expenditure of Zakat. In the modern age, banks have been established for facilities of borrowing. But it has resulted in this that hundreds of private properties of poor people have gone into the possession of these banks. And barring a few, the majority of the commonality has further deteriorated in their financial condition. It has become almost impossible to borrow without liability of paying interest. And it was due to these difficulties that some people have been trying to find ways to make interest permitted through hair-splitting.

But look at the beneficence of Islam how it has managed to save those facing destruction through borrowing.

Undoubtedly, it becomes it to declare usury and interest strictly prohibited when it has provided so many outlets for those badly involved in heavy debts (become insolvent). We must try to remember this tradition about Zakat.

These sadaqahs are the dirt of people. It is not permitted to the Prophet and his kinsmen.

In this prohibitory order are also included the Prophet (PBUH) his family, uncles, paternal aunts, cousins, and their offspring, as also their slaves and slave girls, so that there may not be even a shade of doubt pertaining to the person of the Prophet (PBUH).

Fasting in the month of Ramadan also became obligatory in 2 A.H. and fasting for one month became the fourth item of Islam.

1. Fasting corrects faults in the system and improves health.

2. They inform and awaken the opulent to the conditions under which the socially disadvantaged are doing existence.

3. Placing the well-fed and the partially starved at the same level fasting is helpful in strengthening the principle of equality in the community.

4. Fasting strengthens the spiritual power and weakens the element of animality in man.

5. The Quran has in particular stressed the point that fasting develops and firmly establishes taqwa (fear of God) in man — That ye may (learn) self restraint.

(Q. II: 183).

Bibliography

Ali Kattani, *Muslim Minorities in the World Today.*

Allan Nouvin, *The Gateway to History.*

Amity Etziani, *Hard Way to Peace.*

Andre Beaufre, *General Introduction to Strategy.*

Ann Van Wynon Thomas, *Communism vs International Law.*

Arberry, A.J., *The Doctrines of the Sufis,* tr., of *Kalabadhi's Kitab alta,* Aruf, Cambridge.

Arnold T.W., *The Preaching of Islam.*

Arnold, Sir Thomas, *The Caliphate,* London, 1965.

Athar, Ali, *Mughal Nobility under Aurangzeb,* Bombay, 1968.

Aziz Noomi Kurtha, *Prisoners of War and War Crimes.*

Basham, A. L. ed., *A Cultural History of India,* Oxford, 1975.

Batty and Morgan, *War: its Conduct and Legal Results.*

Bertram Thomas, *Arabia Felix.*

Bird, Major General, *The Direction of War.*

Browne, E.G., *A Literary History of Persia,* 4 vols., reprint, Cambridge, 1957.

Carl Bockleman, *History of Islamic Peoples.*

Christman, *Peace and Arms.*

Clerk Mark, *General Calculated Risk.*

Corbin, H., *Avicenna and the Visionary Recital*, tr., W. Trash, New York, 1960.

Czaplicka, M.A., *The Turks of Central Asia in History and the Present Day*, Amsterdam, 1973.

Dicy, *An Introduction to the Law of Constitution.*

Dorothy Vaughan, *Europe and the Turks.*

Drew Pearson and Constantine Brown, *The Diplomatic Game.*

Earle Meade, *Makers of Modern Strategy.*

Edward Mortimer, *Faith and Power, The Politics of Islam.*

Emil Brunner, *Justice and the Social Order.*

Faris, Nabith A., *The Book of Knowledge*, tr., of Ghazali's Ihya', Lahore, 1962.

Faruqi, Ziya'u-i Hasan, *The Deoband School and the Demand for Pakistan*, Bombay, 1963.

Foster, W., *The English Factories in India*, 13 vols., Oxford, 1906-27.

Fred Joseph, *International Relations.*

Frykenberg, *Land Control and Social Structure in Indian History*, Wisconsin, 1969.

Gabriel's Wing, Leiden, 1963.

Gauba, K.L., *The Prophet of the Desert (PBUH)*

Gibb, *Muhammadanism.*

Gilsenan, Mechael, *Saint and Sufi in Modern Egypt: An essay in the Sociology of Religion*, Oxford, 1973.

Glubb, Major General, *The Story of Arab Legion.*

Gulzar Ahmed, Brigadier, *Defence of the World of Islam.*

Gulzar Ahmed, Brigadier, *The Prophets (PBUH) Concept of War.*

Gustav E. von Grunebaum, *Unity and Variety in Muslim Civilization.*

Halepota, A.J., *Philosophy of Shah Waliu'llah*, Lahore.

Haqq, En'amul, *Muslim Bengali Literature*, Karachi, 1957.

Harley Williams, *The Conquest of Fear.*

Hasrat, B.J., *Dara Shikuh: Life and Works*, reprinted, New Delhi, 1982.

Hitti, *History of The Arabs.*

Holt, Lambton and Lewis, *The Cambridge History of Islam*, Cambridge, 1970.

Howard Michael, *The Causes of War.*

Hussaini, *Constitution of the Arab Empire.*

Ikram, S.M., *Muslim Civilization in India*, New York.

Irfan Habib, *The Agrarian System of Mughal India*, Bombay, 1963.

Izutsu, Toshihido, *A Comprehensive Study of the Key Philosophical Concepts of Sufism and Taoism*, Tokyo, 1966-67.

Jalbani, G.N., *Teachings of Shah Waliyullah of Delhi*, 2nd edn., Lahore, 1973.

Jamil Jaibi and Qazi A. Qadir, *The Changing World of Islam.*

John Green, *Clausewitz.*

John Loffin, *The Face of War.*

Kamal A. Faruqui, *Islam Today and Tomorrow.*

Kernan, Lt. Col, *Defence will not Win the War.*

Khalifa Abdul Hakim, *The Islamic Ideology.*

Lan Brownbie, *International Law and the Use of Force by States.*

Lawrance, T.E., *Seven Pillars of Wisdom.*

Levantin, *The Myth of International Security.*

Lings, Martin, *A Sufi Saint of the Twentieth Century*, 2nd edn., London, 1971.

Luckner, R.C., *The Bhagavad-Gita*, Oxford, 1969.

Ludwig Renn, *Warfare.*

MacDonald, D.B., *The Religious Attitude and Life in Islam*, Beirut, 1965.

Manucci, N., *Storia do Mogor*, l653-1708, tr. W. Irvine, London, 1907-8.

Mao Tze Tung, *Selected Works.*

Mayne, P., *Saints of Sind*, London, 1965.

Meer Hassan, *Observations on the Musulmauns of India*, vols., London, 1832.

Michael Williams, *Outlines of World Military History.*

Milton Shulman, *Defeat in the West.*

Mohaghegh, *Mahdi and Landolt: Islamic Philosophy and Mysticism*, Tehran, 1971.

Mohiuddin Ahmad, *Saiyid Ahmad Shahid*, Lucknow, 1975.

Monserrate, Fr A., Commentary, tr. J.S., *Holy land and annotated* by S.N. Banerjee, Cuttack, 1922.

Montgomery Watt, *The Majesty that was Islam.*

Moreland, W.H., *From Akbar to Aurangzeb*, London, 1923, reprint, New Delhi, 1972.

Muhammad Ayub, *The Politics of Islamic Revolution.*

Muir, William, *Life of Muhammad* (PBUH).

Muslim Intellectual: A Study of al-Ghazali, Edinburgh, 1963.

Mystical Dimensions of Islam, Chape Hill, 1975.

Mystical Poems of Rumi, Chicago, 1968.

Nageeb al-attas, Syed, *The Mysticism of Hazmali Fansuri*, Kuala Lumpur, 1970.

Nicholson, R.A., *The Mysteries of Islam*, London, 1914.

Padwick, C.E., *Muslim Devotions*, London, 1960.

Pain and Grace, Leiden, 1976.

Petersen, E.L., *'Ali and Mu'awiya in early Arabic Traḍitions*, Copenhagen, 1964.

Qanungo, K.R., *Dara Shikoh*, Calcutta, 1935.

Rafiqi, A.Q., *Sufism in Kashmir*, Delhi, 1977.

Riazu'l Islam, *Indo-Persian Relations*, Tehran/Lahore, 1970.

Rizvi, S. A. A., *Muslim Revivalist Movements in Northern India in the Sixteenth and Seventeenth Centuries*, Agra, 1965.

Russel, Ralph and Khurshidu'l Islam, *There Mughal Poets*, Cambridge, Mass., 1968.

Sadiq, M., *A History of Urdu Poetry*, London, 1964.

Saksena, R.B., *A History of Urdu Literature*, Allahabad, 1927.

Schacht, J., *The Origin of Muhammadan Jurisprudence*, Oxford, 1950.

Scholovosky, Marshall, *Military Strategy*.

Shapiro, *The Law: Servant or Master*.

Sharma, R.S. and Jha, V. ed. *Indian Society: Historical Probings*, Delhi, 1974.

Shaukat Ali, *Masters of Muslim Thought*.

Shejwalker, T.S., *Panipat: 1761*, Poona, 1946.

Sherwani, H.K., *The Bahmanis of the Deccan*, Hyderabad-Deccan, 1953.

Smith, M., *Rabi'a The Mystic and her Fellow Saints in Islam*, Cambridege, 1929.

Spear, P., *Twilight of the Mughals*, 2nd edn., Cambridge and New Delhi, 1970.

Subhan, J.A., *Sufism: Its Saints and Shrines*, 2nd edn., Lucknow, 1960.

Tarachand, *Influence of Islam on Indian Culture*, 2nd edn., Allahabad, 1963.

Temple, R.C., *Legends of the Punjab*, London, 1893-1901.

Thomas, R.C., *Legends of the Punjab*, London, 1893-1901.

Tod, J., *Annals and Antiquities of Rajasthan*, Oxford, 1920.

Tripathi, R.J., *Some Aspects of Muslim Administration*, 2nd edn., Allahabad, 1959.

Trueblood Eiton, *Declaration of Freedom*.

Underhill, E., *Mysticism: A Study in the Nature and Development of Man's Spiritual Consciousness*, Paperback, New York, 1956.

Vaudeville, Charlotte, *Kabir*, Vol. I, Oxford, 1974.

Wahed Husain, *Administration of Justice during the Muslim Rule in India*, Delhi, 1977.

Walker, B., *Hindu World*, London, 1968.

Watanmal, L., *The Life of Shah'Abdul Latif*, Hyderabad, Sind, 1889.

Wavell, Field Marshall, *Soldiers and Soldiering*.

Weech, *History of the World*.

Wilfred Seamen Blunt, *The Future of Islam*.

Winston Churchill, *Thoughts and Adventures*.

Wright Patman, *The American Government*.

Yousuf Abbas Hashmi, *Kitabur Rasul (PBUH)*.

Yusuf Iblish, Peter Lambron Wilson, *Traditional Modes of Contemplation and Action*, Tehran, 1977.

Ziadah, N.A., *Sanusiyah: A Study of a Revivalist Movement in Islam*, Leiden, 1958.

Index

❑❑❑